100

THE PASTOR'S WIFE
and
THE CHURCH

THE PASTOR'S WIFE
and
THE CHURCH

By

DOROTHY HARRISON PENTECOST

MOODY PRESS
CHICAGO

Copyright ©, 1964, by
THE MOODY BIBLE INSTITUTE
OF CHICAGO

Fifth Printing, 1974

Library of Congress Card No. 64-23169

ISBN: 0-8024-6360-6

Printed in the United States of America

To my pastor
and the members of Grace Bible Church
who have made being a minister's wife
both a privilege and a joy

Contents

Foreword

THIS BOOK WAS PLANNED just for the pastor's wife, but as it developed, I realized more and more that the wife, pastor, and the church members can't be separated. Therefore, you will find suggestions to the congregation for making a happier relationship between them and the pastor's wife as well as helps and answers to the questions and problems of the wife herself.

While all writers find it difficult to show a true picture of the facts they are presenting in a book, it is much more difficult to give a pattern of the position of the minister's wife, because each church is distinct in its ways and expectations, and each lady who marries a clergyman has her own personality. Mountains of books couldn't cover a subject as large and complex as this one. In order to reach the largest number of church members and pastors' wives, I have chosen to write about the problems of the average church, which, according to denominational statistics, usually has from two hundred to five hundred members. This is also the size of the churches in which my husband and I have had our experience.

God has a particular type of ministry for each of us wives—from sick-bed praying to giving almost full time to the work of the church. He has given each of us the same amount of time which we must plan and budget wisely according to His will. God has also bestowed varied spiritual gifts and talents and brought us into all kinds of circumstances under which we must live. It is not how much we do in a church or how little that counts. The important thing is to find out what God has willed for each of us in this place and do it. No two pastorates will ever be the same.

9

While the "lady of the manse" is what she is because of her personality, background, and spirituality, in a sense she is also what the church makes her. In many cases, the pastor's wife is made or broken by the church people.

My experience has given me an unusual opportunity to see just how this works. My husband and I have been in the ministry for twenty-five years, and have moved almost entirely among ministers' families. We have shared their joys and problems. We are now serving our fourth pastorate. Four types of churches are represented by our pastorates—rural, small town, suburban, and large city. Three of these churches were Presbyterian and one, independent.

I have had as many years as an adult church lay member as I have had as a pastor's wife. Seven of those years came between our third and fourth churches while my husband was teaching school. During this time I was first a member of a church with over one thousand members and then of another with two hundred, in entirely different sections of the country. Thus I have been given a rare opportunity to see both sides of the picture and study the problems that lead to trouble and misunderstanding between the church and the pastor's wife.

My husband is Professor of Bible at the Dallas Theological Seminary and at the same time pastor of a church, and we have watched hundreds of students and their wives go through school, graduate, and return for visits. We have seen them leave happy, hopeful, and well trained for their first pastorates. In a few years, some return the same way, having worked hard and reaped the rewards of their labors—still radiant in the Lord. But there are far too many who come back sick at heart, broken in health, and dissillusioned. And many of the wives feel that they would rather see their husbands dig ditches than return to their churches.

It is obvious to everyone that something is wrong, and there is far too great a tendency for congregations to blame the pastors' wives. They will freely admit that they have made many mistakes, especially in a first parish, but they did what they did because they felt it was the Lord's will and the best for the church and their families, though they may have done it in the wrong way because of lack of experience and clumsy methods. The minister and his wife are equally as guilty, much of the time, in blaming all of their troubles on the church membership.

In all fairness I have tried to show both sides of the picture—from the viewpoint of the church ladies and that of the pastor's wife. Then I have suggested ways that each can help the other and deal with unpleasant situations that inevitably lead to heartache and disappointment unless they are understood and dissolved. This book was written with the hope and prayer that as the minister's wife and the church ladies get to know and understand each other better many of the present troubles will disappear or at least be tolerated in love and godly patience.

All of the illustrations used in this book are true, though some had to be disguised a little. For very obvious reasons, none of them have come from our present church unless I have so stated. I beg my church people to remember that what I have written is not just a reflection of my feelings but of the opinions and reactions of hundreds of pastors' wives. This book does not necessarily express my personal views. Remember, also, that this is our fourth pastorate, and how I felt or acted was different in each church. I hesitated to reveal many of my little secrets and techniques for fear our present congregation might doubt my sincerity and affection. I trust they will bear in mind that these are only my necessary "tools" for serving them better, just as any worker must have methods for carrying on a business.

I would like to express my gratitude to Mr. Wayne Christianson, editor of *Moody Monthly*, for permission to quote part of an article by this writer and published in the January, 1960 issue of that magazine. My thanks go to Mrs. Offie Baylass, who typed the manuscript.

There is deep appreciation in my heart to the ministers' wives who have encouraged me in writing and have made suggestions and asked pertinent questions. Some women have made outstanding contributions by personal interviews or letters. These are Mrs. John Mitchell of the Central Bible Church of Portland; Mrs. Harlin J. Roper of the Scofield Memorial Church of Dallas; Mrs. Alan Redpath, formerly of Moody Memorial Church of Chicago (now in Scotland); and Mrs. Lorne Belden of Knox Presbyterian Church of Minneapolis, who has been quoted several times in this book. Mrs. Milford Castrodale of Westminster Presbyterian Church of Philadelphia, who is a dear friend of twenty years, has given me permission to quote her entire letter on the discussion of the call and the mistakes of the pastor's wife. She trained and helped me through our first pastorate, without which I am sure I would have given up. Mrs. L. P. Mc-Clenny, Mrs. Malcolm Cronk, and Mrs. Edwin Johnson, all of Wheaton, Illinois, have added much to this book through informal discussions of the role of the pastor's wife. Mrs. Johnson was my pastor's wife when my husband was teaching in Philadelphia, and observation of her life as a pastor's wife under all kinds of circumstances taught me more about this subject than any success or failures on my part. Space does not permit me to name the countless others who have influenced the ideas presented, including many men and many laywomen who frankly gave their viewpoint of the problems of pastors' wives and kindly showed me where many have strayed in their attitudes toward the church ladies.

My gratitude goes to the Christian doctor friends who have made special studies of the physical and psychological problems of the ministerial couple—Dr. Henry P. Webb, of Philadelphia, who has contributed his ten rules of good mental health; Dr. Mary D. Varker, a former church member, who first introduced me to the study of psychology by supplying me with numerous books on the subject and then spent hours in earnest discussion on the authors' theories from both the medical and spiritual aspects; and Dr. Marion H. Nelson, a practicing psychiatrist in Dallas, who is never too busy to answer my questions and give suggestions that might help pastors' wives. Dr. Gladys Brown, a Christian psychologist of Dallas, has made my discussion of the problems of the preachers' kids both easy and accurate because of her years of training and experience working with them. My appreciation goes to her for letting me use some of her wealth of information on this subject.

There is no way of estimating the help that has come from the wives of students of the Dallas Theological Seminary who attended a class I taught to instruct and encourage and prepare them for their future roles as pastors' wives. Their intense search for a happy relationship in the churches where their husbands will serve, their almost unbelievable faith that I had the answer to all difficulties they would encounter, and their soul-searching questions kept me studying, questioning outstanding ministers' wives, praying, writing and rewriting, until I felt that I had the best possible answers for the many and varied circumstances under which these young women will have to live. Much thanks go to these girls who have helped me much more than I have helped them!

Looking back over twenty-five years as a minister's wife, many of which have been frustrating and hard, and some very unhappy, I feel they have been fruitful and very rewarding. If I could choose my lifework again, I would still choose to be a minister's wife.

DOROTHY PENTECOST

CHAPTER 1

Is Love Enough?

A TALL, DARK-HAIRED GIRL stood at the door of the classroom, miserably shifting from one foot to another while she waited for the other students to leave the room. Their talking and laughing kept them from noticing that she was alternately picking at her fingernails and too carefully folding and refolding her handkerchief. But the teacher had noticed and sat quietly at his desk until she quickly came up the aisle and sat down in the first chair in front of him.

"I've got to know if love is enough." The teacher was a minister, and the girl was a nineteen-year-old student attending a summer young people's conference at Hampden-Sydney College. "I am engaged to the finest Christian boy I have ever known. He feels called to the mission field, but I don't. In fact, I don't want to go, but I am willing, in order to be with Bill. Is love enough to indicate that God wants me to be a missionary, too?" After a moment's thought, he replied, "Yes, I believe that the Lord is leading you that way by the circumstances of your love for each other."

For the rest of the day, her happiness was beyond description, and she couldn't wait to write Bill that the question was finally settled and they could go ahead with their plans to be married. But that evening, after vespers, as she leaned against a giant oak and gazed at the Virginia sunset, she had to admit, deep in her heart, that the question still was not settled. She had no more peace about going to the mission field now than she had had that morning before class. What had become of that inner urge through the years that the Lord had called her into the work of a helpmeet to a minister? Somehow, reminding herself that Bill would be a minister as well as a missionary didn't help. She knew that something was wrong if she was willing to go to the mission field only for Bill's love, but not for the Lord's sake. She knew she would never go to the mission field except with Bill.

"Let the peace of God rule in your heart" came to her mind as swiftly as though someone had spoken the words. "Let the peace of God rule in your heart." There was no peace in her heart. God was not ruling. This path to Bill's love could not be God's will. The sun disappeared, and darkness descended on the campus and in her heart.

Time, prayer, and the mission board proved that the minister-teacher had been wrong. Human love was not enough for a call to full-time Christian service. Though tears of heartache came freely, and dreams of a blissful future broke one by one like soap bubbles, the engagement was broken before that summer drew to a close. At nineteen, life seemed to be over for her.

A little over a year later I—for I was that girl—became engaged to the man who is now my husband. Dwight knew that he had been called to the ministry when he was eight years old, at a Junior Christian Endeavor meeting. He was interested in the mission field, but the Lord had shown him a number of times that his work was to be in this country. And now God had shown me His mate for me, and peace as well as love filled my heart. My inner desire through the years to be a pastor's wife now became a strong call that nothing could shake. Twenty-five years together, with both of us giving our full time to God's work in pastorates and teaching, has proved that this was the right path.

The question of whether the minister's wife should feel a call to her work has provoked much discussion in Christian circles and, lest I put too much emphasis on a personal experience, I have spent hours learning how trusted Christian ministers and their wives feel about this matter. While they have expressed themselves in different ways, it seems to me that all have come to almost the same conclusions.

The Texas *Baptist Standard* says, "The stresses and strains on the minister's wife are enough to stagger an Amazon" and that she leads an "inexorable fishbowl existence" in which she is expected to be a leader and model in all fields. It blames the failure of many wives on the fact that "most ministers' wives have never heard a divine call, they have simply married men who have." In commenting on these statements, the editor of *Moody Monthly* magazine says that he has met many hundreds of dedicated wives of Bible-believing pastors wherever he travels. "And we suspect the secret of their striking service goes far deeper than personality or even devotion to their husbands." He adds, "Never having been a minister's wife, however, we would probably be presumptuous in attempting a final answer." Then he closes the editorial by asking the wives themselves to write to the magazine to express their opinions. Every letter published stated that the writer had felt a definite call into the the Lord's service as a parson's wife.

My husband, who is now a seminary professor and a pastor, does not feel the wife needs a special call because Scripture gives no indication of its need. He says that if a girl is being led of the Lord into love for a minister, and is willing to make the necessary sacrifices cheerfully, and take on the many extra burdens of being married to a minister for the Lord's sake, then she can consider that, and her love, a leading into the Lord's work. This, of course, presupposes that she understands just what being a minister's wife entails. I, for one, had no idea what was ahead when I stood before our church altar with Dwight and said, "I do." All but a few of those wives who grew up in parsonages have frankly admitted that they didn't either, and some say they seriously doubt if they would have married a minister if they had known what was to follow.

Dr. Arthur W. Hewitt, in his book *The Shepherdess*, feels that just falling in love with a man who is a preacher or who is preparing for the ministry is enough of an indication that her place as his wife is God's call. However, the context of his book shows he assumes the girl is being led of God into that relationship. His message presents such high standards and such a rigid routine for the parson's wife that I doubt if only a human love could hold a woman to such perfection.

I cringe with fear when I hear a seminary student say that he has talked a girl into marrying him, even though she had no desire to be a minister's wife. She will fail in her work for the Lord and in giving him the support he needs unless she has a complete change of heart. The dangers of such a marriage are well portrayed in the novel *The Bishop's Mantle* by Agnes Turnbull. The hero of the story was a minister who made the fatal mistake of marrying a girl who was frankly out of sympathy with his work and only married him because she loved him and he was serving a large, wealthy church in her home city. She showed her true character by her misconduct, unhappiness and outright rebellion because of the time that he spent with his parishioners and in sermon preparation. This theme makes interesting reading as fiction, but too often it is true in real life. Four of the best ministers we know have been forced out of their pastorates completely because their wives by their attitudes and conduct ruined their husbands' opportunities to "preach the unsearchable riches of Christ Jesus."

It is still my firm conviction that the woman who marries a clergyman should have a call, or inner urge, by which she knows that the Lord is leading her personally into His service as the helpmeet of a minister.

When the average girl falls in love, she is just choosing a husband. But when a girl marries a minister, she is not only choosing a life partner but a lifetime career. Other women can train for a profession or career, and if they do not like it, they can change to another or give up working entirely, if they so desire. The pastor's wife has no choice. Her career is carved out for her and it lasts "Till death do us part." There is no change, no retreat, nor escape. She must take her place as an active Christian worker in the church or fail her husband and the Lord.

My advice to you unmarried girls is: Don't marry a minister if you can avoid it! (Dear seminary students, please forgive me for that emphatic statement. It may sound cruel now, but it is designed to protect you, and keep you looking until you find just the God-given girl who will enter fully into all of your ministry because she feels called, too.) There seems to be a fatal fascination on the part of young girls for clergymen. Perhaps it is because they are usually looked up to, respected, well groomed, and well educated. To share this life gives promise of being a bed of roses without the thorns. Little does the average girl know about the thorns in the life of a pastor's wife!

About this time last year my husband advised a student not to marry a girl he loved because she was unsuitable for a minister's wife. At the time the student seemed determined to have his own way. Today a letter came from him thanking my husband for the warning, and telling him how the Lord had spared him from making a terrible mistake. Now he has found just the right girl, the one God wanted for him. She shares his beliefs and his calling into the Lord's service.

I sent part of my manuscript to a dear friend, a very successful minister's wife (her husband is the pastor of a large Presbyterian church in Phaladelphia). She has expressed her objection to the wife's call so well that I secured her permission to quote from her letter.

> There is just one point I sincerely wonder about, and that is your statement that "a minister's wife should have as definite a call to her work as the missionary's wife." I wonder whether that might be upsetting to quite a few who will read it and wonder when and where her call came, and here she is already a minister's wife. Many will wonder, "Just what is a call, what am I to look for? For example, I am Jim's fiancée, the

Lord wondrously led us together, has answered our prayers every step of the way. We are to be married in June when Jim graduates from seminary and now I find that I am supposed to feel a call." She goes on to say, "Human nature being what it is, a love-struck girl can feel a call, or see a vision, or whatever may be the prescribed procedure in order to fill the requirement, and all this quite innocently at that stage of life. I should say, rather, that it would behoove any Christian girl who finds herself either attracted to or dating a man who has been called into God's full-time service to sincerely pray for guidance lest she make the terrible mistake of taking things into her own hands. If she treads very softly, and is wholly yielded to the Holy Spirit's leading, and they are progressively led together and find then that love is binding them together, is that not very often God's way of leading the girl into the position as a minister's wife? So often people get the idea that one's calling must be something mysterious and earth-shaking, when it can be as simple as . . . God's leading is God's calling.

She has so perfectly expressed just what I mean by a "call" to be a minister's wife that I have let her say it in her own words. Lest there be any mistake, may we put the meaning of call into one sentence? A call to be a minister's wife is seldom sudden, or different from a call into any other kind of work. It is usually a slow unfolding of God's will by an inner urge of the Holy Spirit, coupled with circumstances.

Another friend brought up the problem of the girl who feels called to be a minister's wife, but who never meets the minister. Then later, she falls in love with a man in another field of work and marries him. I would say that there is some serious question as to whether the call was a true one of the Lord in the first place. Perhaps it was more of a personal desire for that position. However, it might be perfectly true that the Lord called her only to test her willingness to serve Him in that way, if

He so desired. I had always said that I would do anything for the Lord but go to the mission field. The Lord made me miserable and kept my plans continually upset until He brought me to the place where I said, "Anywhere, Lord, even the mission field." Then I soon discovered that He didn't want me on the foreign field but wanted me to be a missionary as a pastor's wife. He waited until I was brought to the place of being willing to do anything that was His will before He let me know exactly where He wanted me. This same process may have been going on in the heart of the girl who felt called to be a minister's spouse, and later married a businessman.

My deepest sympathy goes out to the women who marry business or professional men, only to have them feel called into the ministry later in life. They have a severe test to face. However, as long as the husband is sure of his call to full-time service, there is no doubt that the wife is called also. God never plans separately for husband and wife. In His sight they are one! The wife must bring her will and desire into line with that of the Lord and her husband. Doing this may be the hardest adjustment of her life, but she must do it willingly, or disaster will usually result.

The seminary where my husband teaches submits many questions to candidates for admission to the school. One of the questions is whether the man's wife feels the same way about his desire to attend school as he does. The school has learned that if the wife is not in sympathy with what her husband is doing, he seldom does good work and nearly always there is trouble. Because of this, the school usually turns down such candidates.

From whatever viewpoint you may look, the job of being a pastor's wife is staggering, and it is impossible for anyone but a super human being to do the required work. For that reason, those who have been questioned about the matter feel that a human love for the husband is not enough to make her find happiness and fulfillment in the work. Some may say that she should have a call, others that she should be led of the Holy

Spirit just as anyone else is led; and others that a love for a minister plus a willingness to make the necessary sacrifices and do the extra things that living in a manse demand are what a girl should look for in herself when she considers marrying a minister. We all agree that being a parson's wife is a different—and many times difficult—job, so that a girl must be very sure that it is the Lord's will for her life if she is to receive from Him the wisdom, tact, strength, and patience necessary for her job.

CHAPTER 2

How to Get Your Training

GRADUATION WAS OVER, our trunks were packed, and our last farewells had been said, and my husband and I left for Philadelphia, where he was under the care of Presbytery. He had candidated in two churches, both of which had called him, and our first big decision had to be made. This is where I learned that my husband was the one to make the choice of the place of service, according to the dictates of the Lord. This was easy, for I had always believed, as taught in the Word, that the husband was head of the home and would make such decisions. In fact, it was a relief to let him have the struggle of knowing which place of ministry was the Lord's will for us.

When we arrived at the scene of our first pastorate, we were entertained for a few days in the home of one of the elders. One evening, he asked, "Pardon me for being so dumb, but just what is a pastor's wife supposed to do?" It was a natural question, for we were following a bachelor who had served the church for forty-two years. My answer is vague in my memory, probably because it was really not clear to me then. A sudden fear hit me that I was in a church, ready for something, and didn't have the slightest idea what a pastor's wife was supposed to do. It was then that this thought struck me: I had spent three years in the shadow of an excellent seminary and though I had received the best Bible instruction and preparation for working with children, I had been given only one piece of advice—and no instruction—for the work of the pastor's wife. It was like sending an unskilled laborer into a highly technical laboratory and expecting him to make the finest products without a mistake. The one piece of advice was, "Take care of your husband, and let him take care of the church." Someone suggested that my husband and I should be aloof from the people so that we would not be accused of having special friends in the church. Much as we loved and respected the man who gave us that advice, it wasn't long before we learned that neither piece of advice was going to work in this church. My husband's only consolation was this: "He was never a pastor himself. His ideas might be very different if he had to serve a pastorate now."

There was no need to worry about my lack of know-how and training, for everyone just ignored me. They could not remember a time when they had a pastor who was married and, frankly, they did not know how to treat a pastor's wife.

For at least six months I was lonely and hurt, waiting for a chance to use my Bible knowledge and children's material in teaching. If I had been trained in seminary, or had had more experience, I would have realized that this was an opportunity to make a place for myself and show the congregation by my actions what to expect of a pastor's wife. This was a golden opportunity to make many visits among the women and to entertain in the manse until they got to know me and I got to know them.

However, no one likes to see wasted manpower, so it was not long after this period that they reached a decision on what to do with the pastor's wife—just to give her all the work nobody else wanted. For several years, I was at everyone's beck and call and, feeling that this was helping my husband's work, I did all that was expected of me.

In the process, it didn't take long to discover that the people were divided into cliques, and when I was doing what one group wanted, I was upsetting another. When I pleased one woman, I was making an enemy of another. As a result of my mixed-up motives, my sense of responsibility to everyone, and pressure from all sides, I spent nine months in bed at the end of our second year there. Physically, I am still paying the price of those mistakes, and probably always will. Had I been schooled for my job and instructed in the ways of churches, there is serious doubt if any of this would have happened. But this was God's way of teaching me a second lesson. What He taught me is perhaps the most priceless lesson a clergyman's wife can learn: We can't hope to please everyone, and should never control our lives by what others demand and expect of us. Our orders are to come from the Lord. Seek the will of the Lord for each day, keep your heart free of sin so the Holy Spirit can freely lead and then, as members of the congregation make suggestions or demands, do what you know to be God's will for you, and only that. It is the only safe way—pleasing God first, and then you will find that you please most of those who also are looking for God's will. The rest would criticize you no matter what you do, so you can be at peace about them. Just trust the Lord to take care of their trouble-making and misunderstanding. Let your joy be that of knowing your way is right before Him.

Stories similar to this have come to me since that time, and the knowledge that so many pastors' wives become ill in their first pastorates has given me the firm conviction that the wife must have some definite training for her career. The amazing thing is that though we wives of pastors are often told that we can make or break our husband's ministry by our conduct and abilities and how we please or don't please the church folk, we are usually sent into the job without any preparation. The wife will be forgiven for burning a few meals, but if she makes one mistake in the church it might lead to a request for her husband's resignation. No doctor would think of trying to perform an operation without many years of training and experience. No lawyer would be allowed to try a case in court until he had completed his educational requirements and passed the state bar examination. Not even a secretary is given a job until she has been taught to type and take shorthand. Ministers are required by most denominations to have four years of college and three or four years of seminary training before they can be ordained. A vast number of men have taken three additional years of theological training for their doctor's degree. But many of us wives have not had the chance to finish college. Seldom do we have Bible training, and in only a few cases have any of us been prepared, or have we had any help, for the work we must do as the partner of a preacher.

It is too late to "un-marry" even if we wanted to, and yet we are daily faced with problems for which we have no answers. But don't let it be a source of added despair. There are many ways of getting self-training right on the job, even though we are apprentices. The best ministers' wives we have known are those who have had no training but have a keen desire to please the Lord and be true helpers of their husbands. God never leaves a seeking soul without assistance. He will guide us in the way in which we should go, in spite of our lacks and mistakes, if we will let Him lead, step by step. Experience is often a hard teacher, but it leaves the most lasting and best-learned lessons.

There are three ways for a pastor's wife to find the training she will need. First, the most ideal time to get the preparation is before marriage, but that is impossible for those who do not realize what they lack until afterward. Second, help can be found at the seminary where her husband goes to school. The third way of preparation is a self-training program for those already in the pastorate, and even for those who have had help in the first two places, because we must keep growing in knowledge, and our thirst for learning how to do a better job should never cease.

At first thought, the idea of getting preparation for the pastorate before marriage will appear ridiculous to some. "Why should I train myself for something I might never do?" Good question! But I know that the girl who plans to be a missionary gears her training in school with the mission field in mind. Most girls have a very good idea of what they want to do in life and of the kind of man they hope to marry, and they include training in things related to that person's occupation. The things that will make a well-prepared minister's wife are those that will also contribute to a well-rounded Christian life, and fit her for any vocation. However, we are thinking primarily of those who become engaged, or seriously interested in a man who is preparing for full-time Christian service. As soon as there is an understanding between the two, the girl should make definite plans to get training that will fit her for her future ministry alongside a minister. If at all possible, she should enroll in a Bible college or institute, even if she can only take night classes. If there is no other way to manage, she can always take excellent Bible courses and related subjects by correspondence from the Moody Bible Institute in Chicago. Her major, of course, should be in the Bible, with any other courses available that are just for ministers' wives. Courses in homemaking are a must for learning how to manage a home, budgeting, entertaining, decorating, etiquette, and the care of children and guests. Courses in English, public speaking, and psychology are essential, too. If she has any talent in music, it would be best to develop such talent and any other special interests of hers.

Dr. Gladys Brown, a Christian psychologist here in Dallas, does 60 percent of her work with ministers, missionaries, and their families. The churches are learning, as the mission boards did long ago, that there are many people who do not have the aptitude and emotional stability to carry on successfully the work of the ministry with its pressures and strains. She has even found some men who were such poor emotional risks that they would probably have had a nervous breakdown in a first pastorate. Four denominations in this area use her services, and they refuse to accept those whom she rejects through psychological testing.

Every girl who plans to marry a minister or missionary should have such tests, which will show where her abilities lie and to what degree her personality and emotional strength will measure up to what will be expected of her. These tests were not available when I was married. If they had been, I would have taken them but I probably would not have received a very good rating. I say this because I now know my great limitations due to childhood experiences, heredity and physical disabilities. The great question then, if I had taken such tests, would have been: Knowing my limitations and the probability of poor adjustments to some strains of pastoral life, should I marry a minister? My answer is easy today. Yes! God called me to be a minister's help-meet, and He put such love in our hearts for each other that we felt we completed each other. Since we knew that we were in God's will, we married. If we had planned on going to the mission field, the mission board would have turned me down, automatically, and there would have been no choice. But the minister and his wife still have a choice, though churches are getting fed up with unsuitable wives, as well as unsuitable ministers, and the day may soon come when only the finest will be accepted by a congregation.

On one occasion a student told my husband that a large Baptist church where he lived had as candidates in their church ten of the best men they could find and, while the ministers were all liked very much, none was called. Why not? In each case it was because of the wife. It would help a lot to know whether these women were truly unfit or if the church was demanding more of the wives than should be expected.

Now, you may want to ask this question: "Since you would have married a minister in spite of the tests, why bother to take them?" My answer holds three reasons. First, the psychological tests would let me know my weak points, and give me help in avoiding the things that would lead to trouble in those places. I would be shown where to put my best energies, and where to say "no" in order to avoid physical and emotional trouble. Second, the tests would have given me time to get help and treatment to overcome my limitations before I was married. In so many cases, an understanding of one's self and a little professional help would have saved ministers and their wives years of emotional sickness, heartaches, and mistakes. Third, I would have entered my work knowing just what to expect. Then, whatever happened would be primarily my own fault. Far too many wives, being merely human, feel that the church tensions are the cause of all their troubles and don't seem to realize that their personality and physical condition might be the major cause of their reactions to the church pressures. The result of the tests would show plainly just where the trouble lay, and the advice given by a trained counselor would give the answer to conquering the difficulties. This method would save much blame and hard feelings on the part of both the minister's family and the members of the congregation.

Since Dallas is the jumping-off place for most missionaries before they enter Mexico for their final screening and testing in the Wycliffe Translators jungle camp, we have come to know a great deal about the severe testings through which these young people have to go before they will be accepted by the mission boards and given assignments in foreign countries. If they can't take the climate, the changes in food, the hard, rugged outdoor life, the mission boards have no choice but to refuse to support them on the field. They cannot spend precious, scarce money on training and equipment for missionaries who, perhaps through no fault of their own, can't stand the strain that a foreign country and a different type of life impose on them.

Many of us have been compelled to learn the lessons of life in a hard, bitter way, but we can also learn through the experience of others. Therefore, it is well that you become as friendly with your present minister's wife as she will let you. If you let her know you want to see a true picture of the life of the mistress of the manse, she will usually be more than happy to help you in every possible way. If you feel that she is not the kind of pastor's wife she should be, then certainly you can find someone in your town who will be a worthwhile model. Baby-sit without charge in the manse, if that is the only way you can be accepted freely there. This will give you a chance to see the kind of home your church provides, and you can easily decide if the pastor's family is getting adequate housing. If it is out-dated, maybe you can do something to make it better. Notice in what ways the lady of the manse has overcome the difficulties of an old-fashioned kitchen, how she has decorated to cover up the bad spots on the walls or floors, or slipcovered the furniture. Offer to help when she entertains so you can see her in action when she has to be maid, hostess, mother and cleaning woman. If she has nice ideas for decorations, menus, and light snacks, get her recipes and make a notebook of all the ideas you would like to use when you have the same responsibilities. Above all, try to draw her out in conversation to tell her experiences, both pleasant and hard, and how she handled any problem. She can tell things that happened in other churches without involving local people or betraying confidences. Find out what she con-siders the greatest handicaps and the finest joys of being married to a minister. Weigh these carefully in your mind to see if you are sure that you still want to team up with a clergyman. If you find out that her life is full of bitterness and frustration, be-ware of her advice, for she may lead you down the same path.

From the time a girl promises to marry a ministerial student until he retires from active work, she should spend as much time as possible in reading materials that concern their work, and that will make her be a better wife, homemaker and worker in the church. This may seem hard for some, but the more you read, the more interested you will become in reading until you will find it much more exciting to read than to look at television. At the present, there are only five books about pastors' wives on the market. All that are available should be read. I suggest that you also read the novels that are written about the minister or his wife or family, because they give an unusually true picture of what churches are like and of the way many ministers' families are treated. Before marrying a parson, or a prospective parson, every girl should read *The Gauntlet* by James Street, which depicts so accurately the church life of a small town that

I could have written in the names of the people of our own church while I was reading it. Another book that should be required reading is *The Bishop's Mantle* by Agnes Turnbull. This is the story of a city church and shows the disastrous results when a woman who is not interested in the ministry, or even sympathetic in her attitude marries a minister only because she loves him. Magazines and newspapers are beginning to include numerous articles that concern the ministerial family, because there has been so much misunderstanding between them and the church people. The Christian magazines are continually running articles that will be especially helpful and interesting to ministers and their wives.

If, after all this preparation, you still feel that you are called or being led into a partnership with a minister, then you can be reasonably sure that you have stood the tests and will make a successful parson's wife. At least, you will have a very true picture of what you are getting into and can decide, with this enlightenment, if this is the life you want or not.

Seminary days should be the best time of preparation, but the working wife finds it almost impossible to get the classes and Bible study she should be having. Surveys show that from two-thirds to three-fourths of the seminary students today are married. It also shows that very few of the girls have had any training for their future work and have no good idea of what the average church will expect of them. If the only way a couple can get through seminary is for the wife to work, I wonder if it wouldn't be much better to delay the marriage until she can get her training before she takes on the job of being the family breadwinner.

My husband and I were married after his first year of seminary, after waiting four years. We were together at seminary for three years. We had decided that I would not work but would devote my time to study and training, as I had not had any opportunities for Bible study or pastoral training in the small town where I lived. I could neither admire my pastor's wife nor bring myself to ask for her cooperation. Though I had attended church all my life, I knew almost nothing about the Bible and had longed for a chance to study the Word under godly men. God answered that prayer by sending me to Dallas Theological Seminary with my husband. We knew that my working would leave me totally unprepared for the future God had planned for me. We went without a car or air conditioner, and bought no new clothes the entire three years, but we managed with only a few hours' work a day that my husband could do without affecting his studies. The sacrifice of material things seemed nothing to us compared to the marvelous training I received here. This seminary does not allow women to attend classes, but there were chapel services, special Bible lectures on the sixteen major books of the Bible, wives' prayer fellowship, and special Bible classes taught at night for the wives. Many of us also took the three years' training course in children's work, and taught classes for experience. My husband and I assisted in a Presbyterian church under the leadership of a seminary alumnus, and later served two years in a student pastorate at a small country church. All that I have mentioned, along with the many hours spent in private Bible study with books from the library and in discussions with my husband, gave me training for my work. I pity the working girl who misses all these blessings. It is sad but true that most of them are working just to gain more material things rather than because of necessity. They do not see their need of training but are carried away with the "cares of this world and the deceitfulness of riches." They feel they must have the things they were used to having at home before they were married. They have to have new clothes, the latest cars, television, air conditioning, vacations, meals out, and all kinds of entertainment, all of which take a lot of money.

Most of the seminaries with which I am familiar offer either the entire course, or a large part of it, to women, thus providing a wonderful opportunity for wives to get all the preparation they will need by studying right along with their husbands. Husband and wife will be trained alike, will believe the same things, and be able to work together in greater harmony in the pastorate.

In an article "The Theological Seminary and the Pastor's Wife," by Louise Blount and John H. Boyle in *Pastoral Psychology* we are given the results of a survey made by questionnaires sent to 122 theological seminaries and schools listed by the American Association of Theological Schools. In the 101 seminaries that sent in answers there were 10,558 married students. Three-fourths of those wives were not enrolled in any course in the schools. All but seven of the schools had clubs, either educational, social, or religious, for the wives. Three-fourths of the seminaries make no provision in the curriculum for a class especially for the instruction of student wives in their future role as ministers' wives. Seven answered affirmatively but did not say what they offered. A number of the seminaries had a special, short-term course each winter on the role of the minister's wife. One had a weekend retreat for the wives' instruction. A few had some lectures by local pastors' wives or night classes taught by the professor of pastoral care or the faculty wives. A number of the schools are making definite plans to include more night courses for the wives, although many others said that they could not expand their work to include the needs of the students' wives.

Since most seminaries do not take the responsibility for training ministers' wives and the wives are not availing themselves, in many cases, of the courses open to them, we still will have another generation of poorly prepared clergymen's wives unless each one takes upon herself the responsibility of seeing that she gets the proper education to fit her for her role as pastor's wife.

Even if the seminary wife must work during the day, she can make good use of her time at night and on weekends. She can attend special Bible lectures, classes for wives, fellowship meetings, and classes taught by local ministers' wives. She can also take Bible study courses by herself, if necessary, or perhaps find enough girls who are interested in forming a night class and securing a teacher. This is also an ideal time to join a local church and become very active in its work. It is well to take a job in the church that might put her in constant contact with the minister's wife, who may be willing to watch and coach her on the job. Always watch the minister's wife to discover the things you like and want to copy. Find out why the church ladies like her so much, and then remember those things. If you see there is some trouble between her and the congregation, observe carefully to see what she is doing wrong, and do all you can to avoid those things when you step into a like position. Carefully note whether any problem between her and the church is her fault or is caused by the thoughtlessness of the church members. All of these things will contribute much to educating you for your future ministry.

Working in a church in an unofficial way will also give you valuable experience in dealing with all kinds of people, learning new and effective methods in church work, discovering how to avoid clashing with troublemakers, and helping gather ideas and materials that will be useful later on.

If you like your minister's wife, and can find a few other girls who are interested in some training, it is likely that she will be willing to teach a class to aid future pastors' wives. I teach a class of about forty seminary wives who meet in my home once a week for instruction on this subject. The class was started at the request of a few of my church girls who knew they needed much training and had no other way of getting it. Most of the girls in the class are not members of our church, since all the wives of seminary students, as well as girls from a nearby Bible institute, were invited to attend if they so desired. Though the class takes much of my strength and time, it will be more than worthwhile if I can have a part in preparing forty pastors' wives for the Lord's harvest field. This training will save them many mistakes and heartaches and perhaps make work which might have been frustrating an experience of real fulfillment.

The seminary library is a "pot of gold" for the seminary wife. Probably at no other time and place will she live where she will have access to books on any subject that pertains to her work. She can acquire for herself a full education for her future by just reading, reading, reading, reading!

Since every pastor's wife is expected to be an accomplished speaker from the moment she steps into the first manse, it is wise to learn all you can about public speaking from books and experience. If it is possible to attend classes, that will help. Put yourself in places where you will frequently be asked to teach Sunday school, or give Bible messages or any other kind of message. This will best prepare you for what is to come later.

Though I had had a little experience in public speaking, I was far from prepared for what was to come. A few months after we took our first pastorate, I was asked to speak at a mother-daughter banquet for the entire town. Needless to say, my fright at the prospect of speaking at such an occasion nearly finished me before I started. I'll never know how I managed to get through it. But I did, and—more important— the guests survived, too.

There are so many adjustments to make when you find yourself in your first pastorate that it will be a blessing if you have gained your main training before that time. However, it is never too late to get the help you need. No matter what your circumstances have been, you should have well-established habits of daily Bible study and prayer by this time. If not, delay no longer! Start right now. These habits are essential. We will also assume that you are familiar with your husband's library and use it. Find your nearest public library and—if possible—theological library, and use them regularly.

It was not until I started my writing career that I learned the wealth of material available through library books and gradually developed an insatiable desire for more reading and more learning. I use my library card more than any of my credit cards. In spite of being a well-known speaker, the study of three or four books last year on speech has improved my messages 100 percent. Studying psychology, psychiatry, and counseling books has helped immeasurably in my work among the church people. Never assume that you have achieved the ultimate in any realm of knowledge. Keep your mind open! Because times are changing fast, keep studying. It is the only way you can keep up with the latest methods and facts in any field. Do this for the sake of your marriage as well as the work. Most ministers have had much more education than their wives and will continue to study and grow. If you bring your acquisition of knowledge to a halt, he will soon outgrow you and be ashamed of your ignorance and disappointed in your ineffectiveness in helping him.

If there is no meeting or club for ministers' wives in your town, why don't you start one? In this way the wives can share experiences, learn the customs of the community, and discover what is expected of the minister's wife in that community. You will usually receive sympathy, encouragement, and advice from other ministers' wives of more maturity. At least you will be with others who understand your problems, and can safely "blow off" the steam of resentments which may build up in your work.

An ideal situation would be to find an older, more experienced pastor and his wife who are of like faith, and let them lead you. In our first pastorate we soon found a wonderful couple in a nearby town who had come from the same seminary. We got together every Tuesday night for fellowship and to discuss our problems. I can never be thankful enough for what that minister's wife meant to me. She carried me through the most difficult church we have had and the most trying time of sickness that I have ever experienced. We could trust them implicitly never to repeat a word we said, and thus we were able to express our feelings of resentment over mistreatment by our church members, and we received the help and advice we needed to cope with these things. In their previous experience they had known many of the same troubles, and hence were able to comfort and encourage us on our path.

Many summer Bible conferences have seminars for the clergyman's wife, in addition to the other messages. Most of the denominational churches have meetings from time to time for this same purpose. Always make your plans to attend these, for they will be a great help to you and keep you abreast of the worldwide work of your church.

Of course, experience is always the best teacher, and every one of us will have to learn some lessons the hard way—by trial and error.

If I were asked the same question today—"Just what is a pastor's wife supposed to do?"—that the elder asked me that bitter, cold October night in 1941, my answer would be very different. The pastor's wife should only be expected to do those things that any spiritual Christian mother who is active in the church does, according to her abilities, time, and energy. Time and experience have taught me many things. I have learned that what the Bible says I should be, what my husband wants me to be, and what most of the churches we have served demanded that I be are often very different and at times contradictory. Is it any wonder that the poor seminary wife is in doubt as to just how she is to find her proper place and work as a pastor's wife?

Some of the most sincere girls here at the seminary, who are getting every available help to prepare themselves for their future ministry, have many soul-searching questions. They want to know why so many church members expect special training of the wife when they make it plain that when they call a man they are calling him, not his wife. She makes no promises to the church, nor they to her. She is assigned no part of the salary, and she is given no official duties nor authority. She is a servant of the church only as other Christian women are, and not in the way her husband is. I wish there were an answer to that question, not only for their sakes but for my own, as I myself have never been able to fathom the reasoning of some churches.

This I do know, that the day when the pastor's wife could get by with a sweet disposition and the ability to play the piano is definitely over. Now she must have a liberal education in all fields of church work, for she may even be considered and called upon to work as the assistant pastor. People seem to have the idea that she can be a wife, mother, and homemaker in the leftover time.

While there is no excuse for demanding so much of the parson's wife, I believe that the trend came along with the changes in our social life. Back in the horse-and-buggy days, few women could get out more than once a week—and then, usually, to attend the church services. Women were not well organized in clubs and associations in the church simply because it was considered best for them to be keepers of the home and good mothers. There were no nurseries and baby-sitters, no cars to speed them to many visits and meetings, so women naturally stayed at home. As modern gadgets were developed the women began to have more freedom for outside activities, and nurseries were provided for every meeting, and women hired baby-sitters. As the work of the church increased, the people expected more of both the pastor and his wife.

Since God's Word is the only infallible rule of life for a Christian, we must see what God has to say about the problem. Many times He gives a definite answer of "yes" or "no" to the question, and in all other cases, He lays down principles to guide us in our decisions. Therefore we can depend upon the leading of the Holy Spirit under these general principles of conduct. Anyone with a very elementary knowledge of God's Word will realize that there are no set rules for the clergyman's wife outside of the reference to a leader's wife in the

chapter of instruction on the qualifications of the elders or
bishops in I Timothy 3. In verse 11 we find this: "Even so
must their wives be grave, not slanderers, sober, faithful in all
things." These requirements apply to all Christian women,
and are repeated in other Scriptural portions. So, it is obvious
that from God's viewpoint the pastor's wife is to be no different from other Christian women. All the added responsibilities
that are placed on her are man-made rules to which a minister's
wife may refuse to submit if she wishes. The older Christian
women are instructed to teach the younger ones what God's plan
is for them. This is given in Titus 2:3-5. Here it is definitely
stated that women are to be keepers of the home, lovers of our
husbands and children . . . and obedient to our husbands. Now,
real difficulty arises when the church demands take time that
should be spent in caring for her children, keeping the kind of
home that will be restful and quiet for the husband's study,
and preparing meals that will be best for his health. We are
also told in Genesis 2:18-20 that woman was made for man,
and that she was to be a "help meet" for him, or a suitable
helper. The doctor's wife helps her husband in one way; the
executive's wife in another; and the pastor's wife in still another.
Each of us has to decide, under God's direction and our husband's guidance, just what we can do to be the best kind of
helper to him.

Now look at the situation from the viewpoint of the pastor's
wife, and you can understand the dilemma she faces. She knows
that it is God's first will for her to be a good homemaker,
mother, and wife. Many husbands cannot find trained leadership, or people who will take responsibility seriously in the
church, so there are a number of duties that he wants to turn
over to her, to be sure that they are well done. Then along
come all the church members with a variety of ideas about
what the duties of the wife should be. Only a superhuman
woman can do all of these things! Is it surprising that she
often lives in a state of frustration and wishes with all her

heart that her husband would leave the ministry? Many a fine minister has done just that because his wife was so miserable in the church he was serving.

The wife who is spiritual must do what is God's will first, and a part of that is being obedient to her husband, whether she has any time left for the church people or not. Such a course of action usually brings criticism and misunderstanding on the part of the church members.

Some surveys show that many women—a large percentage— already in the pastoral life have completely given up trying to be themselves, trying to do any of the things they enjoy, and have even given up God's rule for their lives. Why? For fear of hurting a husband's ministry. They have completely conformed to the demands of the church members. This gives the answer to the often-asked question of why so many pastors' wives are resentful, unhappy, frustrated, and even sick. For many of them sickness, either conscious or unconscious, becomes a way of retreat from the pressure put upon them from outside.

Just a word aside to church folks. If you notice any of these attitudes starting in your pastor's wife, instead of criticizing her, try to find out what is causing the trouble and do your best to straighten it out. Show her kindness and appreciation, and release her from so many demands and expectations. You have already lost a pastor's wife, if she feels this way, and you can be well on your way to losing a beloved pastor if it continues. Because he will not want to see his wife unhappy and, perhaps, sick because of the pressure of the church, and because of his love for her, he may start looking for another place of service where his wife will have her freedom.

Ministers' wives, generally, expect little from the congregation. They are doing their work for the Lord's sake and will receive their reward from Him. But an occasional pat on the back, congratulations on a job well done, a word of understanding and appreciation for all the time she gives, and maybe

a luncheon in her honor would do worlds of good to encourage
her to feel her efforts are not unnoticed. Even an orchid can
change the entire outlook of a pastor's wife. It did for me.
My steam gauge of pressure and resentment was sputtering and
giving due warning that it would soon "blow its top" in spite
of the fact that we are serving a pastorate that is the nearest to
perfection of any we know. I had been sick that summer but,
without telling anyone, I had continued all my church activities.
It was often necessary to get out of bed to listen to an hour-long
recital of someone's problems and sicknesses when it was all
I could do to hold my head up, propped against the wall near
the desk chair. Often those same people would end lamely by
saying, "But you wouldn't understand since you are always in
perfect health." Times like that would only add to my resentment and self-pity, though deep in my heart, I knew that many
of my church people truly cared about me and would have
done almost anything to help if they had known my troubles.
I felt nobody cared what happened to me as long as I per-
formed as they thought a pastor's wife should, listening to
people's woes and helping them out in any way they thought
was my "duty." My husband and my doctor felt that I badly
needed a vacation, in spite of my weakened condition, and so
arrangements were made for me to go to the Canadian Keswick
Bible Conference, where my husband was to speak. On the
day of our departure, the elder's wife who had promised to
take us to the airport handed me a box. When I saw the orchid,
I could hardly keep from crying. Some one did really care
about me, and then my mind turned to Christ's discourse in
Matthew 6, on the "lilies of the field." God cared too, and was
watching over me. That flower did as much for me as the week
of rest and the climate in the beautiful Canadian country, and
I came back restored and ready for my church work with cheer-
fulness and joy instead of self-pity and resentment.

It appalls me to hear how many of the wives of ministerial
students here at the seminary are thoroughly frightened at the

prospect of entering a pastorate. A few have said they pray that their husbands will decide to teach, or go into some other kind of Christian service, for they feel they are no match for a congregation. Several said that they felt the mission field would be easier to cope with than a church in this country. It is obvious that they have seen what churches expect of the leaders' wives, how they are treated, and how many of them become ill. It is time for the church to reconsider this matter and try to make the job of pastor's wife attractive instead of frightening, to express appreciation to her instead of criticism, to let her live her own life instead of trying to press her into a mold of preconceived ideas of what she should be.

Last week our seminary received a letter from a church asking for recommendations of men to candidate for their pulpit. The almost unbelievable letter said they were only interested in a man whose wife could play the piano, sing, lead the choir, teach Sunday school, take charge of the young people, be president of the women's organization, and go calling with her husband. Only one sentence in the letter mentioned the qualifications they desired in the pastor. Of course, all information about the church and the letter writer are confidential, but one cannot help wondering what kind of people would have the gall to make such demands of a pastor's wife. I wonder what they think her salary should be? And what kind of house are they providing for her living quarters? And how many servants do they plan to employ to keep the home and take care of her children?

The future pastor's wife knows that she is facing some serious problems in her work. Most of these young women are sincerely trying to be as well prepared for that work as possible. There is so little provision made for studies in her field of future endeavor that in most cases what training she receives will have to come through her own efforts. The seminaries offer a few courses but at present they are generally not able to do anything on a large scale to train the wives of the students. Even in cases where courses are available, it is frequently impossible for the wife to attend because she has to work or has children to care for. The churches have increased their demands of knowledge and work, but they have made no provision to help in the instruction of the wife. They just expect her to be thoroughly prepared to do their bidding when she arrives. The gap between what the church expects and what the wife is able to find in training has to be filled or we will go right on having serious trouble between church members and the pastors' wives.

If church members could be contented with God's standard for the pastor's wife, there would be little or no problem. However, since most churches have not realized that their demands of the wife are unreasonable and unscriptural, she must seek the best training she can find to try to please them.

The ideal time for preparation is before marriage, while the girl is still free to attend a school that can train her. But if she has not done this and is married to a ministerial student, she should take every available course in Bible and the role of the minister's wife that is open to her. She should be active in a church where she can be trained in the latest methods, get experience in teaching and giving Bible messages, and observe the pastor's wife to see if she is liked or disliked, and why. She can always increase her efficiency by reading available books on the minister's wife, psychology, church work, articles in magazines and newspapers, both Christian and secular, and even reading novels written about the ministerial family.

The wife who is already in the pastorate can find help in studying books, taking any available courses offered by her denomination at summer conferences, special retreats, or at nearby seminaries. Much can be gained by meeting regularly with other ministers' wives for discussions, study periods, or general exchange of ideas, and airing grievances. Perhaps the best kind of leadership can usually be found in an older, more experienced pastor and wife who will take an interest in you and your problems, and who will lead and guide through the rough places. Their advice, based on experience, will often be more valuable than all the theories advanced in books written by experts who have never served a pastorate.

Any pastor's wife who really wants to serve the Lord according to His will can be assured that He will never let her down. In many ways, perhaps unknown to us now, He will send the training and help we need when the time comes.

While I do not recommend any show business, actors have a saying that has often helped me to keep going when I felt inadequate for the job before me: "There are no failures in show business. There are only those who quit trying too soon."

CHAPTER 3

Problems of the Pastor's Wife

BEING A PASTOR'S WIFE is the most hazardous and dangerous occupation a woman can have," says Dr. Marion H. Nelson, Christian psychiatrist and author of *Why Christians Crack Up*. He believes that only the best adjusted emotionally, those who have had full love and security in childhood, and who are thick-skinned will ever come through the experience emotionally and mentally unscarred.

Maybe a brief glance at the problems of the wife whose husband serves an average-sized church might give added weight to the reasons why a girl should feel more than a human love is calling her into teaming up with a pastor and show the importance of being well trained for her work so she can accomplish the most with the least effort and mistakes.

In the average church of two to five hundred members where the minister is the only paid worker, the wife has a full-time job in the work of the church, even though the public does not realize it. A group of ministers' wives kept a chart of the time they spent in work that was in any way related to the church or her husband's position. Nearly all discovered that they were spending forty hours a week, or the equivalent of a full-time job for the average worker. This was spread out over seven days, so the wife had no time that she could call her own, and even when she wasn't actually doing something for the church, she had to be on "alert" in case of emergency. There was no leaving the job and coming home because the biggest part of her work centered around her home. To a certain extent everybody in a clergyman's family is in the ministry. Where else can an employer get a man who will work seven days a

week, most nights, and have his wife work forty hours a week
without pay or benefits? These facts may come as a shocking
revelation to many congregations who have taken their leaders
for granted. It may surprise our church members. All I do that
is obvious to the group is to stand at the door to greet people,
entertain in the manse, give devotionals, attend all meetings,
pray for the members daily, and take a keen interest in my
husband's work because I am not an officer in any organization,
and do not teach a Sunday school class.

If this is true in my church, where our people lean over
backwards to make few demands of me and try to spare me
every possible job and inconvenience, what about those poor
wives who are beset by people who are constantly demanding
their services?

The active minister's wife quickly finds herself enmeshed
in time-consuming activities of her church. If one adds the
meetings, services of different kinds, preparation for and presentation of messages, teaching a Sunday school class (which
nearly every pastor's wife said was automatically expected of
her), time spent taking members to and from activities, time
spent in preparing and helping to serve dinners, teas, coffees,
and so on, entertaining members in the manse, counseling with
those who need help, visiting as time allows, writing notes
and sending cards to the sick and bereaved, taking an extra share
of the care and discipline of the children, waiting meals for a
husband who is delayed, and endless telephone calls, the true
picture of the demands on her time begins to come into focus.
Many wives say that they have to do all the office work, including their husband's letters and church bulletins.

Perhaps the most time-consuming job, which no one seems to
realize, is that of answering the telephone where the calls do not
go directly to the pastor or through the church office. My housework was suffering, so I began to check the time consumed by
incoming telephone calls. Three to four hours a day were used
for that purpose. There are always families who are in distress

and need comfort, and we also get numbers of calls from people who have no church connections or who have not found the answer to their problems in their own churches. I do believe that the two weeks I checked the telephoning time was a little unusual. However, fifteen calls came last Saturday morning while I was trying to clean. They were short and businesslike, but still took a lot of time and steps. Yesterday we had ten telephone calls. We want our people to call us when they need help, but some thoughtless people can do much to hinder our work. Whenever there is to be an unusual service, picnic, or dinner, everyone in our family is given the information concerning the affair so that whoever answers the telephone can give that information. Our girls take our calls when they are at home and can screen out the advertisements, solicitors, and wrong numbers. One morning my husband was very busy getting things ready for a young people's camp when someone called, asking for him. It took so long for him to come from the garage and wash his hands, that I also answered the phone to explain the delay. When my husband finally arrived, the person on the other end wanted to know the time of a church meeting. Anyone in the house could have given that information! All of our church meetings are announced in the newspaper and the church bulletins, so a call of that nature should not be necessary, anyway. An unusual number of calls are from those who ask for the phone number or address of a church member. There seems to be no excuse for that either, as each member of our church is furnished with a church directory, and everyone has a telephone book. Even if the number is not in the book, it would be just as easy to call Information at the telephone office, as to call the manse.

It isn't long after a girl marries before she suddenly realizes that she didn't marry a man, she married a MINISTER! And there is a gulf between that is difficult to span.

For the first few years, while the husband's duties are not too heavy, there is usually a happiness in working and traveling with him and living in the reflected honor and glory that come just from being his wife. The enthusiasm which a young—perhaps well-trained—woman feels will let her overlook those who oppose them, the condition of the manse, and any other smaller troubles that may arise. Being in good health, with only the care of her husband, she has plenty of time for church work, which is usually a wonderful outlet for her training and extra energy. Quite often, it is not until the children begin to arrive that she fully realizes what is involved in her position. The wife's enthusiastic activities and trips and enjoyment of the reflected glory from her husband's success are suddenly taken away from her. Now, her days include long hours of child care, staying at home alone while her husband cares for the work of the church. Many times a resentment of her children, her husband, and the church begins to creep in. She is human, like any other woman. She is often tempted to think that her husband belongs to every member of the church before he belongs to her. Their wishes inevitably conflict with hers, and her husband has to give his time to them first. This feeling is heightened by the fact that there are a few in every church who demand attention they don't really need, when often his wife really needs his help at home. To make matters worse, there are also usually a few who deliberately try to subtly attract the attention of the minister by covering their real motives with many superficial excuses for needing his counsel. One girl made a very true remark, while trying to keep the bitterness out of her voice, "I am surprised that the churches don't demand that the vows in the minister's wedding be different. It is a wonder that they don't make the bride promise to love, honor, and obey every member in her husband's pastorates, because that is what they are really requiring now. I didn't marry a husband; I married a church!"

Along with the coming of children into the family, come added financial burdens. A minister's wife will find that she will have to go without the little luxuries she used to enjoy, because the money must stretch to cover new expenses. Sometimes there are no salary increases and the couple experience real hardship. At least the missionaries receive more salary with each new baby.

Another problem arises with the coming of children. After the first glow of admiration and calling on the new arrival, the church routine settles down into the same rut, and the minister's wife will find that the ladies expect as much of her as they did before the children arrived. In some miraculous way, she is supposed to dispose of the little ones while she continues in her usual duties in the church. It often hurts terribly, when she sees a lack of understanding and obvious indication of that fact on the part of the ladies when she says that she just can't attend a meeting or speak at a conference because she must care for her children. One disillusioned and weeping parson's wife said, "No minister's wife is supposed to have children, especially sick ones. She is supposed to have no housework, no ideas of her own, she must never be tired, never want a vacation or want to have any time to herself." She said much more, but the idea is there! This shows the burdened heart of a woman who is giving every ounce of strength to the Lord's work, only to be pushed beyond her endurance by thoughtless church members. There has probably never been a minister's wife who has not at times dissolved into tears and said, "Lord, I just can't take this any longer."

There is always a day in the life of every lady of the manse when she suddenly realizes that she is required to be four persons in one, besides trying to be herself with some wishes of her own. She must be a good wife who takes care of her husband with special and extra attention to his needs in order to leave him free for the work of his ministry. She must be a good mother who brings up her children as she thinks best, without enough time and strength—and at times—without enough money to really meet their needs—all this under the watchful eyes of the church members, who may have very different ideas of how ministers' children should be trained! She must be a good housekeeper. Ministers' families often live in homes that are old and rambling and inconvenient; yet they must be kept in spotless order and ready for the inspection of church members or the community. She must be a good helpmeet to her husband, doing the things in the church which the congregation thinks are her duties because of her position. It should be obvious to everyone that no human being is adequate for such a schedule.

In case some mystified church members have strayed this far into a book for ministers' wives, perhaps we can explain some things you don't understand about them. In case you think the wives are being unfair in their uprising to recapture their husbands and to be a normal family, just consider a few facts. Statistics of the Ministers Life and Casualty Union show that the average minister works seventy hours a week. This does not include any of the time that his wife spends on church activities. He must be pastor, preacher, priest (weddings, sacraments, funerals), teacher, administrator, and organizer. Many a minister puts in ten hours a day, seven days a week, on the job. If he is allowed eight hours of sleep (which few ever get), four hours for eating, grooming himself, and a few other personal things, that takes twenty-two hours out of the twenty-four. He still must have time for his family, his wife, do some personal shopping and get a hair cut, and so on. That leaves very little time for his family life and his neglected wife, and no time at all for any recreation. This same insurance company has worked out the hours of the ministers, as compared to those of the average jobholder. The minister works seventy hours a week, while the layman spends forty hours on the job and is constantly demanding shorter hours and more pay. For family, household tasks and leisure, the minister has twenty-eight hours a week, and the layman has fifty-eight.

Moneywise, there is a great difference, too. A national survey, made by the National Council of Protestant Churches, reveals that the average minister is paid $4,500.00 a year, besides the use of a rent-free manse, for from sixty to eighty hours' work a week. If we add $1,200.00 per year for the rent-free house, as a part of the salary, the total income of the minister is usually around $5,700.00 a year, or $475.00 a month, or $118.75 a week, or $1.69 an hour. Also, remember that his education includes four years in college and at least three years in seminary, and often more time for additional study. This does not include the wife's work. Maybe this picture will give you some idea as to why the wives are rebelling and are beginning to make themselves heard by the congregations. The minister seldom is able to ask for an increase in salary, even when he is in real need, and most congregations think they are paying enough or can't afford any more. Numbers of fine Christian people feel that Christian workers should not need or want much of this world's material things; these people feel that the standard of living for the minister is different from theirs. It reminds one of the deacon's prayer for his pastor, "Lord, you keep him humble; we'll keep him poor."

The minister has no union to see that he gets overtime for his work, or health insurance, or such benefits as usually come from working for a company. He can seldom afford enough insurance for his old age or to protect his family in case of his death. Only recently has the government included ministers in the federal social security program whereby they can have some old-age assistance. Some of the denominations have set up old-age benefits, but many such programs are completely inadequate. We figured that the denomination that ordained my husband would pay me less than $15.00 a month in case of his death, and only $25.00 for both of us after we reached the age of sixty-five.

Perhaps the minister's salary may seem rather large to some poorer church members, but the expenses of the minister must be taken into consideration. Many ministers spend as much money for gasoline in pastoral work as they do for the weekly food bill, and only a few churches give a car allowance. It takes another week's food budget to entertain members of a church board and their wives for dinner, and even more to have an open house, even when all of the cooking and work is done by the pastor's wife. The pastor and his wife usually have to entertain visiting guest speakers and missionaries and have to maintain a higher standard of dress and more attractive homes than the average church member does. They are constantly called upon to make contributions to charitable organizations and are dunned for money by transients. Last month, my husband got a call from a man who said he and his family were broke and stranded in Dallas. He wanted him to come to a certain hotel downtown and lend the family $200.00. We wouldn't have given them the money if we had had it. A young lady, dying of an incurable disease, whom I befriended by letter, gifts and money decided to let me nurse her and pay her bills for the rest of her life. She was fifteen hundred miles away and did not let me know in time to stop her coming. The Lord took a hand and only enabled her to travel the first five hundred miles. So she hasn't reached here—yet. These are unusual cases but there are many where we feel compelled to help financially.

By far the greatest suffering of the consecrated minister's wife comes from feelings within her that cannot be expressed to others, not from external things, such as the work expected of her, or the difficulties encountered with the conditions in the manse, or even the financial sacrifices entailed. Many a pastor's wife may smile beautifully on the congregation at church meetings and yet be carrying a broken heart. In spite of giving her all to the work, she is painfully aware of the fact that she is not measuring up to what is expected of her. When she is pleasing one group, she is alienating another. What pleases one woman is many times considered wrong by another. There is no such thing as satisfying all the members at once. Most of us can't understand why, when we are doing our very best, we are still considered so lacking by many of the members. Not only is this true, but the pastor's wife is seldom encouraged or thanked for what she does that is pleasing. She is usually taken for granted unless she makes a mistake that brings down the wrath of the congregation. Some wives tell me that they never feel completely relaxed, because they have a sensation of tiptoeing between closely placed eggs, always fearful of stepping on one. If one is broken, the result is always trouble.

Being human, we like praise and appreciation for our work as much as others do, yet most of the ministers' wives I contacted said little was ever done for them personally. Often a pastor is given a birthday party or a special dinner in his honor for one reason or another; he is always received into a new church with a reception, and another is given at the time that he leaves. None of the wives I know had ever been honored for years of faithful, quiet service. Never had a luncheon, or a party just in her honor, been given just to show her that she is appreciated. A baby shower was all that was called to my attention. Only a few had even received cards, notes of thanks, or any flowers for special occasions, either in the church or in her personal life. Is it any wonder that sometimes a minister's wife feels that everything she is doing is in vain?

Another feeling that comes from within the woman is the heartache she experiences because she is usually placed second in her husband's life. His vows to the Lord and to the church must come first, and many church members take advantage of this, making it very hard for her not to feel like a neglected wife. After this goes on for a few years, she begins to think that she is inadequate and inferior and not as attractive to her husband as she once was. She even lets doubts slip in as to whether his affection for her has changed, or if he finds more happiness in church work and people than he does with her. Such thoughts cause one of the most serious marital problems in the manse, often leading to self-pity and a feeling that she will always be married to a man who has two loves . . . and she is second on the list. This feeling is often the basis of the wives' resentment toward church members which so frequently cannot be understood by the congregation. This is only natural, as the wife can't go around scolding the people for making demands on her husband's time that she feels should be hers.

In a novel, *Papa's Wife,* Thyra Ferré Bjorn tells the story of the life of her mother. She was a poor girl who worked as a domestic helper in the manse of a bachelor and later married him. She soon learned two lessons that are just as true in this country as in Europe where they lived. "The pastor's duty to his church always comes first," and "A pastor is supposed to please everyone but himself." The second truth kept her from being overwhelmed by the first. Perhaps her large family, and her ability to make her husband do what she wanted though he believed he was making his own decisions, had a lot to do with her not being overwhelmed.

Still another type of suffering a minister's wife knows, which comes from within, is the lack of understanding on the part of the church women when she cannot take part in every activity of the church. Many women even expect her to be interested in Christian groups outside the church. When we are asked to attend these meetings, or to speak, and have to refuse, we are usually crushed by the hurt tone of voice that says, *Oh, this is just once a month; once a week; once a year; and just this time!* Little do they realize that when she adds all those "once's" together, she would need all of every day to do them. To them the thing they are asking sounds like a small thing, but they have failed to put together the pieces of the day of the minister's wife. If they did, they would see that what they request is impossible.

There is also a deep-seated psychological problem among the church people that causes much suffering for the wife. Dr. Smiley Blanton, psychiatrist at the Marble Collegiate Church in New York, gives the underlying drive that pushes people into demanding that the wife of their parson be perfect. He explains it in this way: "The minister is given the respect and love of his parishioners—which we will call emotional transference—a powerful factor in his work. Strangely enough, the wife usually gets what we call negative transference. The more the parishioners like the minister, the more critical they are of his wife. They hate anyone who takes the minister away from them." They realize that by rights his wife has more call on his attention than they do, and they resent it so bitterly, though perhaps unconsciously, that they take it out on his wife.

The Boston University School of Theology is making a three-year study of conflicts and psychological problems of the minister's wife. They have completed only two years of their work, so of course it cannot be published yet. They have released several things that give an insight into the causes of much heartache. One is the fact that a truly dedicated man often feels that he must make a martyr of himself for the sake of mankind, whether a man is a member of his church or not. His first duty must be the saving of people, many of whom are only using him in some way for their own purposes. In his dedication, he is too innocent to see what is happening. This brings concern to his wife because she sees what is happening to her husband physically and emotionally as he takes on the "problems of the world." It also bothers her to see how she and her family are affected when they are given so little time with him.

And right along this line comes an even more serious problem. Even when a husband makes a conscious effort to take time to be with his family, they are uncomfortably conscious that he is making a special effort, or that while he is with them in body, his mind is occupied with the problems and burdens of the church people, plans for a building program, suggestions to be made at the next board meeting, how to handle a deliberate troublemaker, or ideas for a sermon. And then there's the possibility that the telephone might ring, making it necessary for him to leave for some church duty.

Churches take different attitudes about the ministerial family and the type of person the pastor's wife must be. Some really don't care what she is like and ignore her. Others like her as she is, and still others want to change her a little but don't take it too seriously. Because they love her, they are willing to overlook some of her "faults." But there is always a fairly large group of very active, interested church people who are determined to make the minister's wife over to conform to just the picture they have formed in their own minds. The sad part is that the ones who give advice like a mother are usually the faithful workers, the loyal supporters, the sweet kind ones "who wouldn't hurt a fly." And they make the most trouble. But, because of their position, and because they can't see what they are doing and would be terribly hurt if told, it is impossible to explain all this to them. In reality, they are narrow-minded, inconsiderate, rigid, bound by tradition, and are judging by standards not in God's Word. Though they may not be conscious of it, they have firmly set themselves to correct the faults of the mistress of the manse, cost what it may. And cost it does! When a woman tries to fit herself, or be fitted, into a mold that does not fit her personally or spiritually there is bound to be psychological pressure. Something explodes! Usually, it is the minister's wife! The troubles often come on gradually, so that they are not recognized until they become acute and hard to cure. There is a trapped feeling that leads to self-pity; then resentment leads to bitterness. Frustrations of all kinds that are not dissolved lead to despair and a feeling of depression. Then follows sickness that is often mostly psychosomatic and, finally, nervous and emotional problems that sometimes lead to a complete nervous breakdown.

Recently a Dallas newspaperman, who admittedly is not a member of any church, wrote such an illuminating article on this subject that it is hard to believe that it wasn't written by a minister's wife under an assumed name. His conclusions for the sad relationships between the congregations and the minister's spouse are seconded by my friends. He feels that members of every congregation have an image in their minds of just what they expect the minister's wife to be. If she falls short of that (and in most cases she does, of course, because she is HUMAN!), she is the target of a systematic program to pressure her into the mold that they have set as her standard. He says that, in most cases, the pastor's wife is just what the church makes her. She can easily be a happy, helpful friend to all, or a sickly, nervous, suspicious and resentful woman. Unfortunately, he couldn't give any truly helpful ways of overcoming this fact except to beg the church people to "let the pastor's wife live her own life and be happy." He further advised, "Leave her alone and treat her like other members of the church, expecting no more of her than you would of yourself, or any other member. Remember that she is not a paid servant, to jump at the slightest wish of a church member."

A number of ministerial students' wives, and those who are already in the pastorate, have asked how to bring about a sweet, understanding relationship between the congregation and themselves. There is no pat answer for every situation. Would to God there were. We just have to live very close to God and be led momentarily by the Holy Spirit, doing what He shows is right, and leave the results to Him. If I made any concrete suggestions, they probably wouldn't work with your special problem, anyway, because there are differences in churches as there are in people born in the same family. As long as you know that you are doing the Lord's will, then you need suffer no pangs of remorse, for you know that you have pleased the Lord.

In "Hidden Heartaches of the Minister's Wife," in *Coronet* magazine, Lucy Freeman neatly sums up the problem by saying, "The minister's wife is expected to practice more than their husbands preach; many must make perfect homes; raise perfect children; live perfect lives on less than living wages and often without love or understanding from the congregation."

CHAPTER 4

Double Rewards

I FEEL SORRY for anyone who is not a pastor's wife." This remark by Mrs. Fry, wife of the pastor of the First Presbyterian Church of Dallas, was quoted in a local newspaper at the time the couple came to take up their work. That is just the way every pastor's wife should feel. Now I feel this way, too, but there was a time when I didn't. In our first pastorate, I found it difficult to find joy in my position. I was miserable until I learned, with God's help, to gladly accept my position as a challenge instead of a duty. Then, instead of feeling abused, I wanted to be helpful. I exchanged my resentment against those who did not agree with me—or fought my husband—for a cheerful acceptance of God's planning. I let my heart open with real godly love for the members of our congregation. I learned to pray instead of pushing my ideas through. I forgot self in service. Such changes not only added to my usefulness— to my husband and the congregation—but they brought almost immediate improvement in my physical health.

When we were children, it was fun to place a quarter close to our eyes and see how much we could see of the scenery around the edge before the coin cut off our vision, as we brought it closer to our eyes. Many of us pastors' wives are letting the "coin" of the difficulties we encounter in our work so hide the beautiful scenery of the love and privileges of being in that position that we find no pleasure or fulfillment in the Lord's work.

Before we let the difficulties and problems of pastorates, as portrayed in the last chapter, sink too deeply into our consciousness, let us have a look at the joys and rewards that come from teaming up with a minister in Christian service.

The keenest reward of being married to a minister, is, I feel, that God allowed me to have one of the finest and most godly men for a husband. He is completely dedicated to his work, has a real purpose in life, and puts God's will above all else. Money never enters his decisions, and he never strives for ways of advancing himself. He has taught us through his life to trust God for everything and to leave every detail of our lives in His hands. We know that what comes to us of financial means is just what the Lord in His sovereign will wants, and we never have to worry about our needs, be they small or large, because we know "all things work together for good." No joy compares to being married to a man who knows the Word, feels the same things, believes the same way, and lives before his family the way he preaches. When wives tell me of husbands who are philanderers, heavy drinkers, unsaved, unreasonable, and worldly, I thank God again and again that it was His will for me to be a preacher's wife. I need no greater reward than to know that my husband does only those things that are for the good of his family and others, and that I have been given the very important though often behind-the-scenes job of helping him.

The second cause for such personal satisfaction from my position in life is the knowledge that my children are growing up in the best kind of home environment and have the constant example and training of godly parents. What better place can a child be than in a home where God is Head, where the Bible is read each day, and where prayer is as much a part of life as talking to members of the family? What better place can be found for them to see faith in action, to experience how God can be trusted to work out every situation in their lives and to find that His will is best for their lives? In the manse they can learn to discipline their lives, to share with others, to witness to the unsaved, to give unselfish service in the church, and learn how to live in a way that is pleasing to God. Unless the parents are thoughtlessly neglecting their children, the manse or the parsonage is the best training ground for rearing Christian children and preparing them for future service in God's harvest field.

Growing up in the manse brings many wonderful rewards to preachers' children other than spiritual benefits. They are exposed to the most godly and also the most interesting people on earth. Missionaries are entertained in the home, and the children get firsthand impressions of many countries and often receive unusual souvenirs for their collections. Sometimes they get names of children their age in foreign countries and have interesting contacts through correspondence. Even more important is the opportunity they have to see and feel the need of getting the Gospel out to the far corners of the world.

Some of the ministers whom we know have had as much influence on our girls' lives as we have had and their wives are models which our girls hope to emulate some day. They see that Christianity is not just a "job" for their parents but it is a real and living reality in the lives of many others. They soon discover that there is more real fun and genuine joy among Christians than they ever see in the lives of people who live in worldly ways.

My older daughter has had unusual opportunities to meet people from all walks of life. She has learned early in life to be a charming hostess and not to be embarrassed at meeting anyone. Though she is only fifteen she can talk appropriately to the cleaning woman or to the president of a college. She knows many high government officials, and is constantly thrown into contact with highly educated people such as atomic scientists, authors, professors, and outstanding professional people. She is equally at home with her teen-age friends, seminary couples, adult church members, or millionaires. Poise in meeting people has become second nature for her and will be a valuable asset for her future, whatever the Lord has planned for her to do. Our younger daughter, though only seven, is following right in her sister's footsteps.

A minister and his wife, moving to a new parish, may be pretty sure of one thing: they have been under some critical, microscopic observation and have been approved by all or the larger part of the congregation. Such approval is a kind of encouragement which people in many other lines of work do not receive when they move. This was clearly brought to our attention about a year after we started in our first pastorate. During a dinner party at an elder's home, his wife told me that it was a disappointment to her that I was teaching young people when I had so much excellent training and experience in children's work. What she said came as a surprise since we had never talked to anyone in the church about my work with children. When asked how they found out, she said, "You'd be surprised how much we know about you folks." They had even written to my husband's high school principal about his grades and his attitude in school, and had asked for a general evaluation of the kind of minister he thought Dwight would make. They had people in Philadelphia check on his parents and what his brothers and his sister were doing. They had also received a full report on my background, my education, and my training and qualifications for being a minister's wife.

The minister's family is immediately accepted in a new town not only by the church members but by the community also. They are respected and looked up to and receive many courtesies not extended to other strangers. People may watch you, and even criticize a bit, but at least they all know you and greet you. Likewise the pastor and his wife soon get to know all the church members and many of the most important people in the community. The minister's family feel right at home as soon as they move into the manse. The children are sought out at school and have a host of friends and are asked to all the children's activities without question. Others who move into the same town may find it very difficult to make any friends, or may have to wait a long time to be invited to parties, dinners, and even church sometimes. The parson and his family are singled out for special attention, receptions are given for them, and they are entertained in many of the church homes. They begin to make lasting friends from the day they arrive.

Moving to different parts of the country and living in various kinds of homes is a certain part of the life of the minister's wife. If you are the adventuresome kind of person, such moves can be a real blessing. I pity people who say they have lived in the same city or the same house all their lives, for I am in a position to know just how much they have missed. Going from one place to another gives one a broader view of our country and of life. We not only get to see the varied topography of our nation and historical spots, but we observe new customs, types of people, and ways of doing things. The children get a liberal education in American history and geography the easy, enjoyable way.

At first, we lived in northwestern Pennsylvania, where in the winter we saw a wonderland of ice and snow, with picturesque bobsleds and cutters, pulled by horses with bells around their necks. I saw things that I had only read about in children's storybooks. The moonlight rides on sleds down long hills and the hot dogs and hot cocoa enjoyed afterwards with a crowd at someone's home will be a lifetime memory. While we lived there we visited some of our largest industrial cities, Niagara Falls (much too late for our honeymoon), and the central part of Canada.

We were in the Philadelphia area for over eight years, and during much of that time we lived only three miles from Valley Forge. Taking our frequent visitors there and to the historical showplaces of Philadelphia made us brush up on our knowledge of our nation's history. We were also able to see all of New England, get into the French sections of Canada, and see Washington, D.C.

Now we live in the great Southwest where there are fabulous

places to be seen—vast deserts, rocks, mountains, and gulf coast. We have seen the mesa and the bare, rocky mountains of New Mexico with their ever-changing colors, the Grand Canyon, and all the nearby national parks. Our children have seen more of our country than have any of their classmates and, no matter what part of this great land is studied in school, our girls can make a contribution to the study because they have visited those places. My husband and I have also seen the West Coast many times and hope soon to take the children there with us.

Admittedly, we have had our troubles with the church-provided homes, but that is a real challenge to us, too. We like to see how our furniture looks in different kinds of houses. We enjoy using our ingenuity in planning and fixing up each house we live in. Now that we have a new house, my husband looks around a little longingly for something he can do around the house to change things. Happily, he now has a cottage at a nearby lake that has to be almost completely rebuilt, and he can use his plans and energy on that project. He is making it into such a well-equipped vacation place for us that it could be used for a year-around home.

While moving takes time and is an added expense, each move is worthwhile because we acquire many new friends. We have good friends in almost every part of this country and in some foreign countries. (My husband has had seven speaking engagements in foreign countries.) This entire nation is "home" to us. No matter where we go, there are always friends there to greet us and make us feel as if we belong.

Moving around also helps us to know what an interesting and refreshing variety of people there are—from the cold, reserved New Englanders all the way to the unusually friendly Texans, who receive people on the basis of what they are and not on the amount of money they have. All of these people have added to our lives something precious that can never be taken away from us. A flood of letters from former church members, conference delegates, strangers met while on trips, former students of my husband, wedding invitations and birth announcements, keep reminding us of the lives we have touched and of people we have been able to help.

From a purely selfish standpoint, I feel it is worth the extra pressure of being a pastor's wife just for the opportunities I have been given to have many vacations in this country and in foreign countries. But for my husband's position, I probably could count my vacations these twenty-five years on my fingers. My husband takes as many speaking engagements as he can squeeze into his busy schedule. Usually I am invited to come with him, and I am entertained free while we are there. All of his expenses are taken care of so our only expense is my transportation. His honorarium takes care of that. Since he travels frequently, and to many distant places, I have a nice choice of the places I would like to see and of the time of year I would like to go.

Perhaps my most enjoyable winter was when my husband was teaching at the Philadelphia Bible Institute (he did not then have a pastorate). He supplied a church in Atlantic City the entire winter. We were entertained for the entire weekend in a hotel. There are few people in our income bracket who could afford every weekend at the seashore for nine months.

A most versatile and challenging career is open to every pastor's wife. Her position is a channel and outlet for all of her talents and abilities. Instead of being confined to one chosen work or profession—or just housework—and having to stay in that field for a lifetime, the parson's wife has the opportunity to take part in almost every kind of work open to women. She is not only a mother and homemaker but she can be a spiritual leader, Bible teacher, children's worker, a lecturer, teacher, artist, interior decorator, advisor, counsellor, comforter, telephone operator, camp director, young people's worker, musician, nurse, visitor, a trainer of other women for leadership jobs, writer, entertainer, and official hostess for many wonderful dinners and meetings for the church. And, if she wishes, she can take an active part in all community affairs. The list could go on and on. There is no useful and worthwhile interest of the pastor's wife and no part of her training that cannot be of help to some group in a church.

The minister's wife has another advantage, she can switch from one activity to another as her interest changes or as the needs of the church develop. She can work on one project for a while and then start another. She can stop when she wishes. She can take a few days off when she desires without the consent of a boss, and she can take longer periods for vacations or family needs at any season of the year. Since she is not paid by the church, she can stop doing everything completely, if she wishes, or until she feels like starting again.

A Seattle pastor's wife uses her unusual musical ability to reach hundreds of children. As she teaches them piano, she wins them to the Lord Jesus Christ. The highest ambition of many of these children is to be able to play well enough to play for Sunday school or a church service. Thus she is serving a number of meaningful purposes: She is pursuing her hobby and talent, which gives her relaxation and recreation, which all pastors' wives need. She wins children to the Lord. And she is able to direct them into active service and attendance in the church. The money she earns is of the least importance to her because her husband makes an excellent salary. However, she has been able to give unusual amounts of money to church and missionary projects as well as to assist in paying for the education of their children.

There need never be a dull moment or time of loneliness for the mistress of the manse. She lives in the middle of a steady stream of humanity. Life is so interesting that every day brings a new set of duties, a bevy of pleasant surprises, someone in sorrow or weighed down with burdens that make our difficulties look so small that we are ashamed of any self-pity in which we might be tempted to indulge.

We are constantly told by some of the greatest people of our generation and by doctors that keeping busy and regularly touching the lives of many kinds of people is the real spice of life and keeps one young, happy, and healthy. Therefore, we pastors' wives can be thankful for the place that God has chosen for us to serve Him. We have the greatest joy, the greatest opportunities, the greatest variety of work, and sometimes the greatest burdens. But that is what makes a full and purposeful life.

Many times, as a youngster, I fussed about having chores assigned me in our home. My mother used to say, "Work is the greatest blessing that God has given us." Of course, I did not believe that then, but now I have learned the truth of those words. It is wonderful to awaken each morning with my head full of the things that should be done that day. To have meaningful work gives a real interest in living and a purpose for being. There are days when God has plans for me other than those anticipated before arising. My own plans are set aside because God sends other work for me to do and people who need help and comfort. My prayer on waking each morning is, "Lord, what do You have for me to do today?" Little do I know the answer to that prayer. The day is often changed and full of a mixture of pleasant and unpleasant surprises. Whatever comes, I know that no matter how tired I am, or even if I do not feel well, He will give me strength for the tasks that He sends for that day.

The secret of finding fulfillment and true joy in this type of life is to be flexible and completely willing to let the Holy Spirit be your guide throughout the day. This is not easy for many of us who are not personally constructed that way, but we can all change. I did. I was a rigid person who had to be very systematic in doing my housework. For that reason, constant interruptions, such as those which come to the lady of the manse, were a frustration to me until I learned that it was a lot more fun to live a not too rigidly planned life. I found it was most important to be happy to follow God's will for my life.

Now there is real joy in waiting to see what new activity or experience the Lord will send into my life today. I had planned to write this morning, but the telephone rang while I was typing this sentence and my morning has just been changed for me and, in addition, another engagement has been added for next week.

There are many tired, bored, listless people in this world who retreat into self-pity and psychosomatic illnesses just because they do not have enough interests in life or enough work to do. When my bones ache and my resentment has flared up as a result of some member who has undertaken to set my life straight according to her ideas, or when my nerves refuse to relax after an exciting day of teaching, counselling, or helping others in various ways, I can still be very thankful that the Lord has given me more work than can be accomplished rather than a dull, monotonous job. I can be thankful for many friends and for those who need me and make full demands on my strength and interest. The Lord put me through a period of not being needed and I found life so dull that I was tired, and spent most of my time feeling just as sorry for myself as I had when in a pastorate. It did not take me long to learn what a priceless position I had had as a pastor's wife.

When my husband announced that he felt it was God's will for him to give up his last pastorate and go into full-time teaching (he was already teaching part time), I breathed a sigh of relief and a prayer of thanks because a whole series of events in the church had put me in a rather stubborn mood. There would be no carrying of other people's burdens, no more telephone calls at all hours of the day and night, no more living in the category of "the pastor's wife" instead of being just plain Dorothy Pentecost, no more being a personage who is watched and criticized, but now I was a person in my own right. My time was now my own. No longer would I have to be told that what I did or did not do might injure my husband's ministry. Now we could live in our own home and we could entertain or not, and we could entertain those we chose. All restrictions and requirements were suddenly removed. . . . BUT, so were a lot of other things I soon realized had become a part of the life I loved!

We bought our first home and moved into a suburban Philadelphia town. For a little while my newfound freedom was exhilarating, and the extra hours of rest and just being lazy quickly restored my strength and sense of humor. Most of our free time that first year was spent in redoing our fifty-year-old house, and traveling on the weekends. But that was soon over, and life settled into a dull routine of only housework and child care. The telephone never rang, no neighbor called; not even a church member came to invite me to attend. Nobody needed me or expected anything from me, or even cared if I were alive.

Instead of my husband coming in and out of the house through the day and being home for lunch, he went to town early in the morning and did not return until dinner time. Two nights each week he stayed in town to teach in night school. The quietness of our big house was almost more than my kindergarten-aged daughter and I could stand. She became so listless and sickly that the doctor said she must be put into school and have some friends. I finally persuaded a pastor to let her into a church school, and I went up and down the streets trying to find some friends and entice them, by promises, to come to our home to play with her.

We joined a large, independent church where we knew she would have good Bible teaching—one that could be reached by public transportation, as my husband had to travel every weekend for speaking engagements. We felt it was wrong, after that first winter, to take her from church service to church service without consistent teaching in Sunday school and being in the same church week after week. Having our closely knit family divided on Sundays was the greatest heartache we experienced through this period. We never got used to it, since we were so used to working as a team in one church—our own.

This change in my life not only taught me what it was like to enter a new community as a stranger and be ignored but it also taught me what it was like to be a "nobody" in a new church instead of the pastor's wife. Even the people who sat around me never spoke, and the church was so full of cliques, the members did not show any interest in new people. Though the new members were introduced at a reception for them, I doubt if I met two dozen people—except for the members of my Sunday school class—in the four years we were members there, though I did all I could to make myself known and show friendliness.

In spite of the fact that most of the leaders knew that I was formerly a pastor's wife and a well-trained church worker, they never gave me a job to do. For four years I just sat and watched people move around me as though I was not there. But for the happiness and training of my daughter, and the extreme friendliness of the pastor and his wife, I would have left the church.

When we moved to Dallas for my husband to teach at the seminary, we joined a small, independent church. But to my surprise, the members there ignored me, and it was six months before any of them found out that I was the wife of the professor who was teaching the couples' Sunday school class. In both Philadelphia and Dallas I had to find my Christian activities outside the church. In Philadelphia, I did almost full-time voluntary child evangelism work. In Dallas, I began writing object lessons, articles, and children's stories. This has become a vital part of my life now. While all this was a heartbreaking experience for me, it taught me a priceless lesson—the importance of seeing that each person who joins our church gets a warm welcome not only from us but from many members of our church, and that even the ones who just visit us are made to feel wanted and at home.

Just as I had decided that my desire to be a pastor's wife was gone, the minister resigned to go abroad to study, and my husband was asked to become pastor of the church along with his seminary duties. For four years now, we have been back in the pastorate. In spite of the problems and resentments, the sore feet and jaded nerves, I feel that I have reached "home" again. This is where I belong!

The minister and his wife are aided in many ways with their financial needs, though many of them overlook this fact when they complain about poor salaries. Many churches not only provide a free home, such as it is, but often pay the utility bills and pay for all repairs and upkeep on the manse. We began to realize how much we had been receiving in hidden benefits, when we bought our own house. Now when anything needs replacing or repairing, we have to do it ourselves, or pay someone else for the job. There is no calling a trustee who will send someone to have it done, with the church paying the bill. If those who complain so bitterly would honestly add up the cost of buying and maintaining a home, they would soon shut up. The house they could afford just might not be as nice as the "poor" one the church has lent them.

It is impossible to accurately measure the help that is received, free of charge, from the church people. The love and appreciation that come with the work done mean so much to us. The orthodontist has worked on both of our children's teeth. He worked on one for over two years. Judging from the groaning of friends and relatives who have had to have similar work done, we estimate that the bill would probably have put our budget into orbit. Our family dentist does his best job on our teeth, and he also sees that we get immediate appointments, though we know of others (even his wife) who have had to wait for weeks, or even a month. In the smaller communities all of our family doctors have taken care of our family without charge, and our church doctors here in Dallas do the same.

Many churches carry over an earlier idea that the minister be paid a smaller salary and then receive needed help from the church people, individually, according to their abilities. Sometimes this way of providing for the minister's family makes them seem like beggars with their hands always out for help. We would rather be paid a good salary and pay our own way. In a city as large as this we are seldom treated free, and only occasionally given a discount, which is as it should be, we feel. We happily receive services from our church members, but always pay for others. We feel that it is a reproach to Christianity to expect the public—and especially the unsaved—to help support the ministerial family.

When we moved into this new home, we needed a door in one of the bedrooms. The job was done for us without charge by an excellent workman sent to our house by the president of a construction company who is a member of our church. His wife, who is the interior decorator for his homes, offered to take me to several places where she could buy fabric for half price to be used in decorating our home.

Several of our church ladies type all of the manuscripts of my husband's books "as unto the Lord." They refuse to be paid because they feel this is their contribution to his ministry and want their reward from the Lord. Except for their help, probably only one of my husband's books would have reached a publisher, as he does not have time to do the work himself and could not afford to pay to have it typed. Now they are typing my manuscript, too.

Now that we have a lake cottage near the summer homes of two of our elders, they have helped by hard labor, advice, contributions of lumber, lending tools, fixing meals, and giving us surplus supplies to fix up our cottage.

One church couple paid to have a nurse take care of my baby so I could go to Mexico City with my husband. Another couple paid my plane fare to a section of the country where I had never been, and where I could meet my book publisher when my husband had a conference there.

The list of people who have helped us in some definite way could fill a book. There are numbers of men in our present church who can buy almost anything we need through their companies at wholesale prices. There is a man who uses his employees to work on our cars, lawn mower, and edger. A number of our salesmen give us samples of everything from tape to drug items. We were even given an electric heater we badly needed. A lawyer made out our wills, and a certified public accountant prepares our income tax returns.

Perhaps we receive more or less than other ministers' families do, but in every church there are many people who do things to aid the minister's family. What is done may vary considerably from church to church, but every pastor's wife I contacted named some nice things that were done for them. For instance, my sister is a minister's wife in the state of Washington, and she receives so many gifts from her church people that periodically she has to take an entire day off to write thank-you notes. A couple in a farming area were given so much food, both fresh and canned, that they were sure their food bill was less than half of what it would have been had they bought it all.

We had the privilege of entertaining the seminary commencement speaker and his wife at luncheon this spring. Since she too is a pastor's wife, I asked her my two favorite questions, having in mind the preparation of this book. "What is the greatest joy you know as a pastor's wife? What is the hardest part of your position?" In answer to the first question, about joy, she started out just as all the others had. "Outside of the wonderful spiritual blessings that you already know . . ." And then she told me that her church members were continually doing nice things for them. One man had given her train tickets so that she could come to Dallas with her husband. A lady took her to the nearest large city and bought a complete wardrobe; another who made original hats, made one for her; several women lent her precious items of apparel and jewelry so that she looked like a fashion model in a city known for its well-dressed women.

As a minister's wife, I have been entertained in palatial

homes, exclusive and private restaurants, V.I.P. banquets, and I have often had the thrill of meeting personally, or riding in cars with, nationally and internationally known speakers for special occasions. No life could be fuller and richer than that of the clergyman's wife!

I have purposely left the spiritual rewards and blessings that come from being in the ministry until last because it is hard to explain to any but those who have had the same experiences, and because so many unhappy pastors' wives seem to think that there are no rewards but those that they will receive from the Lord.

My husband and I have lost more sleep over the joys of our job than we have over the persecutions and burdens that come along with it. There is no joy compared to that of leading a person to know Christ as Saviour, or seeing people come to salvation through our church efforts. Sometimes a child is saved in Sunday school, and through his testimony the parents come to church and are saved. A person is often brought to church by a member and is saved as a result. Later that one returns with the family, and in time they are all saved. When my husband comes home at night from a call to say that all of the members of a family have been saved, we are too thrilled to sleep. There is no way to let others know the satisfaction and thanks that fill our hearts over experiences like these. When after a hard counseling session with a person burdened with many problems, that one leaves feeling that you are his best friend and have shown him the "way out," your exhilaration causes the emotional strain and tired brains to be forgotten.

The greatest reward that a minister's wife can have is to know she is needed, trusted, and looked up to as a godly woman who knows the Word and has power with the Lord in prayer. The knowledge that many people will turn to you for comfort, advice, and help, makes life full and gives every church duty real meaning. It may seem like a waste of time to attend a meeting when you would rather have some time alone or pour at a morning coffee when you should be in bed resting, but each of us knows that every pleasant contact with our church people is letting someone know us better so that later that person will feel free to come to us with problems and spiritual questions. At times some of our duties seem so useless, but they are fit into a pattern and we see that everything we do leads eventually to meeting a spiritual need for others. Unless the people know us socially and have a chance to be sure that we can be trusted to keep confidences, they are not apt to turn to us in their time of need unless they are desperate.

It is always "open season" for the pastor and his wife to witness. People expect us to be spiritual and to talk about spiritual things. We do not have to seek out people to witness to, as many of our friends and members do. Instead, people come to us. Not only do our own members turn to us for help but many who have no church connections, or who find no help in their own churches.

Last week a lady from another church called on the telephone to make an appointment with my husband to talk over some of her problems and to hear the way of salvation plainly. My husband was out of town, so the appointment had to be made for a week later. However, I said, "Let's settle the matter of your salvation right now; you don't have to wait until next week." As a result, a stranger was led to accept Christ as Saviour over the telephone. Later the appointment was canceled, because her problems took care of themselves after she was saved and had studied some of the Scriptures I suggested and had read a few books that would help her understand the Word.

I doubt that anyone is as blessed in being remembered daily in the prayers of numberless consecrated Christian people as are the pastor and his wife. We know that our people are backing us in prayer and that God's hand has been moved on our behalf many times because of the faithful prayers. There have been many times when we have consciously felt the power of someone praying, and without this ministry, we might have failed many times in our work, or become physically incapacitated. Our younger daughter was ill so much the first year of her life that the doctors gave up hope for her life a number of times, but our church people refused to let her go. They call her "the miracle baby," and we believe it was their prayers that kept her alive and gave us the strength to endure the trial of our faith and continue with the church work. When someone cares enough to labor in prayer, you know you have a priceless friend in the Lord.

Many women work as hard or harder than I do to help their husbands succeed in business. Some do secretarial work, bookkeeping, or other work in a husband's business establishment. Some women work in other places to have money to increase their husband's business opportunities. But these women are receiving only material blessings for their efforts. They may have a Cadillac, or a fur piece, or a handsome house for their extra work, but that is all. We ministers' wives may have some or none of these things, but it really does not matter, for our real and final reward comes when we reach our heavenly home. The Bible is full of precious promises for those who are faithful in giving out the Gospel, in witnessing to others, in teaching the Word, and in comforting and helping others and in showing love for the brethren. So take heart if at this point you feel your labors are in vain. Even if you never see the rewards of your efforts here on earth, God is keeping the records for faithful service, and your reward is waiting for you in glory.

Many years ago, a faithful middle-aged missionary, who looked twice his age because of the things he had suffered on the mission field, returned to the church which gave his financial support. He was not greeted by anyone, and no arrangements had been made for his food and lodging. He attended prayer meeting and nobody recognized him and his name was never mentioned in their prayers. Later he sat at the window of a third-floor room in a cheap, foul-smelling boardinghouse, trying to catch a breath of fresh air. His attention was arrested by band music and a parade. He watched as the people came by cheering and waving flags and throwing paper. They were welcoming home "Teddy" Roosevelt from a hunting trip in Africa. The missionary broke into bitter tears for the first time. "Why, Lord, why?" he sobbed. "This man is given a royal welcome home for shooting animals in Africa. I have spent my entire life trying to win those people to Christ. I lost my wife and children by disease. Here I am too sick to work, and everything in life is gone, and there is no one to honor me." A still, quiet voice within him answered, "Roosevelt is receiving an earthly welcome that will only last for a day. Remember, you haven't come home yet."

CHAPTER 5

Togetherness

TOGETHERNESS is a word that has been coined by someone in recent years and is frequently used to denote a closeness of relationship. God has given marriage partners to each other to work together in the task He has given them to do. God said, after He created Adam, "It is not good that man should be alone; I will make an help meet for him." Then He caused a deep sleep to fall upon Adam, and took a rib from his side to form a woman, and gave her to Adam. Right then God gave His principle and standard of marriage. "Therefore shall a man leave his father and his mother, and shall cleave unto his wife: and they shall be one flesh."

This close relationship should be a joy and comfort to all marriage partners and especially should it give added strength to those who are in the ministry.

I would like to suggest a few areas in which the minister and his wife must stand together for their own happiness, and for the sake of their work in the church.

First, there must be togetherness in goal and purpose. Seldom does a man take the necessary theological training required for a pastorate unless he is sure that the Lord has called him into full-time Christian service. It is reasonable to assume that once a man is in seminary or in church work his purpose in life is settled. It is just as necessary for the woman who marries a clergyman to have the same purpose and goals in her life. It is easily possible for a girl to be attracted to a man who is a minister and marry him without any thought as to what his type of work will mean to her. She may think of the ministry as the wife of a business or professional man does—as a means to a living, or as the work of her husband only, excluding any effort on her part. In spite of the fact that in reality, and in God's sight, she is merely the wife of a parson, and as such she should not be required to do any more in a church than any other Christian wife and mother, most church people are not contented to have it that way. They think of her, along with her husband, as part of a team of workers. It is natural that in many cases it is necessary for her to perform tasks that come as a result of her husband's position in the church. Unless the wife has felt an inner leading of the Lord to make the sacrifices and denials that are entailed in her marriage, she is apt to be resentful of any demands that are made on her time and of any restrictions on her liberty of action because of possible disapproval by the congregation.

But, leaving the attitudes and expectations of the church completely out of the scene for a while, let us turn to the result of the wife's attitude toward her husband's work, as it affects their marriage.

When a minister knows that his wife believes in what he is doing, is backing him up in his work, is praying for its success and seeking God's will and blessing on his ministry, he is provided with a great incentive to be and do his best. The knowledge that she is cheerfully giving him time and encouragement to do all the work he feels is necessary, even though she might personally want that attention herself, keeps him happy, as he devotes himself to the high purpose of his work.

On the other hand, if the wife's goals for life are contrary to her husband's, she can never be happy with the program that must be carried out by a minister. She will resent the time he spends preparing sermons, calling on the sick, and being phoned at all hours to take care of emergencies no matter what nice plans she may have had for them to go out or to be alone. Unless she shares his ideas of what his ministry should be, she will be miserable. Since a wife cannot hide her feelings well, it will not be long before the pastor senses her bitterness toward him and his work. That gives him a feeling of guilt, and puts him in the awful position of being torn between his ordination vows and his marriage vows. No man can remain emotionally stable when his life is pulled in two opposite directions at the same time. He loves his wife, and wants to please her and make her happy. At the same time, he has been called of God, and called into a church to do things that usually are done only by a clergyman. He must keep the vows he has made to God.

The resentment of the wife and the consequent emotional strain placed on the husband, as he tries to keep two sets of vows at the same time, can create serious matrimonial problems in the manse—the very last place one would expect to find them. Since the minister must be true to his ordination and to God, there is only one major answer to the problem.

Suppose you haven't come to the place where you feel that the goals and purpose of your husband's ministry are yours, too. You are the one who must make the change! It is too late to go back and say that you should not have married a minister, and that he should have chosen his life partner more carefully in view of the exceptional strains on a pastor's marriage. It is too late to get out of your marriage, even though you might wish you could. Your husband must not give up his ministry. You must adjust yourself to his work. That sounds hard and cruel, as if you are expected to make all the sacrifices in life, but in reality God asks all his children to be willing to follow His will. Certainly you cannot be satisfied with the condition of your marriage if you are resentful or unhappy and your husband is in emotional conflict because of it. The answer is to tell the Lord just what the trouble is. Confess your faults and discontentments and ask Him to give you an earnest desire to be the kind of pastor's wife He wants you to be. God remembers that we are dust, and that our flesh is weak. He knows it is natural for us to want our own way. He understands your dilemma better than any human friend or other wives who have been through the same struggle. If you sincerely want to change, humble yourself before God and ask His help in bringing you to the place where you can willingly and cheerfully do whatever the Lord expects of you. Then you can be sure of reality in your life.

It is also well to tell your husband exactly how you feel, and that you want to change. He can do a lot to help you if he just will. He can encourage you in your struggle, pray for you, comfort you when you feel that you have failed in your new purpose. Oftentimes, he can see to it that some of the pressure that especially bothers you in the church is taken off until you are better adjusted to the work. He can go even further to see that you have some regular time alone with him when he will give you his entire attention. He can see to it that you get more, but perhaps shorter, vacations. He can put the children to bed at least one night a week, to give you free time. He can take you out to eat once a week, even for something as simple as a hamburger, coke and ice cream. If your mind and heart are willing and open to God's leading, and your husband's help, many other ideas will arise to help in the growing process until you have a real vision of what it means to your husband, and can mean to you, to back him up in the work he is doing for the Lord.

The old saying, "Misery loves company," is true of many pastors' wives. For every pastor's wife who is miserable, there are many hundreds of others who are going through the same struggle. And many more have come out victorious. I know from experience! Even though I felt called to be a minister's wife, I did not understand what it meant, and I was unhappy and discontented with God's will for me, and often rebellious, but gradually, a change came in my life, just as I have described to you.

A survey taken by a Christian magazine on the subject of the feelings of the minister's wife toward her husband's work and her responsibilities, shows that only about 20 percent of the wives really "felt at home" in their position when they started in their first pastorate. About 60 percent of them have found that adapting themselves to their role as a minister's wife was a complex, difficult, and often painful process, with definite ages and stages through which they had to pass.

Most of the pastors' wives found in the first few years that the range of situations and problems with which they had to cope was simply overwhelming. They had to grow up in a hurry, and ten years after marriage they just began to "hit a comfortable stride." It was a complex adjustment and assimilation process—a hard struggle, but worthwhile in terms of the resulting growth and fulfillment. There is no stage where any of us feels that she has achieved perfection. Even after all these years, there are still times when I feel trapped by the duties my life demands and resentful of things for which I am blamed, and rebellion often creeps in. These things vary from pastorate to pastorate, according to a woman's personality, her health, and for many other reasons. The important thing is not to let resentment and rebellion have a foothold in your heart, or they will take over completely. Remember that the trial is just "for a season, if need be," and this too will pass in God's time.

Conversations heard among groups of ministers' wives give the impression that they feel the pressures put on their marriage and their greatest frustrations come not so much from the demands of the church as from the feeling that they have to take second place in their husband's life. It seems that many of the men feel this is necessary, too. I have heard seminary students, and at least one professor, say that when they marry, the girl must understand that the Lord will be first, and she must be second. These remarks show that the ministerial candidates are serious and cautious in choosing wives who will be a help in the work of the pastorate. May I suggest that it is just as necessary for God to be first in the wife's life, as in the husband's? If they are truly "one flesh" in the Lord, God will be first in their union, or oneness. Happy and blessed is the couple who feel so alike in their goals that God is first in their togetherness!

Second, there should be a togetherness in spiritual growth, as well as in purpose. There is a strong temptation to take care of the spiritual needs of others, and to let one's own needs go. The pressure of work, the numerous interruptions, and the physical exhaustion, all join forces to prevent our spending much time in closeness to the Lord. Since we are studying and teaching the Bible regularly, it becomes so common a tool for us that it loses some of its preciousness, and we do not see the necessity of taking time just to let the Word speak to our own hearts, to talk with God, and listen as He speaks to us personally.

To keep the Lord's blessing on your marriage, and your work, it is important to make a daily practice of reading the Word and praying together as a family. This should be done once a day on the level that can best be understood by the children. This is a time of strengthening the family ties and of showing the children that God is recognized as head of the home and director of all its activities. Then at another time, the two marriage partners should have a private time of reading the Word and praying together. Nothing brings a stronger unity in a marriage than this time alone together. This is the time that you can pray for yourselves, the children, the special requests of the church people that are confidential, the general work of the church, and any other ministries which the Lord has given either of you to do. You simply cannot pray together and stay resentful, or angry with one another. If you are finding it hard or impossible to pray together, please check on your marriage, for something must be wrong!

This togetherness in the Word and in prayer is even more imperative for the pastor and his wife because they seldom have any spiritual counselor. It is even very difficult for the minister to advise his own wife because her problems are usually his, too, and the entire situation is too close to him for him to be able to look at it objectively, and not emotionally. The church member can go to the pastor when he needs counseling; the seminary student can go to a professor; the unbeliever can go to countless kinds of professional counselors; but the minister and his wife stand alone with their problems unless occasionally they can find another, older minister who can be of help to them. At times this seems hard to bear, but really it is a blessing in disguise. It makes it necessary for them to take their problems to the Lord. Every problem and need must eventually go to Him anyway, so it is best to turn to God right at the first, and then there is no possible way of making a mistake by accepting human judgment. For the Christian, the Lord's will is the only solution to every situation, so why not go to Him right from the start?

Learn to lean on each other spiritually. There will be backbreaking problems and burdens for both yourselves and your church members, and each of us must have someone with whom we can share these things. Since you cannot make close friends in the church, it is far better to depend upon your marriage partner for the help, comfort, sympathy and understanding that all of God's servants need so often.

Stand together, and then grow together spiritually. It is pathetic to see one marriage partner grow beyond the other educationally, and gradually become separated because of the widening gulf in their intellectual interests. It is tragic to see one beyond the other spiritually. That is not to say that we wives must study as much as our husbands, or know as much theology as they, but it does mean that we must live as close to the Lord as they, and put His will first in our lives.

Togetherness in your spiritual lives is the backbone and main support of your ministry, and of a happy marriage. If you do not see the importance of this, and let yourself get too busy to maintain it, there will be something seriously lacking in every area of your lives.

Third, there should be a togetherness in love. We have to work to maintain love and a happy marriage, just as we have to work at anything else that is worthwhile in life. Just having the minister say over your heads at a beautiful wedding service, "I pronounce you man and wife," is no guarantee that you will "live happily forever after." We worked hard to win each other before we were married, and then we often let the work of the church and our own personal interests make us slump into the attitude that everything depends upon the other partner to make a happy marriage. We soon forget, or become too tired to remember, the little courtesies and thoughtfulnesses that characterized our courtship. It is natural that love should change from year to year. The burning, romantic love changes into a more quiet, mature love. If it is growing as it should, it will be much deeper and more perfect as the years go by. While we may not spend as much time talking about love, or as much time in each other's presence, we have become more one, and life without the other would be intolerable. Just because marriage partners stay together, does not mean that they have a happy and successful marriage. Many people who are still living together have become separated just as definitely as though they were divorced—and this includes ministers and their wives.

In the many marriage polls that have been taken by psychologists and university professors in their experiments, two factors seem to show up as a crying need in a good marriage. The first was shown in a study of 900 married couples by the University of Michigan. Researchers asked the wives to name the greatest benefit in marriage, selecting their answer from a list of five benefits which was given to them. Overwhelmingly, the wives put companionship in the first place—above understanding, standard of living, and even the chance to have children. The second is shown from the wide experience of Dr. Harold Feldman at Cornell University, a psychologist and marriage counselor. He says, "One of the greatest problems in marriage is the ever-growing need of the wife to talk and the ever-diminishing inclination of her husband to take part or to even listen." Many husbands even resent and criticize their wives for talking too much. One major problem arises from the fact that the husband is with people all day, and when he comes home, he would rather have a peaceful, quiet evening. On the other hand, the average woman is cooped up at home with small children and seldom gets to speak to another adult except over the telephone and the back fence.

On a practical day-by-day basis, talk relieves emotional tension and helps avoid, as well as settle, quarrels. It clarifies a couple's thinking, helps them work and plan together, gives them common ground in dealing with their children, their friends, and the problems of the church. "In talking together seriously, each person receives a little of the other and sends it back charged with new life and meaning," says Dr. Feldman. "It's like the chemical interaction that produces electricity in a battery. This is how we are re-created."

The special stresses and strains that come to the pastor and his wife are often the cause of their gradually drifting apart in the most important function of the marriage, that of talking things over and settling them. We are usually trained not to bring up unpleasant subjects or to mention anything that might start a quarrel, because we are Christians and should live together in peace. The husband has listened to problems and complaints all day. It is almost more than he can take to have his wife start complaining the minute he gets home. If he refuses to discuss things that she considers important, though they may appear trivial to him, she will eventually come to the conclusion that there just is not any use trying to clear up a problem, or that her husband does not care, anyway. If she becomes resentful about some church matter and her husband, the only one to whom she can talk, does not take it seriously or try to help in some way, she just says, "So what?" and pushes the resentment further down into the subconscious mind, and there it grows and festers, and may come out in the form of an unpleasant psychosomatic illness.

The reverse of the case may be just as true. The husband may come home from a busy day, drained emotionally because of the strength it has taken to preach and counsel, feeling the need of talking his problems over with his wife, only to find that her mind is too busy with her own interests to listen to him. She may make a halfhearted attempt, but deep in his heart the pastor knows that she really does not care. This type of thing often grows gradually, and is not recognized at first. Suddenly, one of the marriage partners wakes up to realize that they are not saying anything important, or personal, to each other. Even when they do have a little private time together, they do not have a thing to say that they could not say to a stranger.

One minister's wife said that she would like to meet her husband, as a stranger, on an overnight train trip, and have a long talk with him about the things that she found impossible to discuss at home. Perhaps that way they could break up the logjam of lack of communication in their marriage, and get back to the place where they could freely discuss any problems or interests in their lives.

"Conflict in marriage," Dr. Feldman says, "usually centers around a specific issue . . . sex, money, children, religion. But when you investigate, you find almost always that one of the major underlying causes of the trouble is a failure of two-way communication. When the couple should have confided in each other, they held back. When they should have asked blunt questions and given honest answers, they beat around the bush. Disagreements are inevitable, but when the couple finally get through to each other, they can usually settle their differences."

One husband, who had a very happy marriage, said that when he and his wife stopped talking, he knew that something was wrong. Check on your own marriage and see if you are really talking about everything. It is easily understandable that this is often hard, especially when the husband is out so many evenings, and there are children. If necessary, take the time after going to bed to have the serious exchanges of needed conversation. It is better still if during the day a minister and his wife can find free minutes when they can discuss problems which might bring disagreement and even hurt feelings. In this way, their problems can be all settled before night, when they are tired emotionally and physically and a discussion is apt to keep them from sleeping.

A number of happy, well-adjusted couples in the ministry have made suggestions as to how they keep a two-way communication system going in their homes. One said to draw the other out by asking questions, and *then listening*. All agreed that being a good listener is most important, and taking seriously the other person's attempt to express his or her feelings, anxieties, and gripes, though they may seem trivial to you. Another said, "Take the chip off your shoulder and use your sense of humor, and be able to take criticism and suggestions without being offended." Still another warned that the longer a couple waits to face an issue, the harder it is to get around to discussing it. The result is more hurt feelings. When a couple can freely talk about anything, masked resentments often disappear entirely; if not, they will gradually go away.

No matter how you plan to work out the communication problem in your life, be sure that you do it and do it in the right way if you sense that you and your husband have drifted apart. Take time to make an appointment with each other, and faithfully keep it. Then, hurt as it may, talk over old hurt feelings, unjust acts, resentments, and anything that stands between you. Several intensive sessions may be required to get everything straightened out. When that has been accomplished, decide that from that time on, you are going to freely express your feelings to each other and not beat around the bush, or ignore any hurts, or withhold discussion of anything that needs clearing up.

In many cases where couples have reestablished communication with each other, problems seem to melt away as snow on a warm, sunny day. Better physical condition may also be the result as inner feelings of resentment and repressions are removed, and new and needed energy will suddenly return. It frequently takes as much energy to hold down unpleasantness in the subconscious mind, as it does to dig ditches all day. Children are usually very sensitive to tensions and unhappiness in the family, and the reestablishment of communication between husband and wife will have the effect of giving real parents to the children. Their little minds will be greatly relieved, and they may be in better health, and better in their behavior and school work. Finally, the end of tension between marriage partners often results in a more satisfactory sex life. It is impossible for two different personalities to agree on everything, but frank discussion will enable each to know how the other feels, and to effect a compromise that will keep down friction and hurt feelings.

A minister had to go to a nearby city to conduct a funeral. He asked his wife to go along with him. "If you want me to," she said. "Well," the man said, after a moment of silence, "I'll go alone." Each had been needlessly disappointed. The husband wanted his wife with him and hoped she would offer to accompany him. She wanted to go but, not sure he really meant the invitation, tossed the decision to him. He assumed she was turning him down; she assumed he didn't need her support. And so a couple who wanted to express their mutual love and need wound up feeling each had been rejected by the other.

Dr. Ben Sweetland, who writes the marriage column in the *Dallas Morning News,* gives an excellent prescription for an ailing marriage. We would all do well to follow his advice: For one month, try doing the things that you would do if you were still trying to get your husband to propose, or your wife to say "yes." After you try this a while, you will not want to go back to the old ways. Your partner will like it so much, that he will do the same for you. Real love is responded to with the same love!

Fourth, there should be togetherness in a mutual admiration society. That is not a facetious remark! I mean it! For every young minister who has a swelled head, and an overexaggerated opinion of his abilities, there are at least twenty-five who are often frightened at the responsibilities that are before them.

Many men with years of experience have these same feelings of inadequacy. This is an area where we wives can be a big help.

When I first started having dates, someone told me that the way to be popular with the fellows was to have that "Oh, you're wonderful" attitude. Girls, that works on husbands, too! Many a successful man has said that he reached the top because his wife believed in him. There will be days when your husband will come home as deflated as a pricked balloon. He will feel like a kicked dog with his tail between his legs. That will be the day when everyone seems to have been critical; when the board members have rejected his best plans; and some of the church members have shown their "horns." All he needs to be completely cast down is a wife who says, "I told you so," or "I knew you couldn't do it," or "If you had just done what I told you to," and so on. Your husband's one consolation through all these trials should be, "Well, it really doesn't matter what others think; my wife believes in me."

Many of your church members will largely form their opinion of your husband by your attitude. If you are critical and discuss his faults before them, they will gradually believe you. If you have real confidence in his abilities and truly think that he is wonderful, they will in all probability accept your estimate of him, too.

Many experts in homiletics and pastoral psychology have given us wives excellent advice in helping our husbands improve their work. However, there is one piece of advice that I don't agree with—that is to help my husband by criticizing his messages and making suggestions as to how he can improve the work he is doing. To begin with, seminary men are trained by experts in these fields, and I seriously doubt if most wives are qualified to judge their husbands' actions and to make constructive criticism. It always hurts to be criticized by anyone, especially a loved one, so I doubt if the word of an untrained wife is of enough value for her to run the risk of hurting her husband's feelings.

Acquaintances of ours on the East Coast tell a story about themselves which they think is very funny. The wife takes seriously this advice to criticize her husband's sermons. She even writes down every mistake he makes in English, all the tangled-up sentences, when she thinks he should have an illustration, and so on. On the way home in the car, she tells him all the things that he did wrong. For some reason one day, she was late with her criticism as they started home. One of the children, sitting in the back seat of the car, leaned forward and said, "All right, Mom, tell Pop what was wrong with his sermon." I pity that family! How can a man preach his best when he knows that his wife is listening only to criticize? How can she worship God and get any blessing out of his messages when her ear is only open to mistakes? And how can those children have much respect for their father when they hear their mother criticize him?

I have already anticipated your question. Certainly, some things will need to be corrected. If you honestly feel your husband would profit by constructive criticism, how are you going to do it? First, do not express criticism the first time he makes a mistake. Don't say a thing; just wait. Very likely he will realize what he did wrong and will correct it himself. Second, never talk about his mistake in the heat of emotion. You are likely to say too much, or exaggerate, or even start an argument. Third, do not pick a time when he is hungry, tired, or already overwhelmed with the criticisms of others. Fourth, never never, criticize him in front of others. There is no excuse for humiliating him, no matter how big a mistake he may have made.

There is a little formula I have developed to be used in connection with making suggestions for my husband's church work. I don't! After all, we both desire *God's* will for our church more than anything else, not mine. I just pray about what I feel should be done in our church, and let God do the working. Not only is my formula the easiest, most peaceful way of doing things but it keeps my husband from feeling that I am interfering in his work and eliminates any danger of error in human judgment and misunderstanding. Most of the things about which I have prayed have come to pass in due time. There was one matter about which I prayed for a long time, and nothing happened. I then concluded that it must not be God's will and stopped praying about it. Less than a month later something far better than my plan was started. It takes a lot of patience to follow this way, but it is the most rewarding way.

The husband can do a lot of things to bolster up his wife's morale. She is in a difficult position, connected with his work but not really a part of it. She is often taken for granted, and many times is ignored. It is hard for her to continue in the awkward position in which her marriage to him places her without some expression of appreciation from time to time, to encourage her and to show her that her part of the work is important. Since many church members forget that she needs attention from time to time, it is up to her husband to show his appreciation in ways that he knows will mean the most to her. As an individual, he can follow many of the suggestions that have been made to the churches, such as having a special dinner for her, bringing her flowers occasionally, telling her frequently how much he appreciates her sacrifices and work, seeing that she gets vacations, and making sure that no special pressure, that would be too much for her, is placed on her by some church members. I believe that ministers' wives want most of all their husband's appreciation and his full attention when he is at home, since he must be away so much of the time. Success, and admiration of the congregation give the pastor a wonderful incentive, while the wife stands on the sidelines, even getting criticism at times. Her feelings of accomplishment and success will have to come largely from the way her husband accepts her and shows that he knows she is making a great contribution to him and to the church.

There may be periods of hardship, real trials, and even open persecution in some of your churches, but these will have little lasting effect on you as long as your marriage is a true union of "one flesh." If you stand together in purpose, in spiritual growth, in your love and mutual appreciation of each other, you are ready for anything that God sees fit to send. A happy, peaceful home and a vital unity in your marriage make a refuge from any storm from without.

CHAPTER 6

PK's

CHILDREN OF THE PRESIDENTS of the United States, movie stars, wealthy or prominent people, and ministers have one thing in common. Because of their parents' positions in life such children are seldom allowed to live completely normal lives. It isn't long before they realize that they are considered different from other children and are being watched by people because their parents are constantly in the public eye. There is a consciousness that they must share their parents with others. It seems to these children that others get more attention than they do. They see their lives pushed into a mold that is shaped more by public opinion and the parents' positions than by their parents' personal views. As a result, these children have a very confused and distorted idea of what is expected of them in life.

One of the quickest ways to raise the blood pressure of a minister's wife is to say that all preachers' kids turn out to be bad and all manse children are brats. Such thoughtless remarks are cruel, and there seems to be no justification for statements like these. In my years of watching the newspapers and listening to news reports I have not learned of any children of ministers who have been in trouble with the law. I realize, of course, that in some cases some information might be withheld from the public out of respect for ministers. But lately the ministry has lost so much respect in the public eye that I doubt if a newspaper would hold back printing something done by a preacher's kid which would make good copy. Few newscasters or papers care to lose a good chance to report a juicy scandal.

I have asked a great many people about their knowledge of truly bad ministers' children, and few could remember more than one. A number of people said that they knew of kids who had been considered bad only because they were born to preachers and were judged by a different standard from that used to measure the actions of other children. One lady remarked that she knew of a few now that were on the border line, but ended by saying, "What can you expect of them when their father isn't even a Christian?"

Though my husband and I have moved in ministerial circles for twenty-five years, we have never heard of a preacher's kid that was bad. Of course, we have moved with pastors who believe and preach the Bible—pastors who have taken a real interest in the spiritual training of their children. I can't speak for the liberal ministers who don't believe in the Word themselves. All the PK's we have known have been basically good, and most have grown up to be good Christian parents and citizens, and a large percentage have gone into the ministry or back to the mission field. Of course, many of them were full of fun and spunk and did mischievous things, which is only normal for all healthy, intelligent children.

There are no statistics and surveys comparing the actions of children from different walks of life with those of the PK's and I really am not trying to prove anything along that line anyway. I admit that there are bound to be bad PK's and some get into serious trouble with the laws of our land, just as do children of families in every walk and economic level of life.

There are a number of reasons why remarks about bad PK's have gotten started, but there really is no excuse for letting such talk continue. There is so much comment and discussion about the few preachers' kids who are naughty or really bad that the subject is magnified in the eyes of the church members. The gossip makes it seem as though there are more bad kids than good ones. People's attention is constantly drawn to the few who go wrong, resulting in a poor impression of all of them. Nothing is said about the thousands of precious children who are everything a parent could desire, who quietly assist in the church, who give up their parents' presence many, many times for the needs—and even whims—of church members. These facts don't interest the average person, for there is nothing sensational about good children.

All in the minister's family—including the children—live in a glass bowl. Everything they do is watched and in some measure judged by the people of the congregation. Everyone in the congregation has his opinions, and the leader's family is weighed and often found wanting by the people's own ideas. It is hard for the children to live normally and freely when they are always conscious of being observed by the congregation. They learn this early in life. For instance, our older daughter once wished that she could do something just to shock a lady who was continually checking up on her. A few years later, one woman told me of something my daughter had done, thinking that it was very improper for a minister's daughter. I thanked her with a sweet smile, and told her I would take care of the matter. I never mentioned it to my daughter, as what she had done was something one might wish could be done in front of this lady to give her a jolt and a much-needed lesson. My daughter's action was personally justifiable, thus one for which my child was not going to be punished. I had taken care of the matter, as promised, by choosing to ignore the fact.

The children of the manse also live with the fear that if they displease any of the congregation they are displeasing their parents, and might even be punished for it.

Some of the pastors' wives reported that the pastor's children get correction and criticism from members of the church who feel that they have a right to train the children as well as correct the pastor and his wife. When my children do something wrong in Sunday school or junior church, or in the homes of church members, I expect the adults to correct them. I appreciate such correction. Since I am not there to do it myself, I am happy to have others help me. However, those who have corrected my girls have done it kindly and wisely and not out of spite for us or because of any resentment toward my children. It is important to take into account the attitude of the one who is doing the scolding, and the reason for doing it. Neither of our girls has objected to anything that a member of our church has said to them about their actions. They usually know when they have made a mistake, and kind correction does not bring any resentment.

Many ministers' wives have asked me what to do about people who constantly correct their children, even in front of their parents, and criticize their actions to the mothers. I have never faced either of these problems as most of our church people have liked our girls and would not be so rude.

Only once did I have a problem, and that was when my two-year-old daughter had to have her hair cut to keep it from ruining her eyes because it was impossible to keep the soft, fine hair out of her face. After her hair was cut, none of the lovely curls she had had returned, but my daughter was happy. What were a few curls compared to my daughter's frustration and the danger of harming her eyes? But at least a dozen people told me what a terrible mistake I had made. In those days, I used to try to explain my actions, but I have long since given up doing that. I felt I was just wasting my breath and prolonging an argument. Just drop the subject and keep right on doing what you think is best for your family even if it may disagree with what some church people think. It is not wise to dwell on a disagreement, and there is great danger, in defending your actions, of saying something you might be sorry for later.

There is no surefire method of stopping criticism of your children. First, check to be sure whether it is justified. If so, be sure to correct your children at home. It will be for their own good. If the criticism is not deserved, keep them as far away from chronic critics as possible. If fault-finding continues, the only thing to do is have a quiet, kindly talk with the troublemaker, privately, explaining how the criticism is affecting your children, and ask her to desist. It is far better, if necessary, to lose a church member than your children.

By far the worst situation that the pastor's child has to contend with is where a subtle, insidious person directs his dislike for the minister to his child. It would be nice to believe that such an attitude is always unconscious, but I know of at least two cases where it was not.

Bob and Kate were serving a Baptist church in Alabama when trouble began to smolder in the congregation. A few people were openly opposing Bob's leadership. One day while they were in town shopping, one of the deacons came to the parsonage and destroyed all of their small son's toys. The man ripped up the tires on the boy's bike, bent the spokes, and broke the seat and deliberately hammered all his trucks and cars out of shape, dumped the sand from its box over the lawn and then chopped up the box. Some of the neighbors saw the man and were able to identify who had done the damage. This man's hatred for the pastor had made him sink so low as to hurt a small, innocent child.

A case of "transferred resentment" was enacted in our own family, also. Our older girl loved "church" from babyhood. It was the first word she could say. Suddenly, in the midst of some church disagreement, she decided that she didn't like Sunday school or church. We were perplexed, but took her anyway. The minute we came to the door of her class, she solidly planted her feet down and refused to go in. She cried and clung to my skirt, begging to go with me. Soon she began to develop stomachaches and vomiting each Sunday morning. If I had been wiser in church ways and psychology, I would have connected such symptoms with the fact that the superintendent of her department was the woman who was heading up the trouble for my husband. It took a doctor to show me that my daughter was in perfect health and had developed an emotional illness to keep her from having to go to Sunday school, where she would be mistreated. Later some of the other teachers told me what they actually saw done to my girl by the super-intendent. I blame every woman in that department for not telling us what was going on and not reporting it to the general Sunday school superintendent. No such emotionally unfit person should be allowed to teach any children, especially in a church.

At this point, the Lord moved us again and spared us having to make a "scene" over this trouble. It took a full year after that to get my daughter emotionally adjusted so that she would trust a Sunday school teacher. However, if we had stayed at that church and the teacher had not been immediately removed, we would have taken our child out of her department. If she couldn't have been put into another, I would have taken her to my Sunday school class until the children her age were promoted. We realize that this move would have brought much criticism and misunderstanding, but no child should have to suffer the rest of her life for the meanness and hypocrisy of a church member posing as a Christian teacher. There could have been great emotional scars and even a reaction to all Christian teachers because of the impression made on a little child who looked up to her teacher as a model Christian. I didn't want my girl to get that idea of Christianity!

Some preachers' kids aren't wearing halos because the church people are spoiling them or just giving them too much attention. This is especially true when the children are attractive and pleasant and appreciative.

Donna Manning was a lovely mother and pastor's wife. Her children were popular too. At Christmas and birthday time, they were deluged with gifts. There were entirely too many, but she had to give them all to the children immediately for fear of offending one of the church members. It would have been a wonderful help if she could have handed them out through the year as new toys were needed. The best she could do was to let her children see them all, write thank-you notes to the givers, and then let her children play with the toys in rotation.

That still gave her the serious problem of being sure that when a guest called, the children were using the gift given by that guest. As a result of such generous treatment on the part of the members, the children began to expect to have everything they wanted and showed plainly their preference for the people who gave them presents. Many of the others thought the children were very ill-mannered.

Such a problem never confronted me, since our girls have seldom been given gifts in any of our churches. My biggest difficulty came when my girls were little and were not allowed to eat between meals because they were such poor eaters. Even knowing this, our ladies would fill them with cake and ice cream when we came for a visit and with candy and chewing gum at church. Our little one got in the habit of watching for those who did give candy and gum, and even hung around them, giving broad hints.

All the ministers' wives said that the time their children are most apt to get out of hand is before and after services held at the church. The minister's wife is expected to be greeting people, listening to members' problems or complaints, and giving attention to the congregation. In the meantime, her children are left to roam without restriction. I have seen my daughter doing something at a distance which I wanted stopped immediately, but for fear of offending the one I was talking to, I couldn't leave. Even some of the members, unthinkingly, add to our problem by encouraging our children to do funny things and then laughing at them. Everyone knows that attention of this kind only leads the children to more misbehavior in order to get more attention. A few mothers said that the very ones who think such misbehavior is cute later criticize the children. Those who stand around just watching think the children have been poorly trained at home. An attempt by some to explain the matter to these people did no good, as they misunderstood and began criticizing the mother as well as the children. If people don't understand what they are doing to the children by treating them this way, telling such people seldom does any good. A few ministers' wives said that they do not hesitate to stop in the middle of any conversation, regardless of who they are talking to, and straighten out their children's behavior the minute they see anything out of the way. Then they return to the one with whom they are talking, apologize, and continue the conversation. No one said what the reaction was in the congregation. I seriously doubt if most of the members of the churches we have served would have taken this kindly, and if I had interrupted a conversation, I doubt that I could find the person again afterwards. But I do believe that the pastors' wives who put their children first are doing God's will and what is best for the children in the long run, and will be a good example to other parents. Small children can't be expected to stand quietly by their mothers for a long period of time after sitting nearly three hours in a morning. Furthermore, I don't want my child to hear many of the things that are said to me, and I don't believe the women would feel as free to talk to me about problems if a child were listening.

One of the most distressing and hardest problems for me as a pastor's wife and mother is to keep my children from seeing, hearing, and thinking about the wrong things and later being depressed and upset by them.

There is almost nothing I can do to keep my children from hearing and seeing things that happen right in our home. Women come into our home to talk about their troubles, and I can't keep my daughter out all of the time, though I try. After all, this is her home, and if the guest stays a long time (which is usual) my daughter has every right and need to be here. Many of these members, and others who seek my help, talk very freely about extremely personal things, give graphic descriptions of horrible situations, and so on, in my daughter's presence. My visitors are often so engrossed in their own circumstances that they never think what they might be doing to a little girl who is listening with both ears. Even my end of a telephone conversation from a member in a critical state of affairs, is often enough to disrupt her routine and keep her tugging at my skirts during the long calls, and wanting later an explanation of what I said. I am caught in a trap of trying to give sound advice and help and at the same time put it in words that will not upset my child.

We have even had several men crack up in our living room and become so violent that they tried to attack my husband. All I could do was run out of the house with the children and leave my husband to protect himself. We have decided it would be better to have my husband injured than to have the children see that.

I strongly recommend that there be an office in the church where the pastor can observe regular hours to see members, and that he do all the counseling there. If it is necessary for the pastor's wife to do some of it, the conversations should be in the same study with some one dependable (if possible, the pastor himself) at home to take care of the children. This would keep such harmful things away from the children. I know that this would be hard to carry out, for many times people just drop into the manse on the spur of the moment, and at other times when they come for a visit, they do not plan to discuss their problems.

Right along this line, there is also the problem of taking my younger daughter, who is still too small to be left at home alone, into situations where there has been death or tragedy, because she is easily disturbed and upset, and is never satisfied until everything she has seen or heard is completely explained to her. Sometimes this leads to sickness because she can't cope with situations that are beyond her age. I doubt if other children can either, but instead of showing it, they let their feelings accumulate in their subconscious minds and will probably have emotional symptoms later as a result.

Last summer, the twenty-year-old daughter of a neighborhood couple was killed in an automobile accident soon after her honeymoon. I felt that I must go to see the family—and really wanted to—because they were friends. There was nowhere to leave Gwen, as my mother is out of Dallas in the summertime. (When she is at home, I can usually get her to keep my daughter.) I had a little talk with Gwen before we left, telling only the barest facts and I asked her to please sit quietly wherever I told her to when we arrived. This she did beautifully! It seemed that everything worked out perfectly, but I couldn't have been more wrong. This was the last straw that perpetrated a series of emotional crises which involved many months of expensive treatments to cure. We have decided that no matter how much the need, or what the tragedy, unless Gwen can be left with someone, I will not go to that home. It is the only way we can protect our child from greater troubles.

Why does everyone expect the preacher's children to be so much better than children from other Christian families? This is one question I have always wanted to ask a layman, and I have never received a satisfactory answer. The usual one is, "To be a testimony for the Lord." Shouldn't other Christian children be a testimony, too?

Looking over the Scripture passages that discuss the relationship between children and the Lord and children and their parents, we find that God makes no distinction between children of ministers and of other Christians. God has given one set of rules for the rearing of all children.

We are told to teach our children obedience and honor or respect for their parents. (See Eph. 6:1-3.)

In Ephesians 6:4 we are told to bring up our children "in the nurture and admonition of the Lord." To nurture our children means to feed and nourish them on the things of the Lord, which would be the Bible and the Christian life. To admonish our children means to guide and train and teach them the things of God. Paul has given us a beautiful picture of how this training should work in the home in his letter to Timothy. In II Timothy 3:14, Paul tells Timothy, "Continue thou in the

things which thou hast learned and hast been assured of, knowing of whom thou hast learned them; and that from a child thou
hast known the holy scriptures which are able to make thee wise
unto salvation through faith which is in Christ Jesus." Paul had
already spoken of the faith that was in Timothy's grandmother
Lois and in his mother Eunice, and Paul was persuaded that the
same faith was in Timothy, too.

"Train up a child in the way he should go: and when he is
old, he will not depart from it." If he does depart from it, the
training hasn't been what it should have been. Others feel this
promise has failed them because they have not seen the difference between the meaning of "train" and "teach." Teaching
is imparting knowledge, while training is the sum total of all
the influences that touch a child from birth on. It is impossible
to teach a child much until he is two or even three years old.
But psychiatrists tell us that a child has gotten most of his emotional training and attitudes toward life by the time he is two.
Not realizing this, many parents have neglected the most important years of the child's life because they have failed to see
that everything the baby sees, hears, or senses is training him
even before he can understand words. It may be too late
to go back now, but never too late to start correctly now.

When Moses gave God's warning and instructions to the
children of Israel, he gave the method of teaching and training
children. "And thou shalt teach them diligently unto thy children, and shalt talk of them when thou sittest in thine house,
and when thou walkest by the way, and when thou liest down,
and when thou risest up."

The primary place for carrying out the responsibility of
bringing up a child in the nurture and admonition of the Lord
is the home, not the church or the Christian school. Teaching
and training is to be carried on not only daily but hourly by both
parents from the time they rise in the morning until they go to
bed. This is God's standard for all children, not just for PK's.
The people who point out the flaws in preachers' children had

better check on their own children, since they are to be just
as perfect as the PK's.

While the influence of the congregation on ministers' children often has adverse effects on them, I believe that most of the
troubles that contribute to making preachers' kids bad come
from the parents and the improper type of homelife.

There are four ways in which the minister and his wife can
have the wrong influence on their children. These are: neglect,
pressuring the little ones into a preconceived pattern of what
the model PK should be, the attitude of the parents toward the
church and the demands of the ministry, and the atmosphere of
the home.

There are many ways of neglecting children while giving
them the best physical, educational, cultural, and even spiritual
training. It is often hard for some parents to see, and seems to
be especially true in the minister's family.

There seems to be much evidence that the parents' neglect of
their children due to the pressure of the church work has more to
do with the way they turn out than any other. A lady said to me,
"Rev. and Mrs. So and So certainly neglect their family." I
happened to know from Mrs. So and So that this lady is the
most demanding member of their church. So I quietly and
politely asked, "Has it ever occurred to you that they might
long for more time to be with their children but the congregation is taking so much of their time that they can't do both?"
She snorted indignantly, "Well, I might have known all you
ministers' wives would stick together." With that she marched
away without a thought of the true cause of the situation. But
this is something about which every church member should
ask himself some serious questions: Am I having a part in the
neglect of my pastor's children by thoughtlessness or selfishness?
Am I really concerned enough about them to sacrifice a little on
my part, to take an extra job if needed, to spare the pastor and
his wife needless extra activity and thus enable them to take
better care of their families?

There are many people who can carry on the work in the church but you, pastor's wife, are the only one who can be a mother to your children. God is holding you responsible for the care and training of your children and the care of your husband to better fit him for his work in the church. In most cases there doesn't have to be a choice between the good of your children and the work of the church, but when those few times do come, the children should come first, no matter what the attitude of the congregation may be.

For that reason, I would like to show that in most cases there shouldn't be any conflict between your God-given duties as a pastor's wife and as a mother except when a new baby arrives, a child is sick, or some emergency arises. Church life should be such a definite part of your family life that all are active in its services at the same time, thus leaving the mother free to carry on her work as pastor's wife. The children should be as keenly interested in the activities of the church as the parents so that the family is doing together something everybody likes.

My husband and I avoid going out on the same nights as much as possible. Usually one of us is home with our girls. We also plan our schedule so that we seldom go out together more than once a week—and that only occasionally—unless the children are to go with us. When we do leave, my mother stays with them. Because they love her so much and she is a member of our family, they don't feel neglected. If you are not so blessed, you can usually find someone who will sit for you—often free—and take good care of your children. Don't be surprised if your baby-sitter soon wins the children's love. After our first baby was born, we had a lovely teen-ager whom our little girl came to love so much that she sometimes begged me to go away so Shirley would come and play with her.

Just make sure that your children don't have the feeling that they are shoved around from baby-sitter to nursery to a meeting or any place to dispose of them because the church work comes first. Make sure your children feel first in your life, and then they will cheerfully give up your presence from time to time for the sake of the work of the church.

The elementary school nurse at the school where my daughter attends told me that she had checked carefully on the children to see why they come to the clinic. She found that many ministers' children (and there are an unusually large number in this school district) come to the clinic, that they are constant repeaters, and always seem too tired. Some discreet questioning revealed that they were taken to church meetings night after night and seldom got enough sleep for a school-age child. She wondered why the parents didn't realize they were harming their children by neglecting to see that they got enough rest for their bodies in order to do their best work in school. Apparently the mothers feel that they must attend these meetings, even though it means taking a small child. The child should be at home on school nights either with the mother or a dependable baby-sitter and put to bed at the proper time. What the nurse observed is a very poor testimony in a public school, especially when ministers faithfully preach sermons on the Christian home and the care of children. The people around the minister see that he is not practicing what he preaches.

As long as the mother keeps her God-given place in the home and gives the children proper attention and the daddy gives them at least a little undivided time each day, the children feel that all is well and don't resent the many times when daddy must be out. As long as they feel first in the lives of their parents and are assured that they are wanted and appreciated, they will be interested in the church work and know that it is necessary for their daddy's work, just as many other fathers who are in professional work must be away from home a lot.

I know that my husband is often very tired with several jobs, but he sees that he gives each of our girls his personal attention some time during the day or evening. He is very affectionate toward them, and they dearly love him, even though he is often away from home. When he is home, he is a real father, so they don't resent his being away. They understand his work, pray for his ministry, and are more than willing to do without him that others might hear the Gospel preached. But each night that he is home early enough, he always visits each girl individually and has what our little one calls "our loving session." He goes to their rooms, where they can tell him things without anyone else hearing, and gives them his undivided attention for that time, shows them his love, and leaves them feeling happy, secure, wanted and an important part of the family. As a result of our actions, our girls are very loving persons. Our church people can hurt them most by not responding to their love, which they distribute liberally. I dread the time when they will see what real hatred can do.

You tired, discouraged ministers are wondering how you'll have the strength to give some time to your children. Perhaps they will be noisy and demanding when you come home sick at heart and laden with others' burdens. But your children are an important part of your congregation, as well as your responsibility, and if you neglect to give them some attention, they will blame the church or even the Lord. Unconsciously you will be turning them away from the very things that you are trying so hard to teach them. You may be giving them the idea that Christianity is just something that makes daddy tired and cross, and makes him yell at them. You can't blame them for not wanting that. If you see the need and really want to play with your children, the Lord will give you the strength. It may surprise you to know that some physical exercise is better relaxation than slumping into a chair rehashing the offenses of the day. Dr. Paul Dudley White, the famous heart specialist who cared for former President Eisenhower, has stressed the importance of exercise, and you will probably be aiding your health at the same time, as few ministers get enough outdoor exercise. Your outlook on the church problems will also be changed by the fresh air and seeing the joy you are giving your children. This won't put you in the limelight like church work, or bring honor to you, and it is often hard to find time, but you must include in your schedule time for your children or you shouldn't have any children. I have seen so many neglected wives and children of ministers that it often seems better for clergymen not to marry.

A Christian psychiatrist told me that if a child clings too closely to his parents after the toddler stage, it is a sure sign that he is not getting the attention and affection he should have from his parents to give him a feeling of security. In such a case, it is only natural that the child will in his mind blame the church people and the work of the ministry as soon as he is old enough to understand his father's work. He will unconsciously resent everything connected with Christianity before he fully comprehends what it is or what he is doing. And later in life he may develop feelings of guilt about his attitudes, which aren't his fault. His attitudes go back to parents who neglected him because of the church work, which seemed of primary importance at the time, or because the pressure from the people made it nearly impossible for them to give him the time that he should have had with his parents. Their lack of time with him meant neglect of the spiritual instruction and guidance God demands in the home.

The second cause for ministers' children going astray or becoming truly bad kids may be found in the restrictions put on them by the parents because of the father's position. We have already talked about the proper kind of teaching and training for all Christian children, but now are going to talk about those restrictions that relate only to ministers' children.

Naturally, the ministerial couple want their children to be well mannered and looked up to as good children by the members of the church. This is not always easy, since the children are watched by the congregation, and everything they do is especially noted and often passed from person to person as a bit of gossip. The parents as well as the children are living under this strain and pressure. Sometimes parents, in their zeal to see that the children are pleasing to the congregation, are tempted to use the wrong methods to bring it about.

We feel so guilty about the least thing our children do wrong and are so sensitive to any criticism, that we feel any method is justified if it makes the family into model PK's.

Often our first mistake is to bring up our children by standards we know the church members will approve. Many times what we do is not necessary, but we have to be on the safe side. At other times, we feel what is expected of our children is far above what others demand of their children, but because of the father's position, we must insist on certain conduct. We are given our standards in the Bible for rearing our children, and no matter what the church folks think, our first duty is to train our children by the Word.

Another mistake is often made. This is to suggest by our words and actions that our children must live as a credit to their daddy's profession. Everything they do is weighed on the basis of how it will affect the pastor's ministry—not how it will affect the children. Many times, I have heard a parent say, "We can't let you do that because your daddy is a preacher." Or, "No minister's child can do that without being criticized." And as a girl leaves for a party or a date, she is told, "Remember you're a minister's daughter, so see that you act like one." None of this is calculated to make being in a minister's family very popular.

There is an unwritten rule in our family that no decision of what our girls can or can't do is to be put on the basis of the fact that my husband is a pastor. We make our own decisions of what is right and wrong for them according to our personal views in the light of God's Word. Their lives are governed by the principles given for all Christian children. Our girls have never heard us even suggest that they have to act in such a way as to enhance their father's prestige. He can take care of his own image without sacrificing our children for his benefit.

We all shudder a little at the German legend about Faust who sold his soul to the Devil in order to have all the worldly things that he wanted in this life, but think little of what we are doing to our children for our personal gain. Someone said, "We wouldn't sell our children for a million dollars, but we might as well because we often sell them inch by inch."

One more mistake often made by parents in the ministry usually comes as the result of a conflict in our own desires and feelings as against what our parishioners might think or feel. Most children soon sense such conflicting feelings and are thrown into a state of confusion, and some take advantage of the situation and play one parent against the other, much to the guilt and distress of the parents, thus adding to their difficulty in rearing their children in a cross fire between personal convictions and congregational opinions. Conflict between the desire to bring up our children as normal and active on the one hand and the feeling that they must wear halos before other Christians, puts us in the awkward and serious position of trying to push our children into behavior they don't understand. As a result, not only are the parents often embarrassed but the children suffer emotional injury; they are punished, and become rebellious for just cause.

An illustration might show you better than an explanation. At a ministers' conference in the East, the friend sitting next to me at the dinner table whispered, "Watch what is going on at the next table." We both did. "She is going to wind up by taking him out of the dining room to give him a spanking," was the next remark. Sure enough, after an exchange of words, some demands and tears, mother and son left, with the mother almost dragging the boy, her face red with rage and embarrassment. It was obvious to both of us that the child was being expected to do something the mother thought he should do as a minister's son (though we couldn't hear a word of the conversation) which the child did not have to do at home. It was apparent he didn't understand why the mother suddenly required of him what hadn't been expected of him at home. "It really was her fault," my friend said, and I agreed.

Last, but not at all the least of mistakes made by parents, is the habit some have of correcting and punishing their children in front of the church people. It is terribly humiliating and confusing for the children to be treated so. Some people have the idea that spanking children at church functions is evidence that they are being well disciplined . It is my personal opinion— and that of many in the field of psychology—that resorting to spanking a child in public is a sure sign that the parents are the poorest of disciplinarians. Some of the congregation may get great satisfaction from seeing such a performance, but it really is nothing but a show and the child realizes better than we think that he is the butt of the "joke." I will never give a church member the satisfaction of seeing my child punished. Once, when it had to be done—and it was only once, during a church picnic—I took her to the car, and a good talking corrected the trouble in quick order. Punishment which has to be done at the church indicates a lack of systematical or proper punishment at home.

No wonder many pastors' children are unhappy and confused, and rebel against the church and even against the Lord! However much their parents might shine as workers in the church, they are such poor representatives of a Christlike life in the treatment of their children that the children see only the inconsistency, and often turn against their parents and want nothing to do with the church.

A grade-school teacher told me the story of the son of a minister of one of the our Dallas churches. During Education Week, parents were encouraged to visit the school. The teacher suggested that each child draw a picture of his or her father. The minister's son drew a picture of his father with horns and a tail, complete with a pitchfork in his hand. Needless to say, the drawing was destroyed, but the truth of how that boy really felt about his daddy was too evident to be concealed. He was a boy who was forced to live up to the image that his father had created for himself before the church people, but the father had no time to be a companion to his child. Failing in this, he had lost a son. It is too bad he couldn't have seen that picture, no matter how much it would have hurt him, so that he could have restored his relationship to his boy.

The third influence for good or bad on our children is the attitude we have toward the work of the church and the demands of the ministry. This is one of the most crucial areas for the formation of good or bad impressions of God's work. These will stay with them all of their lives. If our attitudes are good, anything hurtful the church people do will have little lasting effect on the children.

We should show our children that we think what we are doing is the greatest work in the world. If we don't feel that way, we had better change jobs. My husband and I feel that the Lord has blessed us above others in giving us the opportunity to work full time with the souls of people in need, and our girls have adopted our attitude. They are proud of being PK's! Both of them hope to marry ministers. They feel that they have a privileged place in life. Our teen-ager teaches children's church and Bible school, and is active in all organizations in our church of her age group. She loves every minute of such activity. Both girls feel hurt if they are denied the joy of attending even one meeting.

Our children feel that they are a vital part not only of our family but of the church family also. They love our people because we love them. They pray for our members because we do as a family, and seriously take to heart the burdens and hardships of the members. We tell them when someone is sick, when someone has to have an operation or needs special prayer (except in confidential cases and those we feel are not suitable for them to know about). So great is the interest and love of our girls that they remember these same needs again in their private devotions.

Our children are happy and cheerful no matter what goes wrong in the church and are not hurt or burdened by mistreatment or misunderstandings because they see that we are not. They have seen how we trust the Lord to work out the details of our lives and of the church work and wait for God's will. They see that is the pattern for our lives. I do not tell these things to give any credit to us but to show that members of the family automatically absorb the feelings and attitudes of the parents. Children are usually happy and content with that which satisfies their parents.

A large number of fine grown-up sons of ministers said that they found it very difficult to even consider entering the ministry because of their parents' attitude toward the work. They wouldn't have minded budget meals, hand-me-down clothes, occasional mistreatment by church members, and old-fashioned homes, which they said were usually more fun to live in than modern ones. They never would have noticed these things if their parents hadn't talked about them so much and lamented the sacrifice that they and the family had to make because the father was a pastor.

If my husband and I have any complaints about church affairs or any members, we save those discussions for times when the girls aren't around to hear. We expect too much of our little ones if we call on them to bear burdens that aren't theirs but our own. Since they aren't a part of the church staff, they shouldn't have to shoulder any of the responsibilities or heartaches, if it is at all possible to spare them. It is so easy to discuss problems at the table when they listen, and talk about difficulties that they can't change. So often we make a hasty remark about a problem or a person, which we promptly forget as soon as we have let off some steam of resentment, but the children seldom forget, and these things are magnified in their minds as serious troubles.

A pastor's wife had a keen dislike for a lady member of their church. She frequently aired her feelings at home in front of her four-year-old son. One Sunday, after services, the little boy was standing on the brick rail by his mother, who was greeting people. The lady his mother complained about so much came by. The little boy, overcome with resentment for the way this woman made his mother feel, reached over, jerked off her hat and pulled out the feather before anyone realized what was happening. The little fellow was severely punished and because the lady was the church gossip and continually talked about the incident, the child was labeled as a bad PK. In my opinion, the wrong person got punished, and a child was given a reputation in that congregation that should have been given his mother.

The atmosphere of the home is usually the sum total of the three influences on our children which I have mentioned: The attention given to the children by their parents (or lack of it); pressure to live up to an image for the sake of family pride; the attitude of the parents toward the church work. If we have failed in even one of these areas, we can be sure that the atmosphere of the home is not what it should be to produce happy, well-adjusted Christian children.

The big question that every ministerial couple should ask themselves is: "Is this a real home for our children, or just an annex to the church?" If the manse is a place in which to eat and sleep and hurry to another church meeting, it is not filling the needs of the children. If the family discussions are a continuation of the last board meeting, scheming for ways to push our ideas through an organization, a rehash of plans for the women's auxiliary or a series of running comments on the faults of the church members, the family is not being given a chance to have any real fellowship with their parents. If members are constantly dropping in to air their opinions and take the mother's time for nonessentials, the children are not having a proper homelife.

The manse was next door to the church in our first pastorate. Because gas rationing was in effect, the ladies had to walk to the store each day and get the groceries they could carry home. The manse made a nice stopping place to rest and visit on the way home. Many times I would be working in the kitchen, only to be startled by finding a church member standing in the doorway watching me. She had to come through the front door, hall, living room, and dining room to get there. Since the church had no phone, people came in a steady stream to the manse between Sunday school and church to use our telephone and bathrooms, and borrow anything they happened to want. I couldn't lock the doors because no one else in the small town did—even at night. This would have been considered an insult. Every time there was to be a church supper or party at the church, people came to borrow things from the manse, and my day was spent serving them. Sometimes I even returned home to find in my house women who were borrowing things, fixing coffee, or using the telephone. The only way we could be certain that we were dressing in private was to use the bathroom and lock the door. (Now do you wonder why I strongly recommend having the manse some distance from the church?) Happily, our first child wasn't born until a few months before we left this church, so I was able to "take" this routine. Children would have been greatly disturbed by it, and before long they would have thought they lived in the church with the congregation. My time and attention would have been shifted to the church ladies so often that my children would soon have lost any feeling of being important to us; instead they would have felt that all members of the congregation were more important than they.

We make a real effort not to discuss the church at all except just before our family prayer time. When we are together as a family, we talk about the things that interest the children, what they did at school, what their friends said, and things that interest every member of the family. This is healthy for the pastor and his wife, too, since they need periodically to get their minds completely off their work.

We make short trips together, go to dinner together, plan our vacations, and work on our lake cottage together. Our girls get the center of attention as much as possible when we are home as a unit. My husband is home for nearly every meal except for a few dinner meetings and banquets, even though he is a full-time pastor and teacher.

Recently a Dallas pastor proudly said, "I haven't had a night at home for over two weeks." My husband and I looked at each other, for we were at a large social gathering which did not require this pastor's attendance. He could have stayed at home, or he could have brought his wife if he had really wanted to. Either he doesn't care to be at home, or he is working himself and his church members too hard with unnecessary meetings. Lay Christians often have the same problem of how to give their children plenty of time, so it is a shame if a pastor is one who can be blamed for the lack of proper attention to his wife and children. Mothers and fathers can give their children the proper care and attention if they really want to. We always do what we think is necessary. The problem is to make people and pastor see that the homelife is the first responsibility.

My husband felt the need for families to be together some nights of the week so keenly that instead of having something going on in our church every night, he consolidated our programs on Wednesday nights. There is something for every member of the family during prayer meeting time. There are Sunday school, young people's meetings, and church services on Sundays. A person can be fully active in our church by only coming Wednesday night and Sundays. The only other times our church is open is for a monthly meeting of the ladies and one for the men, occasional family night dinners, and Sunday school class parties and board meetings. People schedule their committee meetings either before or after a service on Wednesday or Sunday. No one need neglect his family because of any church activity. Some pastors have gotten on a treadmill of activity, and they either don't want to get off or are afraid to jump. They seem to measure the success of their work by the number of nights the church is open and the number of meetings they can list in their bulletins. With wise planning, they could accomplish the same things in fewer nights and encourage families to have more time together.

A definite time for family devotions on a level understood by the children is the best way I know to provide a good atmosphere in the home. Many complain that it is impossible to find a time when the family can be together. Something is seriously wrong in a home if the entire family doesn't sit down to have a quiet, unhurried meal together at least twice a day. No wonder families are splitting up! Parents should see that the family takes time to eat together and to feed on God's Word together. Those who see the need of reading the Word and of praying, will find the time to do it!

Many of us who are God's special servants are working so hard for Him that we don't have any time to be with Him. We are not only doing the work of the church in our own strength and wisdom but we are often trying to rear our children in just the same way. There should be much prayer on our part for our children and for ourselves that we be given the knowledge and wisdom to guide and train them the way God would have us do. After the first few years, they are away from us most of the day, and many temptations will present themselves. Our prayers must follow them from our home all through the day and all through their lives to hold them steady and walking in God's straight and narrow path. How tragic it is to see a minister's child going wrong when the minister and his wife won't take the necessary time to pray for them. There are some who pray faithfully for the needy church members but forget their own flesh and blood and also forget that they are a part of the congregation, too, and should receive at least the same consideration.

Every ministerial couple has to find some way to have a happy, cheerful home life, uncluttered with church members or problems of administration of the pastor's work. Usually the largest part of providing a happy home atmosphere falls on the mother, who is already too busy with housework, child care, and church activities to have much energy left for seeing that everything is running smoothly and well in the home. This is not quite fair, but is a fact that we must face and do something about. Blessed is the woman who has real emotional and physical strength for the work that is set before her, so that she can be equal to such a full schedule. But I say again, if there is not enough strength and time for all things, put the family first.

It was seemingly by accident, from the human standpoint, that I found the answer of how to teach, train, and show real love to my children and make them feel wanted and important in our lives. Our first baby was only a few months old when we moved to our second pastorate. Our house was constantly full of church members, overnight guests, and relatives. My schedule left no time for my private devotional life. No one resented the time it took me to put my baby to bed, so I took that for my prayer time. Since I am the old-fashioned type of mother, I enjoyed rocking my baby, and it was easy to give her a bottle, rock, sing, and pray during this time. I prayed out loud while I rocked, sang hymns, and put my baby to bed. Then I leaned over the crib and prayed a short prayer just for the baby. Though she couldn't understand a word that I said, she could hear the prayer, and she sensed she was getting some special attention from me. As our girls grew older, I started teaching them how to pray and repeat very short sentence prayers, and I encouraged them to sing with me. They first learned Bible stories by looking at pictures in Bible story books and talking about them. When my girls were older, I read the stories to them.

My older daughter says that her earliest memory of me is my rocking her, singing hymns, and praying. That memory more than makes up for the activities I missed when I took time to put my babies to bed instead of leaving them immediately. The few times that we went out to dinner, the baby-sitter did the same things I did. Because I put them to bed early, it was seldom necessary to miss this precious time together. If for some reason I couldn't be with them at bedtime, my husband took over.

There was a four-year-period when their devotional times at night overlapped, and this helped the younger one mature faster and made an even closer family bond. She also learned a great deal from listening to her sister's prayers, and felt the affection of her sister as she participated with her.

I followed this plan until my older daughter was ten, and I will do the same for the other.

Even more precious results came from this time spent with the girls. It established a regular habit of private devotions which has stayed with our teen-ager; it permitted me to lead both of the girls to Christ as Saviour at the age of four. Without any prompting or suggestion from me, each of the girls was able to lead in public prayer, even before adults and strangers, by the time they were five. Our daughters are not exceptional in any way; they are just average children. But what was accomplished was the result of many hours of slow, loving, patient teaching them to really talk to God and training them from the Bible. This can be done in any home where one or both of the parents are willing to give the time.

"I often wonder why there are not more ministers' children with nervous breakdowns or in mental institutions, who are juvenile delinquents, or in penitentiaries." I stared unbelievingly at Dr. Gladys Brown, Christian psychologist, former head of the Child Guidance Clinic of Dallas and now in private practice. She is a minister's daughter and has a brother who is in the ministry. She works for four denominations in testing ministerial and missionary candidates before their churches will admit them to service under their auspices. She is paid by one of the largest churches in Dallas to take care of the psychological problems of any church member who needs it. Sixty percent of her work is done with ministerial families, so there is no one better qualified than she, both from her experience, background, and technical knowledge, to know the truth of this matter.

Dr. Brown says there are three major factors that often contribute to the difficulties of ministers' children.

First, the father, because of the pressures of his church work and the long hours demanded of him, is usually unable to meet the father needs of his child in a healthy relationship.

Second, most ministers' children lack the comfort of pastoral counsel (which includes spiritual help but goes far beyond that into all areas of life). Unless a very close relationship has been built up between parent and child during the years, it is not to be wondered at if the child tries to find help somewhere else or becomes so insecure that sometimes he misbehaves in order to get his parents' attention. Then, too, the busy church worker either does not take time to encourage confidences or does not take seriously the attempts of his children to get help.

Third, the mother usually does not have the home support of her minister-husband in the care or training of the children nor in the meeting of her own social, mental, and spiritual needs. To make matters even harder, she is usually so pressed for time that instead of being able to cope with the problem of being mother and father to her children, she is forced to hold them off and encourage them to find some other way to occupy themselves to save her own sanity. She is just too busy with the church people or too tired to listen to her children.

Dr. Brown says that there is one message that she would like to get across to every minister and his wife, and so she has graciously given me permission to tell you these things. "Please accept your children just as they are. Don't try to make them over so they will be a credit to your profession and be pointed out as model PK's. The result is always an unhappy, disillusioned, and often apparently bad child who feels insecure and unloved." She told me that she is working with a pastor's son now who, to use her terminology, is a "horrible brat." He just cries in her office and tells his parents, "You don't love me, you don't love me, you don't love me." He had been forced into a way of life and a mold that his father felt was becoming to a minister's child and would enhance the father's work and be a credit to his profession. The psychological pressure was too great for the boy, and he began to strike back at his parents by doing all the mean, ugly little things he could think of to hurt and embarrass them. But the parents are the ones to blame; not the child! But often the true blame goes back even further than that to what is constantly expected and demanded from both the pastor and wife by the church people and the public.

The unthinking and unknowing public goes merrily on its way, expecting more of the ministers' families than angels could give. The public watches and criticizes the minister's family, believing that anyone who grows up in the manse should automatically be perfect, never dreaming that PK's have more handicaps than children whose fathers engage in other occupations.

CHAPTER 7

Home or Just a Building?

ONE OF THE TOUCHIEST subjects which can be discussed in any group of ministers' wives is the manse or parsonage. Judging from the hundreds that I have seen, the usual criticisms of parsonages are justified. Few of them are ever new, or remodeled; most of them are almost impossible to heat comfortably. Many would be a discouragement to an interior decorator with money enough to make any changes he chose. Many a wife weeps bitter tears over the building that is turned over to her and her husband; she knows what a big job is hers to try to make it into an attractive, comfortable, convenient home.

In the book, *I Chose a Parson,* by Phyllis Stark, which is largely a true story of her life, she has included some interesting descriptions of some of the rectories in which they have lived. Perhaps the most dangerous and inexcusable condition of one home was the way the heating system was installed. There was one large, uninsulated pipe running from the basement, through a first-floor room, to the upstairs hall. In order to get to the bathroom, one had to pull in his tummy and flatten himself against the wall as closely as possible, to keep from touching the hot furnace pipe, until he could slide through the bathroom door.

A limited survey, taken here in Dallas, shows that only a small percentage of the church members have ever been through a manse. They just take it for granted, if they think of it at all, that the board members see that a nice home is provided for the ministerial family. Even those who have been to the manse are usually there for open house, and they did not get a good look at the place because there were so many others there. They did not see the kitchen and the upstairs and, of course, had no way of knowing if the mechanical equipment in the house was in good working order. A few minutes of visiting and eating at an open house do not give the church people a real idea of what the parsonage is like.

I would challenge the churches who are now changing pastors to encourage as many members as possible to go through the home they provide while it is empty, and take a good look at it. Just remember that looking at a home and living in one are two different things. Have someone with the proper experience check the furnace to see if it is adequate, and whether it will be too costly to run. See if the water heater really works, and if it is large enough to meet the demands of the family for hot water. Do not forget the plumbing and the kitchen stove. Check the kitchen carefully for conveniences, as the wife will spend a large part of her time there, and will find a modern kitchen her greatest help and joy.

Afterwards, have the ones who took the tour of the manse vote on whether they would be happy to live in that house, and give them a chance to make suggestions as to what might be done to make it nicer. This will probably be a surprising revelation to both the congregation and the members of the church boards. At least, it will open their eyes to what they are expecting the pastor's family to enjoy. It will also give them an understanding as to why the wife sometimes complains, in spite of her determination not to say a word.

Odd as it may seem, some Christians expressed the opinion that such a godly couple as the pastor and his wife should not care what kind of home they have, because that is concerning themselves about worldly possessions. That makes us all feel like we are considered to be very peculiar people! These people have two very obvious loopholes in their thinking.

First of all, the average minister and his wife are well-educated and well-trained people who are used to moving in circles of friends who have the finer things in life. They have an appreciation for good art, music, and so on, and have developed, if they did not previously have it, a sense of good taste and discrimination. It would be an offense to their aesthetic sense to be given just any kind of house which has a roof and four walls, and would have nothing to do with their spirituality!

The second fallacy in this line of thinking is purely for the sake of the church itself. Since the pastor works long hours— far beyond a forty-hour week—and his wife works right along with him a large part of the time, it is almost imperative that the manse be as easy to keep as possible, in order to give them more time to work with the congregation. The harder the house is to keep, the less time will be left for the church. When the pastor's wife gives almost full-time work in the church, without pay, the least the church can do for her is to make the home as nice and as convenient as possible, thus helping to keep her from becoming sick or unhappy and wishing to leave the parish.

If the pastor's wife is constantly burdened with needless inadequacies that keep her cross and edgy and overworked, her husband will gradually be affected. He cannot do his best work when he knows his wife is discontented. His resentment will begin to transfer itself to members of the church and thus the Lord's work may be greatly hindered.

In a number of cases, we know of ministers who are being compelled to take time from church work to assist their wives in the home duties because their home is so inconvenient. She has to have help, and they cannot afford to pay someone else for such work.

In one of our church-provided homes, otherwise very nice, my husband had to arrange to be home every two hours to fire the furnace because the steps to the basement and carrying the heavy coal across the entire length of the house were too much for me. Because we had to use soft coal, and were inexperienced in firing, the fire took constant attention. Even at that, it often went out, in spite of the efforts of both of us. Others who had lived there had had the same problem, so it was not totally our fault.

Before we discuss further what a church can do about the manse situation and what the minister's wife can do about it, I think it best to tell you of the homes in which we lived. You might be tempted to think that what I have written comes from a complaining, resentful, middle-aged woman who is getting emotional release by venting her feelings on all church members for the way she has been treated in the past. That would not be fair, nor true, for I and my husband have been blessed in the homes which have been provided for us—much more so than many of our friends.

My husband is serving his fourth pastorate. The first was during his student days here at the seminary. Since our first manse was in an open field, next to a country church, wood stoves were used for heating and cooking, and there was no plumbing. Therefore, we were thankful that we had to live in Dallas for my husband to attend daily classes. However, this should be said to the credit of that congregation: the manse was nicer than most of their homes.

When we entered our first full-time pastorate in western Pennsylvania, the church built us a new manse. The Board of Trustees had taken a good look at the old one and found that it would cost half as much to remodel it as to build a new house, and they would still have just an old house. One trustee frankly said, when my husband was candidating, "We are not going to let you see the manse because we would feel we were taking you slumming." They rented a home for us while the new manse was being built. It was more than worth the wait, as it was a dream of a home, and we loved it. The fact that the door to the downstairs powder room and the front door were opposite each other and only four feet apart made for some hilarious and unprintable incidents, which we just took as a joke.

It was war time, and the ration board allowed us only enough oil to keep our thermostat at 65 degrees. There are days and months of sub-zero weather in that part of the country, and constant heating is needed nearly ten months out of the year. As a result, we had to close off most of the house. Also, since we could never get my husband's study any warmer than 60 degrees, it had to be closed except in the middle of the summer.

Our third manse was a lovely, twenty-five-year-old suburban Philadelphia home that had been kept in good repair and pleased us immensely when it was first shown to us. After we moved in and tried to run a household smoothly, we discovered that the kitchen equipment and heating facilities were also twenty-five years old. The kitchen stove leaked gas so badly that all my plants died. For fear of asphixiation we closed the kitchen door at night and opened the windows wide, in spite of the weather. The daily diaper wash soon brought to light the fact that, in spite of having two water heaters, we did not have hot water. The heater we were told to use looked like a miniature version of the pot-bellied stoves one sees on the Westerns shown on television. This stove burned soft coal. I washed only when compelled to, even though we had a baby and in order to keep the thing going my husband had to study in the basement while poking the water heater with one hand, until the wash was done. I asked the woman who had worked in the manse how to fire the heater. She replied, "Nobody's used that heater for years. It has never worked because the drafts were not installed right." That left us no choice but to try the second heater, which looked more impossible than the first—and was! My husband is a general handyman, so with some adjustments, new parts, and a lot of scraping of rust, we managed to start it without blowing up the manse. It was a twenty-five-year-old, supposed-to-be automatic, coil gas heater. But the burner was on all the time, and we never had more than muddy, lukewarm water. We operated this heater until we received our first gas bill and discovered that it cost more to have rusty, lukewarm water, than to heat an eight-room house. From that time on, we heated all our water on the kitchen stove and carried it where it was to be used. What hurt most was the fact that my brother had given me a new, automatic Bendix to make my work easier, and it sat in the crate, unopened, in our basement for two years, while I washed diapers by hand.

Now, let us be frank about the situation in this parsonage before we throw any stones. Whose fault was it? It was everybody's and nobody's. My husband should have told the church boards of our difficulties, to see if they would do something about it. I doubt seriously if any but the few to whom we dared speak about it (in an effort to get help) were aware that there was any problem, because later, when they did find out, a new kitchen stove and water heater were installed.

We are not the complaining type of people and, whenever possible, we have fixed up the manses ourselves, and have even done much to improve them. We honestly thought, since we knew some others had pot-bellied types of water heaters, that it was our lack of experience that had caused our troubles. On the other hand, the manse equipment should have been checked before we moved in. It is still a mystery to us why the woman who cleaned the manse did not notice these things and report them to the Trustees. Perhaps she did. If she did, why did they not do something about it before our arrival? It seems that everybody's business is nobody's business.

My husband's hobby is refinishing antique furniture. We use it, but we do not like antique kitchens. He requested the trustees to remodel the kitchen after we had been there several years, but they refused. We proceeded to do it at our own expense. When they were told about that, they did offer to pay for the linoleum, as the old linoleum was so badly worn. They had painted it just before we came, and on damp days our feet would stick to it and make permanent shoe prints in the black paint. It was also gradually ruining our rugs by being carried into the other rooms on the bottoms of our shoes. With the help of a church carpenter and a plumber my husband completely modernized our kitchen at a cost of five hundred dollars, though the men generously gave their services free. No word of appreciation was ever expressed by any member of that church; in fact, no one mentioned what we had done to improve the manse. Six months later, my husband went into full-time teaching, and we had to start all over again in our own home.

Our present church does not have a manse, for which we are indeed thankful! We own our home and maintain it ourselves and therefore we can choose to live where we want to and decorate as we want to without comment or criticism from any church member. Last year we realized that we had to have another house. The church has grown so much that it was impossible to entertain any large groups of church members in that house. My mother suddenly developed trouble that made it impossible for her to live in a two-story house. We found exactly the kind of one-level home we wanted and needed, sold our house and bought this one. If our two-story home had been church-owned, we would have been in a very difficult spot, and it would have been next to impossible, and seemingly unreasonable, to buy another home. Our church, with about three hundred members, had just completed construction of a new church building. They would have considered it impractical to give up a house that was completely modernized, carpeted, draped, and air-conditioned, and located in one of the best neighborhoods of Dallas. Not only would they have considered such a move impractical, they would have objected because of the added expense of the new church building. But we had to move!

A revolutionary new trend is just getting started among churches to give a rental allowance and let the pastor's family choose their own home, as no one house can meet the needs of the successive parsonage families. In our case, one home did not meet our needs while we were serving the same church. All of the ministerial groups, and especially the students and their wives, are thrilled to think that they may possibly serve a church where they will be able to choose their own home.

I can hear howls from some board members over this idea. Those who oppose the plan could give me only four reasons, that are mostly just excuses.

One reason given was that it might be hard to find a home— for instance, during war time or in special industrial or military locations. In such cases, it would be better to have a church-owned home. Second, it has been a long-time habit to have the pastor live next door to the church. As one man frankly said, "Then we can keep a better check on him." That is the best reason I know for letting the pastor live away from the church. Third, some believed that choosing his own home would be an inconvenience to a preacher making a change of churches. That could be easily overcome. The church could get some idea of what the pastor wanted and line up a few real estate people who would show the pastor and his wife homes for rent at the time he comes to candidate. Unless they live a long distance away, they might be able to make several visits to the new city to select a home and to plan for its redecoration before they actually move their furniture. The last reason was that it would cost the church more to give a rental allowance than to furnish a manse. If your church is the kind that pays little attention to the manse, seldom redecorates, and expects the minister's family to live in it no matter what the problems and difficulties, you are probably right. However, if you already are maintaining a nice, proper-sized home, a little study will show that it would cost as little, or less, to pay the pastor a rental allowance. And the Board of Trustees would have less work and worry.

Since my word on this matter would carry little weight, I asked several very successful business men with a thorough knowledge of building and maintenance costs to estimate the difference in the cost of giving a generous rental allowance and owning a manse. They gave me a long list of figures which would only bore you, and would not fit your situation, anyway. But each of them showed me how the average church would profit by giving a rental allowance and not providing living quarters. They figured on the basis of a new home, with a mortgage and a small upkeep. They also figured on the basis of a house twenty-five years old, or over, which would have little or no mortgage, but which would have a very high cost of maintenance, remodeling, and redecorating. In each case, they felt it was better for everyone concerned to let the pastor choose his own home. Just see how this would work in our own church situation, one of the men said they would be better off to give us a three-hundred-dollar monthly rental allowance than to build and maintain a manse for us which would be in keeping with the average homes of our members, and large enough for entertaining church members. Ours is a new church and has never had a manse. The first pastor owned his home when he was called, and so did we.

My next step was to call several real estate agents to see how much it would cost to rent a nice home in a good part of the city. A house with three bedrooms, two baths, den, modern kitchen, central air conditioning and heating, and completely carpeted and draped, would cost from $150.00 to $200.00 per month, depending upon the age and location of the house. Of course, a house with a swimming pool or other luxuries would be more. Just six blocks away, an acquaintance is renting a new home with an all-electric G.E. kitchen, three bedrooms, three baths, den, a utility room (as large as most kitchens, with sink, cupboard space and all laundry connections), large living room, dining room, concrete patio (partly roofed), and a two-car garage with a large storage room. It is completely carpeted, draped, and has central air conditioning and heating. They are renting it for $175.00 per month. Rents and homes may be much different and cheaper where you live, but there is serious doubt if they would be more expensive.

The advantages of a church giving a rental allowance are

well worth their giving serious consideration to such a proposition. They would spend no more; in many cases, less. They would not have to worry about the neighborhood running down. They would save the many precious hours required to maintain the manse and to inspect and replace equipment. This would save meetings and the appointment of a committee. The church would be relieved of numbers of unexpected repair bills when something went wrong in the manse. Other advantages are the elimination of hard feelings and misunderstandings between the pastor's family and the board members and cutting of the red tape which the family frequently has to go through while church members decide if and when they will correct some troubles in the church-owned home. When the pastor can choose his own home, he can never complain or blame them for anything that displeases the family. As a result, there is a happier feeling among the more thoughtful members, who might have guilty feelings if the manse is not the kind of home it should be.

The advantages of this plan to the ministers' families would be many! They would be given a choice of the kind of home they would like to occupy. No one house will ever meet the needs of the successive ministers' families. If there is a large family, they can get a large home. If there is just a couple, they can choose to live in a small home or an apartment. If someone in the family is not well, or cannot go up and down stairs, then a house on one level could be rented. The family can have just the number of rooms needed, arranged in the way that suits them. They can get what will suit their furniture, and their carpeting and draperies, or a home which is already carpeted and draped. Those who like trees and open spaces might find a home on the edge of town. Those who prefer to live close to the church can do just that. Families with school-aged children can live in the districts which have the most desirable schools and shopping centers. Best of all, they can have the house decorated to suit their taste and not be subject to the decisions and ideas of the church members. Also, they can demand that things be fixed or changed by the landlord when needed without fear of offending some church people, or being refused help when it is needed. Then there is a wonderful psychological effect on the minister and his wife: They can be more relaxed and secure in a home which the church does not own, and no one can tell them how it should be used. This will enable them to do some things they probably would not dare do in a manse because of the danger of displeasing some of the members of the congregation. As long as the church folk own the home, there will always be some who feel they have a right to express their opinion as to how it should be decorated, and how the minister's wife should keep it. In such a situation, the wife can never feel completely at home in her own home. Giving a rental allowance might also help some couples who wish to buy a home, to get started. In every instance, where we have lived in our own homes, and improved them, we have sold them for more than we paid and have, in reality, lived rent-free in those houses while we were there. It gives a family more security to be buying a home, and this plan will probably make the difference for some families in realizing their dream. When the pastor leaves a town, he can sell his home, or he can rent it if he wishes.

Since so many churches are lax and show little interest in maintaining attractive, modern homes for their leaders, I believe this plan of a rental allowance will prevent a lot of heartache—and backache—for the pastor's wife, as well as dissatisfaction, and grief. The plan will automatically eliminate one cause of tension and misunderstanding between the church and the clergyman's family and might also keep your favorite pastor from leaving.

About a year after my husband left one particular church to go into full-time teaching, we heard that his successor had resigned. We got the full story from him later. It seems that when they built a new educational building, it required a new, much larger heating system. The trustees had put the old system, which had never worked satisfactorily in the church, in the manse to replace the impossible coal furnace. They never seemed to learn! Their attitude seemed to be the same: "Any old thing will do for the manse." They knew the oil furnace was old and hard to run and not trustworthy, but instead of having it checked, or overhauled, they put it in the manse. As a result, the new pastor spent half of his salary to heat the house. He found another church before the next winter. He had asked the trustees to have the furnace repaired, but they did nothing. When we were there, we had had a number of companies come to estimate the cost of repairing it, but they just laughed when they saw it. It was so old that many of the necessary parts were no longer being manufactured.

Several years ago I was a member of a church which had a large membership. A new pastor was called during that time. The church bought a new manse when they came, as it was too costly to remodel the old one, and it was in a poor neighborhood. Here was a golden opportunity to start the idea of a rental allowance and let the pastor choose his own home, but instead the church just bought another old house. Every time I went to call at the manse I was ashamed of that church.

The house was one block from a busy shopping center, and noise kept the pastor's family awake most of the night. One could seldom find a parking place anywhere near the manse because of the stores' customers. The pastor had to put his car in the garage, even to run into the house for only a few minutes. It was a ten-room house with an old, too-small kitchen. The upstairs was a source of irritation all the time. In order to get to the pastor's study, one had to go through a bedroom. And in order to get to one of the bedrooms, one had to go through another bedroom. Obviously, the back section of the house had been a later addition. There was only one bath for five bedrooms and the study. It may be that the purchase of the house by the church was due to undue influence on the part of several members. To be sure, it was certainly impractical. The wife spent most of her time just keeping that huge house clean and was nearly broken in health when they left.

Last winter we visited this couple several times in another part of the country. They have a darling new house just made for them. It has one bedroom, a bath, combination living and dining room, kitchen, and a recreational room in the basement. She looked better than I have ever seen her, and I frankly believe it is because she has a small home that requires little work. I am not sure that this is a rented home, but I think it is. I certainly hope so, for what would another man—with maybe six children—do in that house, or even we, with our two children, my mother, and our large antiques?

I realize that this is such a new and startling idea that many will reject it without giving it due consideration. For some churches it would be impractical, because they already have a good manse. But it is a good idea for church members to tuck away in their minds against the day when a lot of money must be spent remodeling the manse, or repairing it, or when the neighborhood changes for the worse. Then is the time to sell the old manse, or remodel and rent it, and let the minister choose his own home.

Regardless of how poor or rich the members, how small or large the church or town, there are three things that every church can do to make life more endurable for the minister's wife.

There should be a permanent manse committee. It should be made up of some members from the boards, who can also control the money that is used, and a goodly number of women of discrimination and good taste. This committee should be responsible for the condition of the manse and should be especially active when the manse is vacant. Then they should carefully inspect every detail of the home, run all of the equipment to see that it is in good order and arrange for repair or replacement of defective equipment. It is important to check the wiring to prevent possible fires, also to see that it is adequate for present-day electrical needs. The committee should oversee any remodeling or redecorating that is done, and see to it that the manse is spotlessly clean before the new family arrives. The manse should be completely redecorated, and by that I mean a new coat of paint on the walls and woodwork inside (and outside, if it is needed) for each new family, according to their own selection of colors, unless their requests are too ridiculous to consider, which is bound to happen occasionally. All apartment house owners with nice tenants redecorate every other year, no matter how long a person has lived there, and each time a change is made. Surely a church should not do less.

Some of the Methodist ladies objected to my suggestion of having a manse committee. Churches in their denomination usually have what they call a parsonage committee. They all agreed that this group usually made trouble, and did little good. One of them said that there seemed to be only two attitudes of persons on parsonage committees: "dominate" and "dictate." It seems that this committee made no honest attempt to make the church-owned home like the pastor's wife wanted it, but carried out their own ideas and, in many cases, since they were so determined to have their own way, and could not agree among themselves, the parsonage was a hodgepodge of loud wallpaper, off-colored paint, with no central decorating idea that tied the entire house into an attractive unit. In a number of instances, the committee just bought wallpaper and paint that happened to be on sale, with no thought as to whether the colors were harmonious. To make matters worse, volunteers from the church had done the work, and it was so poorly executed that the ladies who talked to me said they would rather have had it unpainted, and then do what they could, themselves. Often the members of the committees were never changed, so that the pastors' wives were helpless to stop the merry-go-round of hideous decorating.

Being a member of this committee seemed to give some of them the idea that they had the right, after the minister's family had moved in, to stop by at any time and tell the wife just how she must use the parsonage and what the church expected her to do with the things that they had furnished. To dictate seemed to be their greatest delight. They had little regard for the rights or ideas of the preachers' wives.

A veteran of forty years in the ministry with her husband recalled the days when the parsonage was always furnished, and usually with the castoffs of church families who seemed to feel that anything would be all right for the preacher's family. She could remember one place where they had to have umbrellas over their heads on rainy nights when they went to bed. The idea seemed to be that when it was raining, it was impossible to do anything about it, and when it was dry, there wasn't any need. In reality, a church member had promised to roof the house and never got around to doing it. Because he was giving his services free, the parsonage committee was afraid of hurting his feelings by reminding him, or insisting that he get the job done. I think I have already made it plain that this is not the kind of committee I have in mind.

Just as soon as the new man is called to the church, he and his wife can be shown the manse, while they are still in town, and given a chance to select the color scheme which will best suit their type of furniture, carpets, and drapes. Then the committee should oversee the work, and insist that it be completed before the family arrives.

Martha and Dick Brown were called to a Baptist church. They took the offer though there were only two bedrooms in the parsonage. They had three children. The church assured them that two rooms and a bath would be added before they arrived, if the weather stayed good. One of the bedrooms in the parsonage had been used as the pastor's study and church office. Martha and Dick thought they would move the office furniture to the church next door and, if the new bedrooms were not finished in time, they could manage with two bedrooms by having their son sleep on a cot in the living room. The weather stayed good but, when the Brown family arrived, they found only a pile of lumber in the back yard. Even though they were disappointed, they were determined to make the best of the situation. When they tried to move the office furniture to the church, they discovered that the congregation objected, that the church office had always been in the parsonage, and would continue to be there. That left them with one bedroom for five to use. To make matters worse, volunteer workers came three days a week to help with the church letters, bulletins, announcements, etc. Martha not only had to have them in her home, but she was expected to spend three days each week working right along with them. The last pastor's wife had worked with them because her children were married, and she enjoyed having the ladies there for a visit. But it was too much for Martha with all her housework, laundry, and such overcrowded conditions. Work on the new bedrooms progressed slowly because men just stopped to work on them on their way home from work, or came to build in the evenings. There were no plans to follow, so each man just did what he thought was best, according to his ideas, or those suggested by some of the women of the church. There was no one to oversee the work or insist that it be completed. During the winter nothing was done. By the next summer, interest had lagged so badly that men seldom came to work at all. Part of Martha's and Dick's furniture stayed in storage the entire time they were there. A little over two years later they were accepted by a mission board and went to the foreign field. She wrote to her mother that the home there was much nicer than the parsonage they had left.

The minister should be told he is to feel free to speak to the members of the manse committee at any time there is a need, without shame or guilt, to tell them what needs to be done.

For instance, if the plumbing fails to function, he should know whom to call, and that member should see that a plumber is notified immediately. If one of our Eastern churches had had a manse committee, we would not have had to make out with a leaking gas stove for so long, or go without hot water for two years.

This committee should visit the manse at least twice a year, at the wife's convenience, to inspect it and talk over the things the family would like changed. They should not bother the family at any other time, except by request. If there are several things they want, and only money for one, then the pastor's wife should be given the privilege of choosing the one which would help her the most. This method will keep the pastor and his wife from feeling that the church members just do not care how they live; will give them courage to ask for what they really need, without fear of offending anyone, or being criticized; and will make them more content to put up with inconveniences that they know the church cannot afford to change.

Now, to make this committee really effective, there must be a manse fund, or an item in the regular budget that includes money for maintenance on the manse. That figure will give both the committee and the pastor and his wife a good idea of the amount of money available to use for improvements. Having to beg and plead for every cent that is spent on their living quarters is very hard on ministers, and many times they will do without, rather than to ask.

If at all possible, the manse should be provided with carpets and drapes. Perhaps the most expensive part of moving to a new parish, and by far the most disheartening, is trying to make the curtains and rugs used in the previous manse fit the new one. To replace all drapes and rugs, on a minister's salary, every time a move is made, is completely out of the question. How nice it would be if the church could carpet and drape at least the living room, dining room, and den, or study, or any other room that shows from those just mentioned! The carpeting should be plain and in a neutral shade which will go with any color scheme and will not clash with any printed or floral-patterned upholstery. The carpeting, drapes, and walls should be the same color, thus enabling the family to carry out their own color scheme. These are very durable items and would not have to be replaced often.

When we moved into our first manse, it was war time, and rugs were almost unobtainable. We finally found a piece of carpet that would do for our living room. We had two huge picture windows, and nothing to put on them. Being just out of seminary, we could not afford even the cheapest curtain material to cover them. The church realized our dilemma and draped those windows for us.

The living room carpet used in the first manse looked like a postage stamp on the next manse floor. Though this carpet had a floral pattern, as did the wallpaper, and the colors fought with each other, we had no choice but to use the rug, though we knew it looked wrong. The house we have now has such a large living room that nothing we had would do. We found the solution in two similar, thirdhand, Olson rugs, which we used until we could afford to carpet our house.

We have hopefully arrived at a new manse with three nearly new pairs of drapes, only to find that the room they were meant for had four windows, or that the colors of our drapes and the wallpaper screamed at each other. Many times the manse is not well decorated, not because the family lacks taste but because they cannot afford to buy new rugs and drapes.

Our only good rug, given to us after the war, had a floral pattern and a border. When we moved to Philadelphia, it was much too small for the living room, and six inches too large for the dining room. The border on one end had to be cut off, though it looked queer, and we were never able to use that rug again.

No matter what the conditions of the manse, there is no excuse for not having it clean and spotless when the new family arrives. If the church cannot afford to pay someone to clean it, the ladies can make a project of cleaning the manse themselves. Perhaps the worst story I have heard about manses, and know to be true, was told us by one of my husband's students. Their first and only pastorate was in New England. When they arrived, they wondered where they would get the key to the manse. However, there was no need to bother, as two of the doors were swinging open. Unfortunately, some animals had discovered the house was open, too. The young couple lived in a motel while they made the manse sanitary enough to occupy. Though it took them a week, nobody came to see them, or to help. They lost their first and only child through the thoughtlessness and carelessness of unasked-for help. The wife has never been completely well since. The husband went from there into business. We have no right to judge his action in leaving the ministry, but we can certainly sympathize with him.

Though this story may discourage some of you new pastors' wives, it is usually possible to judge the type of people in your church, and the possible difficulties which will face you when you look at the manse. I know it to be true, in my experience, and most of my friends in the ministry will stand behind that statement with me.

You ministerial families can see that these pages are designed to alert the churches to see that you have nice homes. However, it is equally important for you to take care of the one that is provided. It should not be necessary to say this to those in full-time Christian service, but even some of them have the idea that as long as something does not belong to them they do not have to be careful to keep it in good order. Occasionally, the seminary gets a few couples who have no respect for the furniture and the apartments rented at small fee to the students. It is much better for the Christian to take better care of what does not belong to him than his own possessions, for the sake of his testimony for the Lord. As far as your talents and money go, the manse should be enhanced by your living there, and never run down.

Now suppose you have just graduated from seminary and have a wonderful picture in your mind of that first manse being a dream of a home. When you arrive you find instead that you have a barn of a house, and you feel your dreams slowly going down the drain. Do not let these first few moments of disappointment "throw you." You will be surprised what some paint and cleaning can do. Try to imagine your furniture and knick-knacks around, and you will begin to revive.

If you do not have furniture, don't go out and buy a houseful of cheap things. Start with an all-over plan. Know the kind of furniture you want, then buy good, well-styled furniture one piece at a time from a reputable store, as you can afford to. You will need a sofa, several chairs, small tables, and some lamps for the living room; a bedroom set, and a table and chairs for the dining room. You are going to need plenty of rest, so by all means do not scrimp on the choice of springs and a mattress for your bed. You can often find excellent buys in good secondhand furniture by watching the private and estate sales in the newspaper. And of course, if you can make slip-covers, and reupholster and refinish furniture, so much the better. Used furniture that is willed to you will be a great help until you can replace it with the items included in your master plan. Remember that the furniture you buy will have to do for all kinds and sizes of houses, so be careful in your buying. Conservative styles are far better, and will suit more kinds of houses and blend better with furniture bought later. If your floors are bare, a few scatter rugs will do at first. In case the floors are unsightly, rent a sander for taking off the old paint and stains. Any paint store clerk will instruct you in refinishing the floors after they are sanded. This will not be expensive when you do your own work. If your funds are limited, and the windows are bare, curtain them all the same in straight, white, inexpensive material. There are many kinds on the market now, at all prices. Be sure to make them very full, and floor length. Skimpy-looking curtains or drapes will ruin the looks of a room. Even if you have the money, it is unwise to buy expensive material for windows, as you will probably have to replace all of it when you move into the next manse. Always buy plain carpeting, for it may have to be cut down to fit another room.

Study your floor plans to see if it is possible to change the original intended use of the rooms to make things more convenient for you. If it is better for you to have one bedroom downstairs, then move the study upstairs and use the study for a bedroom. If you would rather eat in the breakfast room, and use the dining room as a den to make a large space (with the living room) for entertaining, or for the children's use, then do so.

Make up your mind that this is your home, even though it does belong to the church. In a very real sense, you are paying rent for it since it is a part of your husband's salary, and you have every right to live in it as comfortably as possible.

No matter how terrible the manse is, remember you are there because the Lord willed it to be so. He is sovereign and has a special purpose in having you right where you are. Just keep asking Him for strength to be cheerful and brave. Ask Him to help you make the manse attractive and keep you from complaining to the church members.

When people come to call and start telling you, "This room was supposed to be a study," or "That was not made for a bedroom," just listen, smile sweetly and say, "Is that so?" as if the thought had never occurred to you. There will always be some who will tell you what the last pastor's wife did. Listen politely and say, "Isn't that clever?" if you honestly can. If the idea sounds atrocious to you, say, "Well, I never thought of that." Especially if you are a young pastor's wife, some will sincerely think you need their advice.

Even though you may resent it, listen carefully. You might be surprised. They may really be giving you some ideas you can use. Always listen, and be polite, as there is no excuse for rudeness on your part, no matter how unkind a person may seem to be. Change the subject as soon as you can. You usually can get a woman to talk about herself and her house without much difficulty.

Some will come to your home and you will sense from their attitudes and quizzical looks, even though they may say nothing, that all is not according to their ideas, or arranged as the last pastor's wife had it. Make no explanations or excuses. Try to keep the subject from coming up, and if it does, divert the conversation to another subject as soon as possible. Remember, this is your home for the time that your husband is pastor of the church, and as long as you are taking good care of the manse you should live in it and enjoy it as much as possible in any way you see fit.

It was pure accident from the human standpoint that leaking gas from the stove in the kitchen of one of our manses was discovered while we were entertaining some of our board members and their wives. But if I ever live in another church-provided home, where there is no manse committee to help correct the wrongs, I would entertain some of the board members without trying to cover any difficulty. Let them have a look at things as they really are, and usually some changes will be made. A hint to the wise is sufficient, I hope.

When the women see that you are a good housekeeper and mother, they will soon learn to respect you and forget about the manse arrangement. Perhaps the next minister's wife will have to hear about how clever you were, and how you had the manse so well arranged.

CHAPTER 8

Have You Looked in a Mirror Lately?

WHAT A SILLY QUESTION TO ASK! Of course you've looked in the mirror several times today. But have you taken a serious, detailed look at yourself in a full-length mirror lately? Were you pleased with what you saw, or did you shrug your shoulders and just wish that your clothes were more stylish and better suited to your personality? Have you taken it for granted that nothing can be done about it, either because you do not have much money, or just do not know what you should do, or—and I hope this is not the reason—you just do not care how you look?

While the pastor's wife is not employed by the church, assigned certain duties, or given any special authority, she is definitely one of the most important leaders in the organization and, in a sense, the church hostess. For that reason she should appear as attractively dressed as possible all the time. She represents not only her husband but the church and the Lord. Many times the way she looks may have a great effect on the Lord's work.

Perhaps this is such a conviction to me because of the situation in my home church when I was a girl. Our pastors received a salary of $3,000.00 a year during the deepest depression years (more than the average man in the church), a new home with utilities paid, and car expenses. Many gifts were given them by well-to-do people. Our family lived on a farm, and every time we butchered, or the fruit or vegetables were ripe, we gave our ministers the best of everything we had. In spite of being well provided for, the ministers' wives were so poorly dressed that our church ladies were distressed. From time to time, I could not help hearing the ladies discuss the way the women of the manse dressed. Each time there was an interchurch gathering, or a Presbyterial meeting, the women secretly hoped that something would prevent our pastor's wife from going. They were ashamed of her and hated to admit that she belonged to them.

Even as a little girl I wanted to be a minister's wife and I vowed then that if, in God's will my wish were granted, none of my church ladies was ever going to be ashamed of my appearance. I determined that my ladies would *want* me to go with them to other groups and be proud to introduce me as their pastor's wife.

Some of my church ladies may be surprised to know that I have noticed, on special occasions, when I step into the room they carefully look me over from head to toe. But the little smile of approval and love and acceptance on their faces more than compensates me for any extra effort made to look just right. Perhaps the biggest compliment they pay me is to take me around to a group of strangers and proudly introduce me as "Our pastor's wife." Some of them give me a little hug in public and say, "We are so proud of you." That lets me know that a childhood conviction has borne fruit.

There are several general principles of good grooming that will apply to all, no matter what size the church or the type of people.

Never be conspicuously overdressed, or underdressed. Make it your purpose to look nice but not to draw attention to your clothes in any way. You do not want to draw attention to yourself; just create a pleasant illusion that you are nicely attired.

Judge your style and type of dressing according to the average woman in the church. Do not set your standards by the way the wealthy dress, or feel that you must dress like the poorest. Take the average as your guide.

As nearly as possible, dress in the manner that will make

the church women feel proud of you but not outclassed by you, so there will be no cause for envy or criticism.

There are still some in many sections of our country who feel that makeup is wrong for Christian women. No one has ever been able to prove to me that Scripture forbids the use of makeup, or even infers that making one's face attractive is a sin. However, since some people are offended by makeup, that puts its use in the class of doubtful things. Read the fourteenth chapter of Romans, where Paul deals with the Christian's responsibility in doubtful matters. Though you may feel that something is not wrong, yet for the sake of a weaker brother and because of love for him, you are to refrain from those things. If the majority of your church women feel that makeup is wrong, then you will be offending them by using it, thus disobeying God's Word and hurting your ministry among the women.

I came to Dallas from an Eastern city where makeup was frowned upon by many Christians in some very fine churches, so I was very careful in using it, though I have always used a little. To the surprise of some of you who read this, it is just the reverse in the Southwest. In Dallas it soon became evident that one's testimony was ruined if one did not use makeup and jewelry. If a woman's face is colorless, she is considered some kind of crank by even the most spiritual Christians. If you wear no makeup and try to witness to a stranger, the stranger may give you that what's-the-matter-with-you look. In case you haven't gotten my point yet and are still wondering what I do about it, I wear a generous amount of makeup. I would be very conspicuous if I did not. When traveling in different parts of the country, I am always careful to observe how Christian women feel about makeup and I govern myself accordingly.

Sexy type dresses, tight trousers that outline the body, brief bathing suits, and shorts are not for the minister's wife and, in my opinion, not for any Christian woman. Bathing suits and shorts of the proper kind are suitable for the beach and the swimming pool, but never in the manse or on the streets.

There should be a full-length mirror in the master bedroom of every manse and one near the front door so that all members of the family can be sure they look all right before starting away from home.

Now have another look in the mirror. Would you like to see if you need to make a few changes? Then maybe the suggestions that follow will help you.

When you have some time off, bring out your entire wardrobe, especially those clothes that are worn in public. Try on each dress and suit and take a good look in the mirror. What is right about this one? What is wrong about that one? Note the styles and colors that are becoming to you and those that do nothing for you, or even hurt your appearance. Remember, a dress can appear to subtract or add ten pounds to your looks. Decide what colors look the best. Add your accessories and see if they are really right for you, especially the hats. If possible, give away everything that hurts your appearance or wear them at home. If you do not have the money to replace the ones that do not look right, you will just have to wear them until you can. The main thing to learn is what looks best on you so that the next time you go to the store you will not make the same mistake. When you go shopping, have in your mind a full picture of the styles and colors that are most attractive on you, and do not let any saleslady talk you into buying anything else. Do not let the temptation of a bargain lure you into buying another mistake. Don't buy until you find what is right for the price you can pay. No matter how much of a bargain a dress is, if it is not right for you, it is a waste of money.

Since most of you who read this book will be limited by a moderate budget, you should make up your mind to buy conservative colors and styles. A dark-colored suit or dress can be dressed up or down by the different accessories used with it. I spent a day with one of our church ladies, wearing a black suit. That night, for lack of time to change, I wore the same suit to prayer meeting but changed my hat, scarf and gloves. She looked at me and said, "I like your new suit." By the way, it was three years old, too.

Do not buy the latest extreme style. It may not be accepted by the general public and will soon be out of style; you will be stuck with an outdated dress you are compelled to wear. In most cases, the usually accepted styles are the most attractive on the average figure, anyway. Do not buy a flashy or gaudy print, or a dress with too much trimming. Such a dress will make you conspicuous, most certainly make you look fatter, and once it is seen everyone will remember it from then on. Plain clothes with simple lines and little decoration will always be the most stylish and most becoming clothing, and can be used much longer because people do not remember them.

Before you have the money to renew your wardrobe is the best time to make a hobby of studying styles and trends in clothes. This takes no great effort or time. Just glance through the newspaper every day, read the articles that describe the clothes of well-known women and give the comments of fashion editors and the quotations from the best-dressed women in the country. Study names of labels of good brands of clothing so you will know them when they are on sale.

I think I learned the most about how to dress well by watching other women. I picked out a number of church ladies who were the most attractively dressed all the time. Each time I saw them I studied their costumes. "Why did she look so nice? What style of dress was she wearing? What fabric? Why did it look right on her? Would that same thing make me look fatter or thinner? What accessories was she using?" I learned from the women who most attracted me; they were the best fashion models to follow. I observed that they wore darker colors, plainer styles, and less jewelry at one time than the average woman. Some time later I found out their secrets. Several of them made their clothes. Two widows who have to support themselves have as modest a clothes budget as I. Several others, who can have almost anything they want, money-wise, buy all their clothes on sale. Also, they do not have any more clothes than I do because they have learned the art of making every dress and suit adjustable to almost any occasion by a change of accessories or jewelry.

If you read the women's pages of newspapers and magazines, you will often see a list of the clothes of many famous women who fly to Europe. All they take must be put into one suit-case. If they can go to the many places where they will be enter-tained on one suitcase of clothes, then certainly we can manage on few clothes and have better ones for the same money as used for a larger but cheaper-looking wardrobe.

We will assume that you have decided just what looks best on you, the type of clothing you need for the activities you attend, and have money for a shopping trip.

The first—and a very important purchase—no matter what your size or figure problems, is a good foundation, fitted by an expert. No matter how expensive an outfit, or how small your figure, your entire appearance will be ruined unless you have the right kind of girdle for your type of figure. This may make a serious hole in your clothing allowance, but will be the differ-ence between looking nice or sloppy, no matter what you pay for your dresses.

It is best to consider the type of stores where you can find the best clothes for your money. Often people who have a limited clothes budget go to the stores that have the cheapest clothes. As a result, their clothes look cheap even when they are new, and won't last very long. My husband and I had always had the help and advice of our parents in selecting our clothes until we were married, so we had to learn the hard way how to make the best buys. Because we were almost penniless when we left the seminary, we could buy only what we had to have. Everything we bought the first year was wrong. Our purchases were cheap-looking, poor-fitting, and after one season were worn out.

We changed our method. We started waiting until after the peak demand for the new season's clothes. We bought after Easter, Christmas, and July 4th, when the clothes went on sale. We began to investigate the good shops that carried only well-made clothing, and we discovered that by buying when there was a sale we could have a much nicer wardrobe, better-fitting, and longer-lasting, for the same price that we had paid for the cheapest clothes before. We soon discovered that the expensive clothes, bought on sale, were more of a bargain than the cheaper ones, and they looked nice until they were almost worn out. We built up a little clothing reserve and started a charge account so we could always take advantage of the best buys even if we did not have the cash on hand.

We anticipated our needs. If we knew my husband needed a new overcoat for the next winter, we went to the end-of-the-season sales the spring before and bought the coat much cheaper, and often for half price. In fact, even though such carefulness in spending is not now necessary, we buy very few things that are not on a half-price sale, except the children's shoes, and we buy at the best stores in Dallas.

In many of the large cities there are what are called "outlet" stores, where sample clothing and shoes are sold at a greatly reduced price. If you have studied fashions, fabrics, and the labels of good clothing, you can often have several dresses for the price of one bought in a regular department store. But watch out, for you can be fooled in these stores unless you know how to choose the right thing. They will mix a lot of trashy, gaudy, unsuitable things in with the good ones, and those who cannot pick a good garment had better beware.

I buy many of my dresess, except those that are made at home, in one of these outlet stores, and I have had complete satisfaction from them. Recently, I passed another store that was just opening and saw a rack of dresses for $2.88 each. I could not believe my eyes, but thought there was no harm in looking. I bought seven dresses at once and four of them had the labels of expensive dresses in them. It was an opening enticement to customers, of course, and unusual but true. I got all the dresses I liked from size 12 to size 16 that could be altered. I have had more use out of those dresses—and more compliments —than any others.

After you have shopped for a while, you will soon learn the approximate time the department stores have their sales, and you will come to know a few of the clerks well. Many times the clerks will take special pains to give their customers the best buys, and some have even called me to let me know ahead of time that there is going to be a sale.

My husband can get all of his clothes in one store. It is one of the best men's stores in the city. As soon as this store is ready for a sale, a church member who works there often sets aside a few suits and calls my husband so he will be sure to be there the first morning of the sale. As a result, my husband gets all of his suits at half-price sales. They look expensive and fit perfectly, and always look nice until they are nearly threadbare. The clerk knows him well enough now so that he tells my husband exactly what he should wear, matches his ties to his suits, and so on. He completely dresses my husband for half the retail price of the clothes.

My problem is different; a woman cannot get all she needs in any one store. There is one place where I can get my shoes for $5.00 a pair on their final sale, another store where I buy coats and suits. I have learned where to make my best buys and always go to those places. Occasionally we pick up little items from all stores, but we are careful what we buy. Usually the small store, with high pressure sales personnel, means cheap garments that are not worth taking home.

My mother was buyer for ladies' ready-to-wear in a large department store on the West Coast for many years. She says that without fail it was lack of taste, knowledge of what makes a good buy, and when to buy, rather than a limited amount of money that made many of their customers have cheap wardrobes. In most cases she could have taken the amount of money they spent for cheap, gaudy garments that did not look right on them, even when they were new, and could have outfitted them in a perfect wardrobe. Many times she would point out a dress that was twice as good for only a few dollars more, but they refused. They thought the cheapest dress was a bargain. "Penny wise and pound foolish," as the old saying goes, is true in buying clothes as well as groceries. Her two other biggest problems were to get women to select clothing that suited their figures and personalities, and to get clothes that fit correctly. Sometimes she lost sales because she tried to steer them into correct buys, for being a Christian, she could not tell a woman that she looked nice when the dress was all wrong for her. She soon found the answer to the second problem of size. A woman would come into the store and ask to see a certain kind of dress in size 14 when at one glance mother knew she wore an 18. After the customer tried on a few 14's and declared that the store was wrong about the sizes, and made a few more unpleasant remarks, mother would say, "I think I know what you would like, let me go out and select a few dresses for you to try on." Mother chose size 18 and removed labels. The ladies were thrilled with her choices. She had many customers who returned to her as long as she was at the store and let her select their clothes. What they did not know did not hurt them and certainly improved their appearance.

By now you probably have me pictured as an unspiritual, fashion-crazed pastor's wife who spends most of her time shopping and thinking about her looks. Nothing could be further from the truth. I dislike shopping most intensely! I only go downtown about twice a year, and that is when some special sale is on only in the downtown stores. I seldom make more than a few planned shopping trips in a year. I just keep my eyes open for specials in clothes as I go about my regular duties at home and when doing other necessary shopping. I put on a dress that is suitable for the occasion and then forget about my clothes. Sometimes when a woman compliments me on my dress, I have to glance down to see what I have on.

Another thought is probably running through your mind. Living in a big city, we have more opportunities to buy clothing for a good price. That is true, but you can do almost as well even if you live in a little town. Subscribe to the newspaper in the nearest city and watch for the advertised sales. Make an all-day shopping trip if necessary to stock up on the specials. This is where the charge account (if you know how to control one) is handy, for the stores will notify you ahead of time of the sales and it will also enable you to get all you need at the time of the sales and take advantage of the special prices.

God has promised that He will meet every need. There was a time when my husband and I thought that meant that it would be met with new clothes. But we went through many years when we all wore mostly hand-me-down clothes. We discovered that refusal to cheerfully accept God's provision through others was a matter of pride. There are those who feel that it is degrading to accept clothing from others, and those who do are belittled in their sight. But since that is God's way of meeting some needs, it is not only foolish but wrong not to use these things. God had to teach us that lesson the hard way.

When we moved to Dallas eight years ago it took every penny we had to get settled here, and we lived from hand to mouth because we had an extremely ill baby for a year. Medical care for her took all our savings and even part of my husband's life insurance. We all wore hand-me-down clothes, through the kindness of our church clothing exchange, which provides good, donated clothing primarily for missionaries and seminary families. My husband even supplied the pulpit of the church where we were members wearing suits that had first belonged to a man in the church. It was a humbling lesson for all of us, but one for which we are indeed thankful. Even now that my husband is pastor of the church and we have no need of assistance, there are a few ladies who delight in giving me a fancy hat, or a specially nice dress they have outgrown. I accept such gifts in the spirit in which they are given and thoroughly enjoy wearing them.

Every pastor's wife should learn to sew—at least well enough to alter her clothes. This is especially true if you must wear used clothing, for you will want to make it fit and look as nice as possible. Perhaps taking off some trimming, or adding a flower or a collar will make it seem new to you. Some women have a wonderful talent for sewing and therefore can have many more clothes than others. They can take the money it costs to buy a dress and get expensive materials, and have dresses that look like they cost over a hundred dollars. I have several friends who do just that. However, if your sewing turns out homemade-looking dresses, please, please forget the whole idea. There is nothing so pathetic-looking as a homemade-looking wardrobe.

Not too long ago, a pastor of a large church in the North came to Dallas for a special speaking engagement. His wife came with him. She had a new dress for every occasion but I never saw such grandmother-style, homemade-looking clothes in my life. They stuck out like a sore thumb in a fashion-minded city like Dallas. She just must not have taken a good look in her mirror, as they came from a city larger than Dallas and, judging from the size of his church, money was certainly no problem.

Now may I speak kindly but firmly to you few who may not care how you look? You are not being spiritual. You are hurting your testimony and shaming not only your church people but probably your husband. May I remind you that your husband is constantly with well-dressed women? A mental image of you, slouching around home in a robe and slippers is not very good protection against those few women every minister must contend with who deliberately try to attract him, and the occasional one who tries to break up his home or entice him into a secret love affair. Ask God to give you a real interest in looking right; then enlist a friend or clerk to make shopping as painless as possible.

It seemed foolish to me, at the time this book was planned, to take so much space to talk about dress and figure control (next chapter), since there is so much prosperity and fashion-mindedness now. But several things have happened in the past that jarred me into thinking this might be very important. One illustration of the homemade clothes has just been mentioned.

Some time ago a group of women came to me from their church to ask if I could help them by talking to their pastor's wife about the way she looked. It was difficult for me to imagine one so careless. She usually came to every activity, whether church services or social gatherings, in a skirt and blouse or sweater, in flats, and without a hat. Because she was so fat, she should have worn a foundation, but apparently she did not wear one of any kind. Her husband made an excellent salary and was considered a fashion model even when caught by surprise relaxing in his study. It was also known that she had a private income of her own, so lack of money was no excuse. No one could understand unless she just didn't care. Needless to say, I declined the invitation to help her, for no matter how gently given, there is just no kind way of breaking a woman's heart by letting her know what her church ladies think of her. But that experience gave me the final decision to include these chapters on the appearance of the pastor's wife. Perhaps this story is multiplied many times over, and no one has the courage to tell the pastor's wife. Maybe from reading this book she will see herself as others see her. It is far better for her to be angry at an unknown author than at some of her friends or church ladies.

Being poorly dressed may be the sign of a number of difficulties, but it is definitely not a sign of spirituality! We are representing the King of kings and should look our best at all times for the sake of His testimony. We do not seek to win people to ourselves, but we do want to present an attractive appearance as we seek to lead them to our Saviour. No princess would think of leaving her bedroom unless she were properly attired as a child of the king of the land. No Christian, and especially a leader such as a pastor's wife, should think of shaming her Lord, her husband, or her church people by failing to be as well dressed as possible.

While traveling this summer, I learned that several seminaries and Christian colleges have had to put restrictions on the way the wives and female students dress. The largest problem seemed to be the lack of clothes rather than the style. Since then, I have seen some things here at our school that have shocked me. I felt that the younger women who will be going into pastorates need a few words of advice on how to dress properly. In spite of the heat in this part of the country, there is no excuse for a woman old enough to be married to appear in shorts or with a bare midriff on a campus where there are 325 male students, plus the faculty and staff gentlemen.

No matter how poor a minister's wife is and how limited her wardrobe, there is no excuse for slovenliness (even at home)—for crooked hemlines, poor fit, or soiled garments. Start right now to make a lifetime habit of completely dressing yourself for the day before you leave the bedroom in the morning. If you like to sleep until that last minute, as I do, then plan the night before what you will be doing and lay out the clothes you want to wear in order to save time in the morning. Get up a few minutes earlier to remove those curlers and bobby pins, and have your hair neatly combed. My husband often laughs at me because there are times when I even put on my lipstick before I take off my nightclothes. However, he often says how much he appreciates the fact that I look as well dressed and properly groomed at breakfast as I do when he returns home for dinner. My effort to look nice gives him a pleasant picture of me to carry all through the day. I also make up my bed the minute we crawl out. By doing this and using the suggestions you will find later in the book for keeping your house in order, you will be ready for any early morning callers. You need never be embarrassed, no matter who comes, or how much of your house they see. The only things out of order will be those necessary for breakfast preparation, and everybody will understand that those are necessary.

About eleven one morning, I went to call on a pastor's wife in a wealthy suburban town. She came to the door wearing a tissue-thin dress, and no slip. She was not the least embarrassed and made no attempt to excuse herself to put on a less transparent dress, or a slip. The visit was very disturbing to me, and I couldn't help wondering what she would have done if a man had come to the door.

Last month a charming minister's wife spoke for our women's fellowship group. She was perfectly dressed and had a lovely hairdo, but the hem of her dress was shorter in the front and showed an inch of lace beneath. Most of the women there were constantly looking at the lace, in spite of trying to concentrate on what she was saying. Another time we had a speaker who wore such sparkling earrings that we could not keep our eyes off them, and her bracelet jingled every time she moved her arm until it became thoroughly annoying. Still another wore a dress that had writing all over it and many remarked afterwards that they could not keep from trying to read the printing on her dress while she was speaking.

Coaches in public speaking suggest that a woman speaker wear a plain, dark or soft-colored dress, being sure that it hangs right and fits correctly. Her dress should make her feel comfortable so she will not be conscious of her clothes at all. She should wear small earrings that do not flash, her wedding and engagement rings, and a watch, which she will need in order to stay within her speaking time. A small, appropriate pin is all right for the dress if it really belongs there and looks right. Pastors' wives will do well to take heed to the following suggestions to all women concerning jewelry, made by a top fashion expert: "Put on all the jewelry you think your costume needs and then take half of it off, and you will look much better." If a speaker wears a hat, which according to etiquette is proper in church circles, it should be plain and one that will not cover or shade the face.

Being well groomed does not depend so much on the amount of money spent but on knowing what is becoming to you and what to buy for the activities you usually attend, knowing what is proper for each occasion, and knowing how to match or contrast the costume with accessories. Being well dressed is not so much a matter of having a lot of clothes as having garments which can be changed by the addition of jewelry, hats, gloves, and other accessories. The darker and more muted colors and the plainer styles are always correct and more becoming to most women.

CHAPTER 9

Do Calories Count?

SOMETIMES WE BECOME so used to seeing our image in the mirror that it might take a good look at a snapshot to see our real defects and notice that we are overweight. I detest having my picture made, probably unconsciously, because I know it will show me as I really am, and not as I like to imagine.

Oddly enough, it took a game at a Christmas party to make me see how terribly overweight I was. Each person was told to draw a picture of someone in the room. The pictures were then put together and we were to guess who was represented by each one. Looking at an honestly drawn, amateur picture of myself was enough, but to make matters worse almost everyone there guessed who was "me." That gave me determination to take off weight. A year and a half of careful dieting resulted in my losing forty pounds, which I never regretted.

If the snapshot test does not move you to action, and you need further convincing, just look at the average weight charts. Doctors tell us that since the people of this nation are gradually gaining in weight, these charts can no longer be trusted as a guide to proper weight. They only give the average weight of adults in the United States but not the average of what we should weigh. If you find your average weight on such a chart, and then subtract ten pounds, you will have approximately your proper weight. An even quicker way, and probably more correct, is to allow yourself 100 pounds for the first five feet of your height, and then add five pounds for each additional inch above that. For an example: I am five feet, six inches tall, so my weight should be 130 pounds. However, I find that I have more strength and energy, and I generally feel better, when my weight is 120 pounds. This is the weight I have maintained most of the time since losing the original forty pounds.

Why are people overweight? Let us start by getting the excuses out of the way. My very sympathetic, naturally trim sister-in-law tries to console me by saying that ministers and their wives can hardly keep from being overweight when they are entertained so much and fear offending a hostess by not eating all that is prepared. "Thanks for trying to be helpful, but that is not a legitimate excuse." In the first place, we don't know of any ministers and their wives who are entertained so much that they need to put on weight. We seldom have more than one invitation a month to dinner with church members. However, I do attend a few luncheons each month. As far as we are concerned, the overentertaining of the minister and his wife is a myth. Most people are too busy these days to be bothered. The other occasions when we eat with church people are: fellowship dinners, women's luncheons, morning coffees, and teas. At these, all of the members are subject to the same temptations to overeat as we are. Second, we are usually allowed a choice of the kind and amount of food we eat when we are at church homes. If we take too much, it is only because we enjoy it and not because we are forced to eat that much. I have been to many coffees and teas at which I have nursed a cup and plate in my hand for an hour or more without anyone, including the hostess, knowing that I have had nothing to eat or drink.

We have also learned from experience that as long as we eat correctly at home, what we eat when we go out to meals will not add pounds. There is no rule of etiquette that says you must eat all the serving on your plate, though we usually do because we enjoy it, and feel our enjoyment of the food compliments the hostess. If we do discover, when we step on the bath scales, that we have overdone a bit, we just eat a little lighter for the next few days. Ususally overeating only happens when we spend a week at a church conference and arrangements have been made for us to have dinner with a different family every day.

The most overworked excuse for obesity is gland trouble. When I questioned several doctors about this, they laughed heartily. Each one agreed that only about one person in a thousand has any gland trouble which causes excess fat. When there is a difficulty of this nature there are other symptoms that make it necessary for the person to be under medical care, and the trouble is easily diagnosed. Unless a doctor has stated this as a reason for overweight, and is treating a patient, it is next to impossible to be overweight because of gland trouble! So if you are fairly healthy and overweight, you will have to look for another reason for your obesity. You will have to face the fact that you are overeating.

"I am just naturally the heavyset type. The tendency to overweight comes from my family. Everything I eat puts weight on me." That is no excuse either. My husband and I are just like that, too. But we were fat because we let ourselves get that way. A number of reasons contributing to this will be discussed a little later. We often say, "It seems that if we just pass by some food and smell it, we put on weight." While that is meant for a joke, it almost seems true at times. We have learned to accept the fact that God has made us this way, and do not complain. We have stopped feeling envious when we look at the thin ones who can eat all they want and never gain an ounce. We have known people who were too fat, and some who were too thin, and we feel that the thin ones are more to be pitied, as no matter what they do it seems very difficult for them to gain weight. The rest of us can lose by cutting down our calories, if we just will.

Some people find it very difficult to diet alone. They feel dieting is a type of punishment. Many have said to me, "It would be so much easier to diet if my husband would do the same. You are lucky not to have to cook a lot of good food just to see the others eat it." That is just another excuse, for a proper reducing diet is really just eating the proper amount of the right kinds of nutritious foods. Oddly enough, it is much easier for me to diet alone. That way the family can eat the high caloried foods that might be sent to us without my conscience being hurt by throwing them away. When we diet, since we do not go in for major changes in our food habits, I can eat the same things that I prepare for my family. I avoid the desserts most of the time. I take no second helpings of food unless I am very sure that it is low-caloried, or unless I feel a little more dinner is a safety measure to keep me from raiding the refrigerator later.

Another favorite excuse for overweight is that the food budget will not stretch enough to get all the expensive things required for a diet. We find that we save money when we diet because we just eat less of what we are accustomed to buying and eating. The financial angle may be a very pressing reason for not dieting if you think you have to buy some expensive, bestseller book, and follow a routine of steak and other expensive foods. Some folks have the idea that the only time people can lose weight is when they make radical changes in their eating habits. Even the typical list of foods for a diet recommended by most doctors might involve a few items that cost more, BUT eating less of what you serve your family will not cost more.

An excuse that goes right along with this one is, "I don't have time to fix two meals, one for the family and another for myself." This has already been answered. Just eat less of what the family has and no desserts. Just to disprove this most commonly used excuse for being fat, I tried two types of eating regimens for a year, while writing this book, even though my weight was well under what it should be. The first was the one I suggest to most people who ask me how to lose weight. As long as you are feeding your family properly, you can eat what they do, omitting second helpings and skipping the dessert, except occasionally. The same applies when you are invited out to dinner, or are at a restaurant. I lost about two pounds a week, and sometimes three, over a period of three months. After I let my weight go up again so it would be safe to start reducing again, I decided to eat everything my family ate, including desserts, cereals, waffles, rolls, and potatoes. I ate only what would satisfy but not fill me up. Over a period of four or five months, I lost approximately a pound a week, several times two pounds, and a few times no weight in one week. So it is my firm conviction, acquired both through years of experience and through this special test for this book, that one need not buy extra food or cook a different meal in order to diet.

The main difficulty lies in the fact that most people want a "get-thin-quick" type of diet so they can go right back to eating like they always have. They are not content to take a long-range, slow method of dieting. Many people come to me for diet advice, and when I tell them the simple truth, they are disappointed because they are not willing to diet in this way. This method is often harder than a "crash" diet, but it has several real advantages. It teaches one to eat only the amount of food he needs for health and strength. Since a person's appetite is conditioned to desire less food and he makes a habit of eating less, there is much less temptation to go back to the old ways of overeating and using fattening foods than if he used a "crash diet."

Unfortunately, some of the articles, books, and doctors who are encouraging reducing have a way of making it seem as hard, unattractive and expensive as possible. Depending upon their suggestions would discourage anyone from trying. One popular doctor's diet, at the time of this writing, goes something like this: Have two raw eggs mixed in a glass of milk for breakfast. The idea of eating raw eggs turns my stomach at any time, and especially before breakfast. For exactly the same number of calories you can have two lightly scrambled, boiled, or poached eggs and a piece of toast, lightly buttered, with coffee or tea with a no-calorie sweetener if you want them sweet. For a change, two crisp pieces of bacon can be substituted for one of the eggs and you will be having the normal, well-rounded American breakfast which every member of the family should have. For lunch this doctor suggests yogurt and fruit. The usual size of yogurt sold in our markets contains 320 calories and is overly salty. Salt is undesirable for one who wishes to lose weight. For the same number of calories a person can have an attractive, satisfying luncheon and feel as if she has had a meal. A three-ounce hamburger is only 200 calories and a large, tossed vegetable salad with lemon juice or low-calorie dressing is only 100 calories. Add fruit for dessert, and you will have no more calories than the yogurt and fruit contain. Two hot dogs, a two-egg omelet, a large shrimp salad, fruit and cottage cheese combined, and other things can be substituted for those who like variety. The tossed salad can be changed to almost any two vegetables except potatoes, corn or lima beans (one half cup each), eaten raw, or cooked if you have time. Dinner should consist of a large serving of lean meat, baked or broiled, two vegetables, and fruit for dessert. Get a twenty-five-cent book that gives the calorie count of all foods and work out the menus that appeal most to you, but stay within your allowed limit.

Liquid or formula diets are a new fad. Most doctors agree that they are safe, and I know many people who are trying them. However, all said that they did not feel satisfied because they hadn't had the pleasure of "eating" something. The liquid "meal in a can" did not seem like a meal. Many dieters became nauseated after constant use of these products and had to give them up. Most of them discovered that as soon as they went back to their normal eating, they gained weight again, and what they had suffered was in vain.

While we are thinking about fad diets it might be well to warn people again, as our doctors and the Food and Drug Administration so often do, that most of the best-seller diet books are not worth the paper they are printed on and are often incorrect and harmful. Their only consolation is that the suggestions are so foolish that most people never wholly follow them. I know a number of individuals who seem to follow every new diet as a hobby. After carefully noting the latest books and diets they are following, I begin to watch the papers and magazines to see what the experts say about the method. The claims for most of these diets have been proved false, and some diets have been proved harmful. The harshest denunciation came from Dr. Fredrick J. Stare, head of the Department of Nutrition, Harvard University, about a book which stated that calories do not count and that we can eat all we want and still lose weight. Though many of the new fads have been denounced by experts and government agencies responsible for the protection of our food, yet some people never seem to learn and will try anything that seems to promise an easy way to reduce.

Sadly, two friends of ours did take one of these fad books seriously and followed the instructions so meticulously that they ruined the linings of their stomachs and will have to follow an ulcer diet the rest of their lives.

Doctors have been giving us free dieting advice for years, but most of us do not want to follow it. They say that we must find out just what our bodies need for our type of work and eat only enough for strength and energy, and then stick to that type of diet for the rest of our lives.

When we were about twenty-five, my husband and I began to realize that we were having a weight problem, and we knew something must be done about it as we grew older. We counted calories. That never worked very well as it took too long to figure up the count, and we often lost the papers on which we were keeping our charts. We went on a very strict diet, being hungry and unsatisfied all the time. We lost some weight, but then we went back to our normal way of eating, and all the pounds returned. Our efforts had been in vain. After years of this, and other types of diets, we woke up to the fact that doctors mean what they say when they state that one has to change his eating habits permanently. And that is just what we did. I gave away the deep fat fryer. We looked over a good calorie list and found the foods that added the most weight, and yet gave the least nutritional benefits. Those foods were taken off our menus permanently. Of course, we eat them occasionally when we have guests or go out to dinner. Foods we know we should not eat just stay in the store, where they belong, and in that way we cannot be tempted to use them. We do without gravies and sauces, which have real taste appeal but little food value and often contain more calories than the food they cover.

Perhaps a few of the tips we learned through the years will help you in your crusade to have a nice figure. We have found out that we can feel full, enjoy our food more, never refuse anything that is offered by others, and feel more comfortable and have added energy by eating a healthful diet. Yet we have no problem with overweight.

If we diet together, which is seldom, I cook just the amount of food we should have for that meal and serve it on our plates. We know what we have to eat, and there is no more. That way we cannot be tempted to take second helpings, and we have no temptation to eat food just to keep from wasting it. We have fruit for dessert, except that once a week we have a good baked dessert just to celebrate the weight lost that week.

Try, as nearly as possible, to serve food you are used to having instead of entirely new, untried, or questionable and expensive foods. Just cut down on the amounts you eat. A diet can be filling most of the time, and does not have to be different, unattractive, or expensive if you will just take some time and thought in planning your meals.

Magazines and newspapers abound with attractive menus for those who want to lose weight. Study some of them for new ideas and ways of fixing foods and for finding out how to plan so that your calorie allowance includes the most nourishing and filling foods.

Try not to talk about your reducing plans, either at home or outside. Those who talk the most about dieting are usually the ones who are doing the least about it. It embarrasses your hostess and the other guests if you discuss your dieting when you are being entertained, and makes overweight people who are present uncomfortable. At home, it just increases your self-pity and leads you to those little excursions to the refrigerator when no one is looking. What you eat on a binge is often as much as your entire day's calorie allowance—or more—so think it over twice before you do it!

Don't think in terms of the "months" that you have to diet. Think of one day at a time. Tell yourself, "I only have to eat this way today. Tomorrow, I can go back to my usual way of eating if I wish." Then say the same thing the next day. If you fail one day, don't be too hard on yourself, but determine to start the diet again the next day. After seven satisfied years of being from fifteen to twenty pounds under the average weight charts, I can promise you that if you will stick to your diet for a month you will lose that desire to overeat, and you will feel much better and realize that you have been uncomfortable, without realizing it, from overeating. You won't ever want to go back to the old eating habits. You will find that the smaller amount of food will be just as filling as the larger amount, and much more enjoyable.

You can do much to control your weight, or that of other members of your family, without their realizing it. Stop frying foods and adding shortening to meats; broil or bake them. Stop buying the prepared meat and fruit pies and other things rich in fats and starches. Invest the same amount of money in meat and vegetables, though it takes longer to cook them, and substitute fruit, fresh or canned, for the pies. Skim the excess fat from gravy and soups; it will never be missed. Forget to buy the starch-laden vegetables and get leafy ones. Don't use potatoes every day, but serve them in rotation with other vegetables. Try to leave bread off the table. Salt makes the body hold liquids and often adds uncomfortable weight. Since salt is not needed, and gives no hunger satisfaction, gradually add less and less salt to the food you cook. Doctors tell us that we can drink all of the liquids we wish as long as we keep down the salt in our systems. Those who want to lose weight will find it best, however, not to drink during the half hour before a meal, and the hour and a half afterwards.

The most important aid to dieting is a real desire and determination to lose weight. Without that it is useless to start. The whole matter of keeping one's weight at the proper level boils down to one thing: willpower! Maybe you feel like the man who said, "There's no use talking about willpower, what I need is won't-power."

Now before launching on a full-scale diet program, it will be well to analyze your reasons for overeating. Many people honestly try to stick to a diet, but they become so cross and depressed and dissatisfied that they soon are eating more than ever before. Perhaps there are causes for overeating which they have not faced. These things have to be corrected before successful dieting is possible.

Overeating is often just a habit. When we middle-aged folks were children, it was thought that a fat child was a healthy child. Therefore we were encouraged to eat even more than we wanted and often forced to eat when it would have been better not to. In our families, we were compelled to eat some of everything on the table, and we were forced to eat everything on our plates. It was considered sinful to waste any food. That became a habit with us, and we find it difficult to overcome years of early training. It still hurts us to see any food go into the garbage, so we often eat what we do not need or want, instead of throwing it away. Now we say, "It is better to have it go to waste than to waist." I remember the day when I suddenly realized that I was eating a piece of pie I actually did not like or want. I was just going through the motions of eating through habit. Make sure that you are eating what you really want, and only what you need, and that you are not bound by some long-time habit.

Medical authorities attest that it has long been an established fact that overeating is of a psychological and emotional nature. We overeat because eating is a comfort to us and a compensation for something or some things we feel we are missing. This has nothing to do with our actual physical need for food. Food soothes the stomach and gives the body a relaxed feeling and lets us forget for a while the gnawing emotion that drove us to the food.

Dr. Karl Huber, in a magazine article on overeating, presented an excellent discussion of the emotional patterns that lead children and adults to eat more than they should. He says pressures that are too hard to take lead us to find comfort in food. This is often true of those who feel themselves a failure. But it is also true of the apparently successful man because he is afraid that he cannot maintain the success and standing he has. So when a person feels insecure, he turns to food for reassurance and comfort.

We have seen this work in the lives of a number of ministerial couples. If all is going smoothly in the church, their weight is no problem. Let a serious problem come up in the church, or a disappointment in their plans, or in people whom they trust, and they have a tendency to start overeating to comfort themselves. In most cases, they do not realize why they are gaining weight.

Find out what makes you want to eat when you are not honestly hungry. Then try to have something creative and interesting to do to keep from thinking of food. My biggest temptation comes when my husband travels. When he departs, I start out very bravely on a strict diet, intending to lose a few extra pounds while he is away. After several days I finish all the tasks I had planned to do in his absence. I become lonesome and restless, and often a little self-pity creeps in and I begin thinking that I'm always the one who is left at home with tasks I could get a cleaning woman to do for fifty cents an hour, while my husband is out traveling and meeting interesting people and eating out. Then I begin to think about how good something in the kitchen would taste, and down I go! I yield to eating to make up for an emotional need. Any pastor's wife could suffer with this just in the evening and eat to find comfort while her husband is attending a board meeting, or out making calls.

There are always a few women who feel the need to excel in cooking to make up for some type of inferiority complex. Every church has a few of them. They are not only often grossly overweight themselves, but try their best to force good food on others, whether it is wanted or not. They insist on your taking large second helpings, not because they want you to enjoy yourself but because unconsciously they want to recharge their own ego and meet their emotional needs. This is where the pastor and his wife get into some difficulty. I have seen my husband lose a night's sleep because several women have insisted, at a picnic or a church supper, that he have some of everything they cooked. He knew he was overeating and was miserable, but he couldn't very well refuse. However, in most cases, we find that a small serving of all food offered us, along with honest but flattering remarks on how good it is, will usually be enough to save the day for both the cook and for us.

Look over once more these reasons for overeating and try honestly to face your emotional need for too much food. Then make a systematic plan for avoiding those periods by not being near food or by doing something that interests you more than food. Put the energy of preparing and eating extra food into some worthwhile project. Dr. Huber gives his answer to the problem in one sentence: "When overeating assumes a pattern, when we are compelled day after day to dull all our other senses with food, life becomes a rather joyless affair; we should look for something more emotionally satisfying than food to fill our emptiness."

Some people meet their emotional needs with alcohol. The compulsive eater eats to find comfort and reassurance. The alcoholic drinks for the same reason. He just happens to be afflicted with a more dangerous and less socially acceptable way of expression. Both the alcoholic and the overeater need help and redirection to fill the need that creates the appetite. An overweight person acts in the same pattern as the alcoholic only under the guise of respectability, and hence can never point a finger at him in criticism.

The matter of weight control is a concern of God. We get so in the habit of thinking that weight control is only a form of vanity that we have forgotten the admonition of God's Word. Our bodies are the temples of God (I Cor. 6:19-20), and anything we do that harms the body is sin. Since we have been severely and repeatedly warned by doctors that we are harming our bodies and shortening our lives and making ourselves much more apt to develop killing diseases by overweight, then it is a sin in God's sight.

Overweight is a sign of a spiritual lack. Read carefully the fruit of the Spirit in Galatians 5:22-23. You will notice the word "temperance," which might better be translated in present-day English as "self-control." When the Holy Spirit is given complete control of our lives, as God so wills, He will manifest His fruit in us. It is rather obvious that in most cases of extreme overweight, the Holy Spirit is not having His way in the life of that person.

Several years ago the former dietitian at the Dallas Theological Seminary felt led to diet, solely because of the leading of the Spirit. She cooked for her husband and three big boys at home and planned food for over a hundred men at the school. She did not talk about her plan; she did not change her style of cooking, or the type of food. She ate just as she felt led of the Spirit. In short order she had lost twenty pounds, and she now keeps an attractive figure in exactly the same way. The easiest way to keep your weight normal is to live constantly under the control of the Spirit. I, as well as others, have found that this is the true secret of any type of self-control, including eating.

Recently my husband and I went to hear a well-known minister. The message was powerful and his knowledge of the Holy Spirit seemed limitless. He was so fat his neck hung over his collar and his stomach rested on the pulpit. On the way home, we made a few comments on the message. Then there was a long silence. Later I asked, "Did you get a blessing from the message?" The answer was "No." "Neither did I. All I could think about was how fat and sloppy he looked. I know that what he gave us was a head knowledge of the Holy Spirit and not what had reached his heart. If he had no more control over his eating than that, his message will never mean anything to me." My husband agreed. If there is an obvious indication that the Spirit is not producing self-control, there is serious doubt that He is allowed to manifest any of His other fruit in a life.

Overweight among ministers and their wives is almost expected for some reason, and it almost seems there is a conspiracy or game among Christians to keep them that way, when the minister and his wife should be the ones to lead the way in self-control. Many a minister has ruined his testimony by his apparent lack of control over his eating habits. My husband says that he would watch his weight for the sake of his ministry even if there were no other good reason for doing so. Many times he puts on a little weight when he travels, but the minute he returns home he takes it right off no matter how tempting the dishes on our table are. He practices what he preaches.

A few years ago, one of the most charming and spiritual widows in our church looked me straight in the eye and said, "I killed my husband. Please don't kill Dwight!" The shock made me speechless, which is most unusual for me. "Don't feed Dwight pies and cakes and foods that are too refined. Feed him what he should eat. My husband died of a heart attack brought on by overweight. I thought I was showing him my love by baking for him, but in reality I killed him, as definitely as if I had poisoned him." That impression has stayed with me through the years and made me see that the proper feeding of my husband is one of the important contributions I can make to the Gospel ministry. My husband is a full-time seminary professor and a full-time pastor of a church of 300 members. He travels from the East Coast to the West Coast and from Canada to Mexico on speaking engagements. Sometime in between, he manages also to write books and be a good father and husband. He often tells me that he knows it is the good care I give him in well-planned meals that keeps him going. And because we have lived on various salary levels, I know it can be done on any salary level.

Doctors have warned some of my best friends in Christian service that they are digging an early grave because they are dangerously overweight. I may have caused some resentment in them by expressing what is written here. I pray that the Lord will use this to show them what they are doing to their testimonies in misuse of their bodies, and the poor example they are setting for their church people.

Last night we received the shocking news that my husband's roommate during his first year at seminary had died of a stroke. They are the same age. He had had dangerously high blood pressure for some time but he just would not reduce as the doctor had ordered. His remark was, "He died an early death from carrying around too much blubber for too long."

CHAPTER 10

Counseling

THERE IS A REAL DIFFERENCE between counseling and just
listening sympathetically to other people's troubles and resentments. The average minister's wife will find that there are few
times that she will have opportunities for true counseling, but
many, many hours of time will be spent listening to people who
feel that she should be interested in their feelings, misunderstandings and symptoms, just because they have no one else
who will listen, and because they feel that it is their privilege
to use her whenever they want to "let off steam."

Most people who have serious problems want to discuss them
with the pastor, a doctor, or some trained counselor. They seldom feel that the pastor's wife falls into one of those categories,
which is generally true. Increasing numbers of people have
mental, emotional and marital problems, so it is a blessing that
most of these do not come to us. If we are not trained to
counsel people with such problems, we should turn them over
to trained counselors. However, there are a few basic rules
of counseling that the pastor's wife and all Christians should
know in order to be prepared for the times when they can
be a help to others.

Three problems must be faced: (1) You must know yourself as counselor. (2) Know, or find out, as much as possible
about the person in need, the counselee. (3) Have a good
method for finding the trouble and leading the person to see
the true problem and to make a definite decision for solving it.

Perhaps the biggest problem we face is ourselves, as counselors. The first place to check is on our attitudes. If it is our
habit to live a life of rigid rules, we must be careful not to at-

tempt to make the one who comes for help conform to those rules. They may have a very different background, be just as pleasing to the Lord as we, yet not live by our lists of dos and don'ts. So many Christians and churches have made long lists of what is right and wrong which are not stated in Scripture that we are reminded of the Pharisees in Christ's lifetime, who added many requirements to the Mosaic law. Many sincere Christians think that unless another believer is living by their particular standards of what is wrong and what is right, he is not living by the Word of God.

Since we have lived in different parts of the country, we can give many examples of just how this works. While living in the East, we found it was considered by many fine Christians to be wrong for a woman to wear makeup. In this part of the country, a woman's testimony seems not so readily accepted if her face is colorless. In the East, those who would not wear makeup would appear on the beach in the briefest of bathing suits and parade themselves up and down the boardwalk before men as well as women. Here, many Christians feel that "mixed" bathing is wrong. In case you do not know what that means (we did not until we moved to Dallas), boys and men, girls and women go swimming separately, and they do not stand around watching each other. As children, we grew up playing dominoes as a perfectly innocent game. While doing young people's work in a Dallas church years ago, my husband let some of the kids play dominoes. He was called before the board of stewards and told that what he had done was wrong. It seemed that dominoes was a gambling game and there were gambling parlors, much as the gambling casinos in Reno.

We must also be sure to listen carefully, without showing shock, no matter how terrible the story that is being poured forth. If we show a horrified attitude, the person who needs help will be afraid to tell us the full story, and may depart as soon as possible. We must be able to accept the facts of the case without showing any personal feelings, no matter what we might feel inside.

When a person on top of a tall building is threatening to jump, the policemen and doctors do not spend their time telling him what a sin and crime it would be to jump, but they quietly and calmly, without condemnation, try to coax the person back into the building. Adding to the needy person's guilt will only make the situation worse and might bring about immediate disastrous results.

We must not let ourselves become identified with the person in trouble. Your first reaction may be: "That's not very sympathetic!" There are sound reasons for not letting ourselves become emotionally involved with the person's problem. First of all, we cannot stand aside and view the problem without letting it be colored by our own emotional background and reactions. That keeps us from clear thinking and reasoning and prevents us from asking what the real problem is; what brought this person to this condition; and what I can do about helping him.

Second, it takes too much strength and energy to counsel when we identify ourselves with the one who is being counseled. Many ministers and their wives in spite of their detachment, become exhausted from helping emotionally and mentally disturbed people. But since we women are more inclined to let our feelings rule than our hard common sense, we especially must watch this point.

It is important—by reading all you can, attending any classes that are available, and by talking to psychologists and psychiatrists—to get a rudimentary knowledge of how to recognize the difference between physical, mental, emotional, and spiritual problems. We have often affirmed that God's Word has the answer to all the needs of the Christian. True, but we must face the fact that the Bible cannot heal a broken leg. Quoting scripture verse after scripture verse to a mentally or emotionally disturbed person will do little, or only temporary, good. If we find a purely spiritual problem, then we use God's Word to show the person God's will, either by showing him the actual command in the Bible, or the principle that should govern that person's conduct.

Never give your private opinion on spiritual matters; always turn to the Word for the answer. A girl came to me to talk about her marriage. She was a Christian planning to marry an unbeliever. Her case was simple. I turned to II Corinthians where we are told, "Be ye not unequally yoked together with unbelievers." It became obvious that she knew more verses that forbade her marriage to that young man than I did, but by talking to me she had hoped to get my approval so she could go ahead with a clear conscience.

Most cases of counseling are not that simple. We usually find a combination of troubles, often spiritual and emotional. Some of these people are helped from the Bible, but the emotional problem remains until that one gets professional help. There are others who will not admit that they have emotional problems, even when diagnosed by a doctor. Many counselees, because they will not face the true facts, resist treatment by trained counselors, and turn to the pastor and his wife and expect an immediate cure by hearing a little of the Scriptures. They feel the Bible has some magic touch that will miraculously remove heredity, background, and past and present circumstances.

There are others who are so mentally upset that it is impossible to help them with spiritual truths at all. Their minds are unable to reason, and the more we give them the Word, the more confused they become. Such persons should be turned over to specialists who must cure the mind before they are ready to explore, to find if there are spiritual problems involved, too. When they have been cured, then they can receive help from the Word and from the spiritual leaders of their church.

In the minds of a lot of uninformed people, the minister and the psychiatrist are synonymous. Such people honestly believe that each can do the same things. Nothing could be further from the truth! The public will have to learn that the doctor takes care of physical ills; the psychiatrist, the mental and emotional troubles; and the minister, the spiritual problems.

Dr. Harold Ockenga, pastor of the Park Street Church of Boston, gave several hours of counseling to a stranger who just walked into his office and requested to see the pastor. When he left he said, "Thank you for your time. I came to you rather than going to a psychiatrist because I knew you would have to take care of me for free." Once you have been able to recognize the trouble of the person who needs help then do all you can to arrange for him to see the proper professional counselor. I talked for hours on the phone to a woman who was a regular visitor at our church. It took quite a while before I could find out just what her problem was, though she thought it was her husband's lack of spirituality. For hours, days on end, we went round and round in circles, until she had me exhausted. It was not long before I realized that the Scriptures were not doing her any good, and that she knew it as well as I. My husband took over and we both did some undercover investigating. Finally we were able to get her to visit a psychiatrist, who had already told us, from our description, that both husband and wife needed special help. We even arranged through the doctor to let her have free treatment at the hospital where he worked, only to have her back down at the last minute. Her husband said, "They are the ones who are crazy, not us," and they promptly left the church. The tragedy is not that they left the church, but that they are going on in their misery, and leading their children down the same path. Since that time, they fooled the next minister for a while until he put a stop to it by telling them the truth and now they have moved to another church.

Probably the greatest temptation of a counselor—and I think this is especially true of us women—is to talk a lot, express our opinions, and even give advice. That is little or no help, and often dangerous. If we do not learn to listen quietly when the other person is speaking—only rewording what they have already said when it is necessary for us to say something, we are apt to miss the most important part of the trouble. When we express opinions we merely lead the counselee to fear, guilt, or wrong impressions which may destroy the desired results of our counseling. Never give advice—or seldom, shall I say?—unless you are forced to, or honestly feel it will help. To begin with, most people do not want advice. They come to us with their minds already made up, and do not intend to change in most cases. They only hope, by talking to us, to get us to agree with them and thus salve their conscience. Some want you to take their side in a family or church disagreement. It is dangerous to take sides in any dispute, because in so doing, you are judging from one person's viewpoint alone, and that is probably very biased. Invariably, you are going to make the person on the other side angry, and he will feel you are meddling in something which is none of your business. If you give advice, and it does not turn out right, you will be forever blamed for it. If it does turn out right, *they* will take credit for it.

The counselee is as much of a problem as yourself. You will have to study the personality of the person who needs help, as well as listen to what he has to say. You will probably know considerable about the person if he is a church member who needs help. Facing the fact that all of us really live on two levels will be a big help in determining the nature of the problem. We function on the emotional and the intellectual levels, the conscious and the subconscious levels. Many people do not realize this when they try to express and face their problems. Ask yourself several questions: Is he telling me what is really his problem, or just the last thing that happened to upset him? Is he facing reality, or adding imaginary things because of his attitude toward the trouble? Is he blaming another person or circumstance for something that is his own making? Blaming someone else for our problems is universal and it takes a strong person to admit that he is his own biggest problem. But the person must be gradually drawn out by questions, and by your restating what he has said, to see for himself that he must take full responsibility for his situation. Blaming circumstances and others is the easiest way of escape and gives a person the feeling that there is nothing he can do about his problem unless those outside things are corrected. Even if others are to blame, he must make an adjustment to the difficulty, and that means facing reality and making some definite decisions.

Even when we face reality, in all truthfulness, we find that different personalities see the same thing from different viewpoints. Niagara Falls, in reality, are tons of water going over massive rocks. To the tourist, the falls are a breathtaking scene of beauty; to the engineer, so much electric power generated by that water; to honeymooners, the next step to heaven; and to the artist, a blend of colors, light and dark shadows, and a challenge to make the perfect copy on canvas. Though they are just so much water, the falls present a different aspect to the different viewers in the light of their background, training, and personalities.

Suppose a woman has come to call upon you. You are not sure whether she is making a social call or is leading up to a discussion of a problem she has. So just let her talk about the things which are on her mind. Before long she will begin to show if something is bothering her. Women tend to be less reserved and more emotional than men, and often begin to cry and state their problems as soon as they feel at home with the pastor's wife. Perhaps she may say, "My husband doesn't love me any more." You may be perfectly positive that he does, but instead of saying so, just reword what she has said. You might say, "You don't think your husband loves you?" That gives her just the chance she is looking for to tell all the mean things she can think of. If you had tried to assure her that you knew her husband loved her, you would have brought the interview to a close. You would have been no help to the woman, for in her state of mind nothing you said would have been accepted. Let her talk freely, as long as she wishes. Sometimes, just having an opportunity to vent her resentments will make her see how ridiculous they are anyway, and she will go out laughing, realizing that she has no problem after all.

But if a woman does have a problem, listen carefully for any sound reasons she might have for thinking she does. Try, by short questions, to lead her from the supposed injury to what may have some truth. Eventually, you will find the key to the whole problem. Perhaps the husband has refused to let her have a charge account at the department stores. There must be some good reason. Sooner or later, in her anger, she will trap herself by saying that he accuses her of not knowing how to manage money. You might try to lead her to revealing the truth by asking how she manages her household money, and the truth will out. Then you know the true difficulty in that family. She either is a compulsive spender, or she refuses to live within their income. Therefore, the only way the husband can keep from going bankrupt is to keep temptation out of her way by retracting the privilege of a charge account. After hearing her troubles spoken aloud and releasing her pent-up emotions, she will begin to see that, instead of blaming her marriage partner, she is the one to blame, and that he is protecting their very livelihood and home, and helping her to resist temptation. When she has come this far, she can usually see—maybe with a subtle hint from you—that as soon as she proves to him that she can be trusted to use a charge plate wisely, he will be glad to let her have one. His refusal to let her have a charge account doesn't mean he doesn't love her.

A case of this kind is a very typical one for the pastor's wife. First, she might not be sure that the lady who is calling has a problem; she might be making just a social call. Second, the originally stated problem usually has no bearing on the real one at all. Third, when the real problem is exposed, the blame is always put on the other fellow. Fourth, the person has to accept the solution to the real trouble on the emotional level. When one accepts an answer on the intellectual level, little or nothing is done about the problem, but when it is emotionally accepted, it is almost certain that some constructive changes will be made and the difficulties will be cleared up. This is why just passing out advice, excellent as it may be, seldom does any good.

The methods used in counseling are varied, but some of the following general suggestions are used in nearly every case: Let the person who needs help decide when and how he will tell his problem. Let him set the pace of conversation or actions. In most of the cases of counseling I have had, the girl or woman has visited with me about other things for about a half hour before she got to the problem, even when she had called and asked to come to discuss a problem. If I asked, the minute she arrived, "What is your problem?" she probably would never have told me. Only the most desperate ones start with their problem immediately. The half-hour visit is, in a sense, wasted time for you, but it is usually necessary preparation for the one with the problem.

Do not try to argue the person out of her problem, such as in the example just given. If I had tried to assure the lady that I knew her husband loved her, she would not have accepted what I said anyway, and would have left before I got down to the real problem.

No matter how wrong, or outrightly sinful the deed someone has confessed, do not start condemning her or suggest that her behavior is wrong. Usually she already knows this, and if she doesn't, you will have to gently and slowly lead her to such knowledge.

Usually you can get enough facts to find the answer, but even if you cannot, do not start probing into things which are none of your business. Please respect the other's dignity and rights. Sometimes asking three or four questions at once and observing which one is answered first will give a definite clue to the trouble.

Whenever a spiritual problem is involved, or the Bible has the answer, always turn to it and show the one in need what God has to say, then try to lead him to accept God's will instead of insisting on his own will. If you are talking to an unsaved person, he should be introduced to Christ as his Saviour and only hope. Where you find someone who will not accept the Bible as God's Word, it is almost impossible to be of spiritual help. You just have to help as best you can on the human level.

Do not commiserate with the individual, or tell of some of your experiences that were similar. You are apt to be telling your troubles and not listening to or helping the other fellow. Be as unemotional about the problem as possible. You can give sympathy and comfort about the problem, when needed, without telling what others have done in the same situation. The end results in those cases might not be the answer to this person's problem at all. Commiserating with a person makes her feel worse, assures her that she is right even when she might be wrong, and often makes her feel that her problem is much worse than she thought it was when she came to see you. Whatever you do, do not let the counseling session turn into a two-way conversation, or just an ordinary visit, as a result of your talking about yourself and your troubles.

Perhaps the hardest thing to do is to avoid using pat Christian phrases and answers. We Christians often just parrot what we hear others say or what the minister uses in a sermon. Or we use a few Scripture verses that are probably as familiar to the one we counsel as they are to us. And we seldom help the counselee when we give such responses.

My husband travels a lot and always by plane. For some reason, I suddenly developed a fear of having him fly by jet—when they were first used. One summer a series of dreams that he was killed in a plane crash while landing here, upset me. Since a minister's wife has no pastor, I discussed the matter with a seminary professor. I could see that committing my husband to the Lord was not the problem and that I was trusting Him in this matter and had come to the place where I could say, "Thy will be done." That interview taught me more about counseling than all the training I have had and the books I have read. He started right out by saying, "Let's talk about exactly what you would do if he were killed." Then he proceeded to outline a program of necessary actions for any eventuality. He knew I was familiar with all the Bible verses that promised protection and with the pat Christian answers to fears and doubts, and that I had been counseling others longer than he had. He shocked me into facing the reality that there would still be life and purpose even if the Lord did take my husband home to be with Himself. He made me face reality, make a few decisions, and then forget it. Though he offered to delay his trip another day in order to go to the airport with me when my husband was due to land, I refused with thanks, for he had done such a thorough job in counseling that I did not need to lean on the counselor any more but could trust myself to lean only on the Lord. Since that day I have never had the least fear of my husband's traveling. Incidentally, the next day my husband's plane landed before I realized which one he was on, so the Lord spared me even the temptation of doubting for a moment.

The purpose of counseling is twofold: to help with the immediate problem and to help the person learn to solve his problems alone. There are two ways of getting a tot from room to room. One is to teach him to walk, and the other is to carry him. Our purpose is to help when necessary, but also to train the person to find his own answers for himself, and not to continually lean on another for advice.

Life is a matter of choices. Each day we all make little and big choices, and we must learn to weigh the facts and the consequences and decide which path is the best, or the safest. Like the tot who learns to walk by walking, we learn to solve our problems by reasoning and thinking them through, and making decisions even though they may be wrong ones at times. Most of us learn more from our mistakes than we do from our successes.

The easiest person to help is the one who comes with an open mind, ready to discuss his problem in full. In most cases, the major need is for him to be able to express his need out loud to someone who can be trusted. In having to explain it to another, he sees the answer for himself. Such a person usually goes out thanking you for settling his troubles, when you did not say a thing. All you did was to act as a sounding board for his thoughts, and he made his own decisions. That is the best kind of counseling. Happy is the counselor who can help a person to see what his real problem is, and then bring him to the place of facing it honestly and making a constructive decision for himself of what must be done, and DO it.

Webster says that the word "counsel" means to "give advice or to consult; to exchange ideas or to talk things over." The pastor's wife may not counsel in the strictest sense of the word, but often, where there is no assistant to the pastor, she will spend many hours just listening to people tell their troubles. They do not want any advice, or exchange of ideas. They just want someone with a sympathetic ear to listen to their troubles. They think that they honestly want help, but too often, when it is given, they refuse it or feel highly insulted that it was offered. Many of them cannot be honest enough to face their own problems and are too emotionally immature to do anything about them. Their only relief and recourse is to find someone who will listen to them repeat, over and over, the problems that baffle them. Since their friends get fewer and fewer as they rehash their troubles, they turn to the pastor's wife because she usually cannot refuse to listen to them.

This puts the pastor's wife in a real dilemma. She has to decide just how much time she is going to give to people of this type and what she can do to stop their calls when she sees that nothing can be done to help that person.

In my case, most of these people talk to me on the telephone. Because we live in such a large city, it is difficult for them to come to our home. That explains why I spend so much time on the telephone, as has been mentioned in the second chapter of this book. This has some definite advantages, as it is easier to terminate a telephone conversation than a visit. On the other hand, it is too easy for them to reach for the phone, so sometimes they phone daily, whereas visits to the manse would have to be much more limited. Another disadvantage is that those who use the phone can call at very inconvenient times, like when I should be preparing dinner so that my husband can get out early for an evening of calling, or a committee meeting.

Making it even harder to decide how to handle those who just want to talk is the fact that they are seldom members of our church, but often attend. We even have people in a large city such as this who just look for a sympathetic pastor's wife who will listen to them, and then they greatly overdo that privilege.

The first thing to do is to listen to these people and try to help them. Telephone counseling is nearly impossible, especially when a stranger is involved. When you are sure that she will not receive help, and there is no possibility of getting her to people who can help her, then start tactfully bringing your conversation to an end by telling her frankly that your child needs you, or it is time for you to get supper. For about a month I had four people of this type calling me every day, with the result that I was not getting my work done and was exhausted from listening to other people's troubles. That is when my doctor and my husband both laid down a few rules. My husband said to tell them that he was the pastor of the church, and he wanted to talk to them himself. He would be glad to make an appointment with them any time they wished. That put a stop to most of such calls, since these people knew they could not take the pastor's time to just talk, and they could not be bothered to go to his office. Since most of these either were under a doctor's care whose advice they would not follow or had refused to see one who could help them, we felt that it was impossible for us to help them further. My doctor told me to tell them that since I was not trained to treat their types of troubles, I might do more harm than good talking to them, and thus put an end to the conversation. Remember, though, I never do this until I am sure that these people are beyond help from either me or my husband.

At one time, I thought I was helping a fine Christian through a period of prolonged illness by listening to her at least an hour every day. Soon we found out that she was under the care of six doctors, all of whom had recommended institutional care for her as a necessity. After she talked to me, she would feel better, and for several days she and her husband would feel that the doctors were wrong because she seemed to be better. This went on quite a while until I found out from a Christian psychiatrist that each day she delayed entering the hospital was making her case harder to cure. In my ignorance, by listening to her problems every day I was not helping but hindering her getting the proper medical care.

My husband and I have an unusual opportunity in having a Christian psychiatrist in our church who has offered to discuss any problems with us, and he has done a lot to help us recognize the real sources of trouble. This has helped us to know which cases can be helped by us and which can only be helped with medical care. He will screen out the emotionally affected and the disguised cases, and even arrange care for those who need it and will face the fact that they do. This is most unusual, and few pastors will have a specialist to decide the mental and emotional balance of those who need help. With the Lord's help, seeing that giving them the Word repeatedly will not help, or that they refuse any help or advice, you can soon know whether they are just using you to vent their feelings or whether they can really be helped. No matter how sorry we may feel for these people, there is a limit to the time and strength that a pastor's wife can give to those who are just wasting her time. Her husband, family, home, and church members need her and one woman cannot do all of these things. You have to be firm and turn down those who sap your strength and keep you from important things which need to be done.

Real counseling is a challenge for those who want to engage in it, but it takes fortitude and courage to put an end to wasting time and precious energy on those who are only using you to escape facing their real problems.

At any rate, do your best to find out the true problem, and help if you can. If not, turn the person over to someone who can, starting with the pastor himself. He can take over and decide, after hearing the person's story, what can be done to help him. You are not the assistant pastor, and all of these people are first and foremost his problem, not yours.

CHAPTER 11

Mistakes of the Pastor's Wife

LISTENING TO A GROUP of ministers' wives, one would get the impression that they are the most persecuted, mistreated and overworked people in the world. It seems impossible to discover why they should feel this way. Apparently, they have not looked around to see what is expected of other wives, or they would not hold this attitude. They live like an ostrich with his head in the sand, thinking that what they do not or will not see does not exist. It has been an eye-opener to me to check with other wives whose husbands have different types of occupations, to see what their problems and difficulties are. To my surprise, I found that almost every one of them has nearly the same problems that we ministers' wives have.

One of the commonest complaints of the parson's wife is that her husband does not have enough time to be with her and the children. However, other women have this problem, too. A surgeon, at whose home my husband conducts a Bible class, had not been to bed before three in the morning, for three consecutive days, and he had to be at the hospital at seven every morning. His wife told me that prior to that he had been home to dinner only three times in two weeks. A psychiatrist's wife told me that she not only had to run the constant risk of having the women patients fall in love with her husband and try to attract him, but she and the family had to weigh every word before they spoke because he would interpret their thoughts and actions in the light of his knowledge. A certified public accountant stopped by our home at dinner time to give my husband a message, so I asked him about his schedule. He had not been home for dinner in two weeks, and was going home early that evening only because his wife was sick, and they had two small boys. He told me that he left home in the morning before the children were up, and had not returned before they went to bed for several weeks. His older son asked, "Have you had a letter from daddy recently, Mommie?" He thought his daddy was out of town.

An elder and his wife, in one of our pastorates, started a store together. She worked as many hours as he did, and also took care of her children and her home.

Quite a number of men in our church are traveling salesmen, and many of them can only be home on weekends. A few men are out for two weeks at a time. We also have a number of airline pilots who have most difficult schedules. Sometimes they are out for several days, then in for a few, and as soon as they are used to one routine, their schedules are changed, and the entire pattern of homelife has to be rearranged.

Farmers' wives have to work from sunup to sundown, right along with their husbands, and they usually do not have all the conveniences that we city-dwellers do, to help in their work.

Perhaps the hardest case I observed was that of a man who had just started to buy his own gasoline station. Because he was limited in funds, he could employ only one helper. That meant he had to work from five in the morning until ten at night. Since their youngest children were in high school, his wife went back to work to help bear the expenses until he had a paying business going.

Many more such illustrations could be given. Usually, except in cases where a man works in a factory, or in other places of employment where he has an eight-hour, five-days-a-week job, the business and professional man works as many hours as some ministers, and sometimes even more. These men also give a generous amount of time to church work, free. They have the same problem of giving more time to their wives and children as a parson does. However, I noticed with interest that none of the persons interviewed on this subject complained or resented the situation as pastors' wives do. The long hours were accepted as a necessary part of living.

We will readily admit that there are two differences. The lay wife is only working for her husband, or one employer, while the minister's wife tries to please hundreds of people. There is also another difference; the wife of the business or professional man is either directly earning money for her work, or is getting the financial benefit of helping her husband or giving up the pleasure of his company for many hours. Few ministers and their wives are ever blessed with financial remuneration commensurate with the education required for their work and the amount of time they put into church work.

The second most prominent complaint of the minister's wife is the lack of adequate finances for their needs. More often their complaints stem from the fact that they cannot live as nicely as the people around them. Many are very free to mention the seemingly small salary they are receiving from the church, but they usually fail to tell that they are also getting a rent-free home, and many times even the utility bills are paid for them. They fail to add in the savings that come to them by gifts given by the congregation; the doctors' and dentists' services that are free; baby-sitters who make no charge; help with food when entertaining; contributions made toward vacations; and even fees paid for the children's schooling. These benefits vary, of course, according to the church situation.

So many wonderful things have been done for us that we often wish I had written a book of remembrance. My office is a corner of what is really my utility room. I just happened to glance around, as I was writing this, to see what was in the room that came from the church people. The typewriter came from a pilot; the filing cabinet, to my right, from a business executive; the fancy plate hanging over the chest of drawers from a teacher; a hand-painted vase from an elder's wife; the unusual calendar on my wall from another lady; the picture of praying hands, right at my eye level when I look up from my typing, from another member; and the flowering shrubbery and the trees outside the window from the entire congregation. How quick we are to forget the wonderful friends God has given us in our membership!

The third, and the most serious, complaint of the minister's wife is the state of her health. Since there are so many who feel overworked, tired and sickly, this is understandable but not justified. No one wishes to hear about another's health, even though it is customary to ask, "How are you?" Just say "fine," and let it go at that. If a special friend presses you into an answer, then say as little as possible about your condition. No one wants an "organ" recital, even if you feel it is necessary to be completely truthful. Remember II Corinthians 4:16. Even when the "outward man" may be giving you a lot of pain, the "inward man" should be renewed by the Lord, day by day, as we let Him do it. We have to listen to the health details of many members of the congregation, whether we wish to or not. They need someone to give comfort and sympathy, and you are probably the only one to whom they can go. I admit that we need the same help, but we must find our comforters outside of the church. Our husbands should be a help to us in this matter but, since they must listen to so many problems during the day, it hardly seems fair or wise to start in with our complaints as soon as they get home.

A college classmate of my husband married a lovely girl who had every promise of being a fine pastor's wife. She complained so constantly about her health that he had to move quite rapidly from one church to another, until finally her reputation went before them and no church would give them a call. His ministry was ruined because she had nothing better to think about than herself, and nothing to talk about but the way she suffered physically.

All of us who have a tendency to complain about anything in our lives should stop to consider just what we are doing. We thoughtlessly consider that circumstances are against us, but in reality we are blaming God for the problems, and are rebelling against what He has sent, in His will, for our own good. It is good to read and reread the story of the serpent in the wilderness to remind ourselves just how much God hates complaining. The terrible scourge of poisonous snakes that He sent among the children of Israel should teach us a solemn lesson (Numbers 21:5-9).

Many ministers' wives resent the fact that they have to be "looked over" and approved by the congregation before their husbands are called. They feel such a procedure is only followed in their case. However, many corporations will not employ a man until some of the directors have had a chance to look at his wife to see if she will fit into his type of life. She is expected to measure up to standards the company has set for the wives of their employees. If she does not measure up, the man fails to get the job. Or if he is already employed, he often is not considered for advancement on account of his wife. She is expected to take part in community drives, and help with charities. In many business organizations, she must belong to certain clubs to be acceptable. She has to dress in a certain way, drive the right kind of car, and see that her children attend the best of schools. Even if she has a private income, she is not allowed to live above the standards of her husband's superiors, or to belong to the same country club. These responsibilities are imposed upon her without any regard for her wishes, home duties, or health. Unless she complies with the requirements and helps her husband in these ways, he seldom advances in salary, and is often passed over when there are chances for promotion.

Executives' wives have as much of a problem entertaining, though perhaps in different ways, as we ministers' wives do. We are limited because of lack of funds and of household help, but we can entertain Christians, or those who at least act like gentle people when they are in the manse. Many fine Christians are compelled to entertain officers and visiting clients in their homes, only to have their homes invaded by bottles of whiskey and have the air made blue with swearing and cigarette smoke, with unbecoming behavior increasing as the evening progresses. One of our elders refuses to furnish liquor, so out of respect for his Christian testimony, the guests have also stopped bringing their bottles with them, but come well "tanked up" ahead of time, so the entire affair is a vexation to his righteous soul. We pastors' wives entertain the Lord's people and shall receive our reward from Him, while many other Christians have to entertain just because of their business.

Much harm has been done in the church—by both the wife and the pastor—by trying to change things too quickly. When the new parson arrives, the church members are usually perfectly happy with the way things are going, and expect the incoming couple to feel that they have a nice organization. They are cruelly hurt when the ministerial couple starts picking their work to pieces and suggesting changes. They feel—and justly so, I believe—that this is as unkind and rude as visiting a friend's home and starting to criticize his furniture, pictures, children and the food that is served. We all resist change, so we shouldn't be surprised when the people show resentment, or outright rebellion. It gives them the impression that their ways are not right, and that the new couple feel they know how to do things much better than those who have run the church for years. This is usually true, but it is much better to carefully study each phase of the work; see where the first change is most needed; and ignore, for a while, the areas where changes can wait without serious damage. Be perfectly honest and ready to see that it may be best for that particular church to leave some things just as they are.

Along with much prayer for God's guidance, you will have to move slowly and carefully, working through a few of the people (perhaps some of the ruling board members) who support you wholeheartedly and who also see the benefits of making some changes. Make suggestions or drop hints where they are most likely to be acted upon and, if possible, let someone in the church think that the change is his own idea, and let him get the credit for it. Of course, where there are things that are scripturally wrong with the church, a change *must* be made, but even that should be done kindly, after a careful explanation of why it is necessary.

The pastor's wife should never make any changes! Those should be left up to her husband and the members of the church board. Most of the ministers' wives who are in serious trouble in their churches have gotten into trouble by taking things into their own hands and running ahead of the men. Women who think that they can run the church had better rethink their position in the light of God's Word. God says that women are to keep silence in the church and not to usurp authority over men, and this applies to the clergyman's wife as well as to the other ladies (I Timothy 2:11-12).

Right along this line, there is a serious temptation. A wife who will not openly run the church may try to work out her plans and schemes through her husband. Please do not try to push your ideas through the pastor. At the right time, you might be able to make some constructive suggestions, but do no more than that. If he does not feel these ideas are best, just forget it. If he wants to work some of them out, he will probably discuss them with you later and may even ask your help in carrying them out. It is his church, and he has to do what he feels is best, whether you approve or not. Just keep praying about the things that concern you, and God will see that they come to pass if they are within His will.

In talking to laymen about ministers' wives (either friends who would be honest with me, or strangers who did not know I was a pastor's wife) I found that two criticisms are held against them more than any others. These are: The pastor's wife either completely takes over the church, as if she owned it, or she stays completely out of everything, as though she were not interested in the work at all. "Isn't there any middle-of-the road attitude for ministers' wives?" asked one who was brutally honest with me.

Do not take over in the church, as if you thought you were the only one who could do the job right. If you do, you will give others the impression that you think they are inferior, and that you have an overdose of ego. These people ran the church before you came, and they will be able to run it for years after you leave. Stand aside for a while, and see how they like to do things. Then later, if you are sure you can be of help, carefully make a few suggestions.

Do not be hurt because you are not asked to be president of the missionary society. Perhaps you have complained to the ladies of the church that you have so many responsibilities and are exhausted. They are probably trying to help you by not placing more work on your shoulders.

I have no official job in our present church. Even so, the people know that I am interested in them as individuals, and in the church organizations, and I attend all meetings. They know that they have my prayers and that I give my husband 100 percent support in his work. It does not take a hurried, worried, worked-to-death pastor's wife to make a church know that she is interested. In fact, my ladies prefer that I be free from church work so I will have plenty of time to meet all the needs of the pastor and our family. They want to know that I am well, rested, and available when there are special needs in the church family. They would much rather know that I am praying for them than to have me serve as president of the women's society.

Other wives apparently stay out of sight as much as possible, and try to avoid any responsibility. They feel that since the church called their husband, they have no more work to do for his success than does the wife of the businessman who goes to his office in the morning and leaves his wife at home. Other women feel that they want a career of their own and so seek outside employment and are too tired and too busy at home to take any active part in the church work. A very few pastors make it plain to the congregation, often by announcement from the pulpit, that the wife is not employed by the church, and does not expect to have any work to do. These women are usually those who would be misfits in any area of life, and would drag their feet in any activity except those that are their special hobbies. They make it plain that they regret being married to a minister, but are not going to let that stand in their way. In all fairness, in spite of the one who told me this, I believe that these women are few and far between. I can honestly say that in the past twenty-five years, though I have lived in ministerial circles, I have only met one like that. In this case, it seems evident that the cause is more physical and emotional than spiritual. For all I know, the person who made this observation may be including me in this second group since I have no official office, but, generally speaking, we find that the ones who give their time to their husbands, their home, their children, and individuals in the church, are more successful and better liked than the ones who take over so much of the church responsibilities.

We have been told so many times that we can either make or break our husband's ministry, that often we take that too literally. We find that we take ourselves too seriously and feel that we are indispensable to every activity in the church. That is a mistake, too. No one is indispensable in any work. Even when a person dies, his or her place is soon filled. Remember that when you are tempted to try to do too much.

One big secret of real success as a minister's wife is to be your real self! Live in the home and before the church people as naturally as possible. In this way you can feel relaxed, sure of yourself. It will keep you from making mistakes in etiquette, from saying something hastily that you will regret later, and from seeming to be snobbish and unloving. It is useless, and often disastrous, to try to be like the last minister's wife, even if she is held up to you as a model. The parishioners neither want, nor expect you, to be like another person, no matter how much they liked her. While it is well to learn what you can from wives who are successful, it is never wise to try to copy them. To be your best self, you must be yourself.

In this connection, we might say here, do not take your *faux pas* too seriously. Some pastors' wives, who are not too sure of themselves, often smart over a minor mistake they have made for days, feeling they have offended a church member. We all have made mistakes, from large to small, and probably will continue to as long as we live.

I try to know all the people who come to our church. Since we have numbers of visitors, and nearly four hundred who attend regularly, it is difficult, and the mistake I make most often is getting names and faces mixed up. It is embarrassing, but I have determined to apologize, laugh at myself and forget it. There is only heartache in rehashing such errors and feeling guilty about them. As long as the people know you and your interest in the church, they will quickly forget any mistakes you make. You only make things worse by trying to explain, and usually the more you say the worse you make the situation.

Some ministers' wives carry a chip on their shoulder. They start in the first pastorate frightened, and so full of advice that it is hard for them not to be on the defensive. Do not assume everyone has it in for you and that what is said and done is to deliberately hurt or humiliate you. Many times what I thought was an insult turned out to be a misunderstanding on my part, and I suffered needlessly, and found it hard to be nice to the one I thought had offended me. That just makes life hard and is often so useless. Even if an offense were intended, if you go over and over the incident, no useful purpose is served. And you suffer from feelings of resentment. The sooner the incident is forgotten, the easier it will be for you to work with that person later.

Remember that your husband needs a real wife and companion and a neat, efficiently run home more than he needs an assistant pastor. The children need a good mother (even though she often has to take on some of the father's duties), more than the church needs another worker. So, no matter how much you feel wanted in the church, do not overlook the needs of your family. If the homelife of the manse and the people who live there go to pieces, the work of the church will not progress very well, and the children might truly turn out to be bad PK's (Preachers' Kids). Be sure that you save plenty of time and strength for the most important place—your home.

It is just as important for the minister and his wife to learn to keep everything confidential as it is for a doctor, or a lawyer. It is often a temptation for the minister's wife to gossip because she knows so much about the church people and the things that are going on in the church. There are times when you feel that information you have can be used to defend a person, and you long to use it, but you must not if it has been given in confidence. We women are not noted for keeping secrets, so sometimes it takes a long time to show the church folks that we can be trusted with information. If one confidence leaks out, your usefulness as a counselor is over. No one wants to discuss her private affairs with a person who will gradually let it get back to all the church members through her special friends.

All ministers' wives I contacted felt that having special friends in the congregation is a serious mistake. My husband and I know from experience that it never works. Church members have a father and mother image of the pastor and his wife, and are unconsciously jealous when it is felt that one, or a few, of the "children" are getting more attention from the "parents" than they are.

It never works to entertain individuals, couples, or families in the manse. It is impossible to get to entertain all who belong to the church. Even if you succeeded in reaching every one carefully, you would be criticized because of the order in which you invited them. No matter what you do in this matter, you can not win. We entertain in groups, such as Sunday school classes, the board members and their wives, prayer groups, morning coffee for the women of the church, Sunday school board, young people, and—once a year—open house for the entire church. In this way, every one who wishes to can come to the manse on invitation, at least once a year, and the active members usually come several times because they are members of the groups that are invited.

Once I invited a family consisting of the husband and three small children to dinner twice in one week while the mother was in the hospital, just to help them. This was during the time when my husband was not the pastor, but was just teaching the adult Sunday school class. Many months later, the remark got back to me, when it was too late to explain, that I had entertained this family twice and had not yet entertained the complainer.

"While the minister's wife has a perfect right to have opinions of her own, and to vote in congregational meetings, it is best that she not take sides in church issues unless it is a doctrinal stand of right and wrong in God's sight," wrote a Minneapolis minister's wife. Once a minister's wife takes a stand, that automatically puts her in one group and turns another group against her. She cannot afford to divide the church, no matter how much right she might have to express her feelings.

Perhaps the basic reason for our other mistakes is that we try to please all the church people, and to take our orders from them. Instead, we must live so close to the Lord that we take our orders from Him, and Him alone. That way we can make no mistake. It might not please some of the members, but you might as well dismiss the idea of pleasing everyone; nobody has ever done it! You will have the joy of knowing that you are being led by the Lord and are pleasing to Him, so what little criticism He allows should not bother you at all.

Try not to show your antagonism toward those who disapprove of you, or who are fighting against your husband's plans and program for the church. It is easy to turn away from them, or try to get even with them for hurting your husband. If you do that, you are stooping to their childish level, and are no better than they. Instead, try being a little more friendly, even though you find it difficult. Go out of your way to speak to them, to say any nice things you can honestly say about them, and let them get to know you better by calling at their home and, if possible without discrimination, invite them to your home with a church group. So often, those who deliberately make trouble for the ministerial couple do so because they do not know them very well. Do anything you can to show them how friendly you both are. A number of times we have done this, and after they really got to know us well, they became fast friends and staunch supporters. The trouble all started through misunderstanding of our ways, or intentions, because they did not know us well enough.

If, by any chance, their complaints and criticisms are well founded, you and your husband would do well to correct them. It will be for your own good and the good of the church. This is much better than holding grudges, bearing resentment, and criticizing members who do not agree with you. What do you expect of your church members when you give them such a poor example by your own behavior?

Even though it may be hard for you, listen to the advice given by those who honestly think they are helping you. You will soon distinguish between those who are just griping all the time about the same thing and those who will give you real help. Do not assume that you know it all; you might get a surprising amount of help from those members who know the church and the people better than you do. Never be rude. Listen carefully. Then pray about what has been said. Disregard and *forget* what has been mean and thoughtless and useless, and act on those things which will help you and the church.

A successful minister's wife, who lives in Philadelphia, wrote me that she thinks "our 'favorite sin' as ministers' wives is perfectionism." By that she means that "we are apt to be thinking and expecting that everything in connection with our husbands and the church work must be perfect. Since that is impossible, we usually keep ourselves tied up in knots, straining through our husband's sermons from the pew, as though it could help him in preaching. It never does any good and only leaves the minister's wife drained and exhausted after each service. We think our motives are pure in wanting him to reach people's hearts for the Lord, when many times we honestly know that we just want him to be liked and considered a success in his ministry. The second way in which we want perfection is in ourselves. That is impossible, even for the best trained, the well adjusted, and the physically fit, and even harder for those suffering handicaps. When we make a blunder, or feel we have failed in neglecting our duties or what we think is expected of us by the church people, we blame ourselves for our failure. We often make ourselves miserable over things which cannot be helped or changed. The churches we serve will never be perfect and if they were, we would never be called to serve them.

"I am trying to learn by practice to put aside the desire for perfection, which I know neither of us can produce, and just do what each day demands as I can, and leave the real job to the Holy Spirit. It is true that we can waste much strength and energy in apprehension before a given duty or event, and still more in striving for perfection while doing it, and then go home all burned out—or up! Again, along with our faith in overcoming these things, we need good common sense to do our best as the Lord enables and leave the results to Him." This is the answer to the problem that she has found for herself.

The perfect minister's wife has never existed, and never will, though happily many church members feel they have found the best one. There are a few obvious mistakes and pitfalls the minister's helpmeet would do well to avoid.

She should not complain about her husband's working hours,

the salary, manse or her health. She will make a serious mistake if she tries to make sudden changes in the church or to rule the church directly or through her husband. It is equally serious for the pastor's wife to feel she has no responsibility to the church, or to seek a private career. Each wife should be herself and live as normal a life as possible. It is best for a clergyman's wife to refrain from having intimate friends among the church members; she should be equally friendly with, and interested in, all members. The pastor's family should not entertain individuals in their home but entertain as many as possible in groups. Try to win troublemakers and those who oppose your husband's program by kindness. Plan ways of letting them get to know you better. Many differences of opinion are a result of misunderstanding and can be cleared up in this way. Many who give advice are sincere in hoping to be of assistance, and their suggestions may often be a help. No matter how critical a person may be, there is no excuse for rudeness on the part of the pastor's wife. There will never be a perfect church or ministerial couple, so the sooner we all face the fact and go on as best we can with what we are, the happier we will be and the greater will be the progress made in the work of the Lord.

CHAPTER 12

Persecution for Christ's Sake

TRUTH IS STRANGER than fiction," someone has said. I am taking the liberty of changing this statement a little. "Truth is sometimes harder to believe than fiction." For that reason it is almost necessary to use in this chapter illustrations from my own experience or that of those very close to me, because what is written here will be so hard to believe that I would doubt it myself if we had not gone through these trials ourselves.

God's Word gives the only answer to why these things have happened. "Yea, and all who will live godly in Christ Jesus shall suffer persecution" (II Tim. 3:12). "For unto you it is given in the behalf of Christ, not only to believe on him, but also to suffer for his sake" (Phil. 1:29). While Christ was still here on earth, He warned that since the world hated Him it would also hate Christians, those who would live for Him and serve Him. (See John 15:18-21.) John tells us in his first epistle, "The whole world lieth in the wicked one." Do you really think that the world and the people who live worldly lives are going to happily accept you, especially when your life is a reproach to them? If you are pleasing to God, and declaring His whole Word, don't be surprised if you are persecuted and misunderstood by the unsaved and even by some of your most active church members.

Somehow, my husband and I had the naïve idea that all our church folks would be Christians, trying to please the Lord as sincerely as we; therefore we thought there would be little trouble. We thought in terms of small personality clashes, and problems from those who coveted certain prominent jobs in

204

the church. We never dreamed that we would have open, deliberate persecution for preaching the Word of God.

Our first shock came the night we arrived in our first pastorate. We were entertained in the home of an elder who was also superintendent of the Sunday school. Soon after dinner, he and his wife announced that they were going to the Saturday-night dance at their club and invited us to go with them, though we had driven about four hundred miles over mostly mountainous roads and Dwight was to preach for the first time in his first church the next morning. Not wanting to antagonize an elder the first day, he declined for those reasons, but they weren't accepted. The elder was stubborn and wanted to know how my husband felt about dancing. There was then no choice but to tell him. This man had voted on the pulpit committee to call my husband. But, because of my husband's views on dancing, this man turned against my husband and never supported anything that we tried to do in the church in the five years we were there. We were distressed, but we were never sorry that we made a stand that was important right at the beginning of his ministry.

Usually if the pastor and his wife aren't having some kind of trouble, it means one of two things: Either they have an unusually godly church, or they might not be making a strong enough stand for the things that are right.

Since you know what to expect when you enter a pastorate, it will help you if you have some idea of the reasons and the methods used. If you find the true reason for troubles or can classify the type of personalities and persecutions, you will save yourself much heartache and greatly relieve guilty feelings of failure on your part. We had to learn this by the hard way of experience. When you start in your work, you will be tempted to take these things personally and be terribly hurt by them or to feel that you have failed in some way. Usually, you haven't. Nearly always there is something else behind the problems that come to the ministerial couple.

A few examples might help you to understand some of the problems that may confront you.

There have been a few men who have made unreasonable amounts of trouble for my husband. We later discovered why. One was driven by an inferiority complex because of his background, though he was a very wealthy businessman and in no way inferior. However, his habitual insistence on having his own way and bossing others kept him from being elected to the office of elder, which he wanted very much. Without those dogmatic traits, he would have made a wonderful officer and he was a faithful worker and supporter of the church.

An officer felt it was imperative that everyone of his suggestions be used. If they were changed in any way, he took it as a personal insult and a vote of lack of confidence in his work. This was far from the truth, and many times, my husband tells me, ideas were changed or discarded in session meetings without others feeling offended. We became better acquainted with the family and found out that his acting as he did was the result of his home and business life. He had a very bossy employer who was seldom satisfied with his work and a wife who ran their home and showed plainly that she was not pleased with anything he did around the house. Then we knew that his unpleasant ways at board meetings came from a necessity to vent his pent-up resentments and to have his ideas accepted by someone rather than from any personal feelings held against my husband.

There was a woman who went through periods of criticizing me for no apparent reason, and then there would be times that she was very friendly. At first, I took it all very seriously and worked hard to find out what was wrong. Then I noted that every time there was real trouble brewing in her family life, which was often, she would pick on me. Some members of her family were doing things that she frankly admitted to us were wrong. But every time they were indulging in unscriptural ways, seeing us and knowing how we felt was a reproach to her and her loved ones. Therefore, she seeemed to get emotional release from criticizing me or my husband to me personally. She was torn in conflict between what she knew was God's will, and at the same time she sought to protect the ones she loved. When I came to a full understanding of what lay behind her treatment of me, then I could show real sympathy for her.

There are three types of persecutions that come to the pastor's wife that I believe not even the pastors themselves, much less the church people, understand.

In a sense she is a partner in her husband's work in the eyes of the lay members, but in reality she is only the wife of a preacher. She is in the middle of everything that happens in the church, but has no power or authority. She has to take any unkind remarks about her or the pastor in a gracious manner and forego the right to express her feelings or tell what she knows that will put the blame squarely where it belongs. She may not have the faintest idea what is wrong or who caused it, but she is criticized for it, anyway. She is often blamed for things she never heard of until the time she was confronted with them. Because she knows nothing about these things, naturally she can't defend herself. When she tries to explain that she doesn't know what they are talking about, it is often obvious that many think she is lying to get out of something she has done wrong.

The average husband goes off to work, and his wife is free to pursue her housework and other interests. She seldom knows what is going on in the office or store or on business trips unless her husband chooses to tell her. Even if some things go wrong, she isn't blamed for them and she hears about them so secondhandedly that they don't hurt much. She doesn't have to have her husband's business associates criticize her or her husband, or listen to the boss(es) bawl him out or tell her his mistakes. A businessman can usually accept or reject a few customers if they act angry. One client or patient more or less makes

little difference to a lawyer, doctor, or certified public accountant. The wife seldom has to shoulder his burdens and rarely
has to do anything to please her husband's clients. But—the
pastor's wife must please all of the church members!

The preacher's wife has to work side by side with him; see
everything; hear everything; and even take the blame for things
with which she had nothing to do. She often has to hear her
husband criticized for things that he either didn't do or had
to do for reasons unknown to the critics.

One pastor's wife said, "I feel like the colonists and the Tea
Tax. It's 'taxation without representation' for us preachers'
wives, too." By that she meant that we are not given any authority or privilege to sit in on board meetings, to make changes
in the church policies, or to express any of our views, but at the
same time we are responsible for everyone else's actions, we
must accept the blame for what displeases a member, and help
to keep the members happy and coming to church.

In every church we have served, there have been things that
made me as unhappy as were those who blamed me for them,
but there was nothing I could do about it. There are even times
when my husband can't change things for which we are both
criticized. This puts the parson's wife in the helpless, frustrated
position of having no more power or rights than those granted
all church members equally, but she is expected to carry out the
wishes of those who feel changes should be made in the church
and who talk to her about it instead of going to the pastor or
board of elders.

A second persecution that is vexing and often puts the minister's wife in line for criticism is some members' expectation
of getting her to make decisions about church policies and
actions and also to give her approval of every plan a member
might wish to suggest. Getting my approval of a plan gives no
more promise that it will be done than getting the approval of
any other church member, but for some reasons, many church
members never seem to learn this. When the wife occasionally

steps out of line, in desperation, to change something in the work, usually the first ones to blame her are the very ones who asked her to make a decision about something she had no right to decide on, or who asked her to give her approval for something they wanted done. Too often the very ones who push a preacher's wife into a corner about decisions are the first to howl —if they later get a pastor's wife, who is in the habit of being bossy or running the church—because things aren't done their way. Nobody seems to realize what a position they are putting the wife in, and they wonder why she refuses them or goes to pieces or resents these church members.

My stock answer to all who come to me as though I were the assistant pastor or a church executive is to tell them to talk the matter over with the pastor or a member of the ruling board. Together they will decide what is best for the church. There again, we see misunderstanding on the part of some, and even if we aren't frankly told, we know that the members are thinking that we are just shirking our duty or they take offense because they think we don't like their suggestions. Many times I have fervently wished I had the power to make the suggested changes, for often I agree with those who come to me with the problem. When the things they suggest aren't immediately put into effect in the church, they feel it is my fault, and their misunderstanding is hard to bear.

When my husband is traveling because of speaking engagements, many unexpected things arise, and it is the impulse of some members to call me to insist that I make a decision concerning them. I kindly explain that such a decision is not my responsibility and I tell them that the ruling board will have to make the decision. They should call the clerk of the session and ask him to discuss the matter with the elders. Seldom are the ones who call satisfied with my answer, and a very few tell me frankly what they think of me for being so uncooperative. They complain that it is too much trouble and it takes too long for the elders to handle the matter, and they see no reason why the pastor's wife can't care for it on the spur of the moment. I wonder what would happen if I decided against what they wanted? They fail to realize what a mess the church would be if ministers' wives were given the privilege of making important decisions in the absence of the pastor.

Judging from the comments of other clergymen's wives and my experiences, the hardest persecution we have to bear is to see our husbands mistreated for things they don't do which others think they should do; or things they do which they feel are needed but which some members think are unnecessary; or changes they feel they have to make for Biblical reasons. It is much easier to take criticism ourselves than to hear others pick our husbands to pieces in our presence or to hear such criticism through church gossip. The mother instinct is brought out in us, and we wish we might claw out a few eyes or tell people what we think of them for a change. We feel as protective of our husbands as we do of our children. We can demand that things be made right for our children, but have to keep a dead silence as far as defense of our husbands is concerned lest we make matters worse by reproaching those who are making the trouble and telling others who is really at fault. There is a justified resentment, even in God's sight (Eph. 4:26), of wrong treatment both for ourselves and our loved ones as long as we don't let that lead us into sin. When we have no way of expressing our resentments and feelings, and feel compelled to suppress them, something frequently erupts.

The best-adjusted, happiest minister's wife I knew lived near us in the Philadelphia area. Some trouble was brewing in their church, and some of the members had openly opposed the pastor. At a congregational meeting, most of the members voted against the plans of the minister and showed that they would like to have him look for another place of ministry. His wife stood up in the meeting, screaming and pulling at her hair, until a few people kindly helped her out and took her home. A doctor gave her a sedative and from that night on she was perfectly normal. Being friends, we learned the full story later. The doctor said that she had lived under constant pressure for so long without being able to express her feelings that she reached the point where her nervous system couldn't take it any more. We all have a limit beyond which we can't go. She had reached hers. She was perfectly well physically, and strong emotionally, but she had come to the breaking point from seeing her husband persecuted. Suddenly without her control, her emotions, which she thought were well suppressed, took over when the last straw was added to her burden through a congregational vote showing a lack of confidence in her husband. They soon moved to another part of the country, and in the more than ten years which have elapsed, there has been no repetition of such a loss of control.

Now let's turn to the persecutions that come to the pastor's wife just by virtue of the fact that she married a clergyman. What affects the minister affects his wife because they are so closely related in their work, and what affects the wife affects her husband. So we will now be talking in terms of what affects them as a couple rather than as individuals.

One form of persecution for the ministerial couple that leads to much heartache is the lack of reasonable cooperation from the church leaders. In a friend's church, the entire Sunday school met together for opening exercises, which took far too much time and were entirely over the heads of the children. The pastor slowly and gently tried to work a change through some of their trusted leaders; he wanted to let them think that it was their idea to have a departmental system in their Sunday school. The only reason anyone could give for having everyone together was that the adults "liked to see the little darlings and watch the funny things they do." Now Sunday school is not to amuse the adults; it is for instruction of both the children and the adults in the Word of God. These parents were sacrificing their children for their own amusement, and it was years before the pastor was able to bring about a change.

In every church we find people who will resist change no matter how much it may be needed. They have the idea that what was good enough for Grandpa is good enough for them. They seem to forget, the minute they enter the church door, the changes they have made in their homes and businesses. They want the church to work by a system that was outmoded a generation ago. The ministers have a joke about such a situation, referring to it by the old hymn, "As it was in the beginning, is now, and ever will be." It is too true to be funny in most cases.

Our first pastorate was in a very small town where recreation for the young people consisted of going to the pool hall and theater, and hanging around in gangs in cheap cafés. My husband was concerned about this and asked the church boards and women's organization to help him in a project to provide something in the church for the young people. As organizations they all refused because they couldn't see the need. After all, *they* grew up without any planned church program of recreation! But quite a few individuals offered to help. They donated games and tables, and a number of ladies offered to make and serve refreshments each week. Most of the games—ping pong, shuffle boards, etc.—were made by my husband (alone!) because we were just out of seminary and didn't have the money to buy these things, and the church wouldn't. The young people appreciated all he and others did. Word traveled fast, and young people from all the churches in the town came to our recreational program. It was mostly a time of playing games, and the evening ended with a hymn sing and a five-minute Gospel message given by my husband, followed by refreshments. This program was planned for a night when no other church had a meeting, and was not carried on in the name of our church. My husband's motive was solely to give the young people something wholesome to do. No pressure was put on anyone to join our church. Even the toughest young people of the town came and enjoyed the program, and many of them were saved.

Opposition to this program began to brew right in our own church. Involved were those who couldn't bear to see my husband succeed in something that they wouldn't support. In two years this became open persecution. The operators of the pool hall, the theater, and the cheap cafés, and the Romanist priest got together and demanded that our young people's program be stopped. Since our board members knew they couldn't stop my husband and even the parents were not able to keep their own children away, a diabolical plan was made to force him to give it up. The board of elders told him that unless he had a juke box installed (at their expense) and let the young people play bridge, they wouldn't let him use the church building for his recreational program. We doubt that most of our elders wanted to do this, but they were so afraid of a few businessmen that they gladly sacrificed our young people for their financial gain. Their plan worked because Dwight wouldn't give an inch on his convictions. Fortunately, the Lord had other plans for us. We soon moved to another church, so we didn't have to see the results of such a move. We have heard many sad stories of sin and disgrace even among the young people of that church since then. Though such reports break our hearts, we know we did the best we could for them, and must leave the results to the Lord.

My husband has always faithfully preached the Word wherever he has been. The church where we encountered the opposition I have referred to told him that the previous pastor gave ten-minute sermonettes and book reviews; also that on good, sunny days when he wanted to get out to the golf course early, he didn't have a sermon at all and dismissed the congregation early. One of our boards criticized Dwight severely for being so busy in church work that he was hard to find sometimes. They could always find the last pastor—on the golf course!

When we left seminary, we decided our attitude toward each

church would be: "This church belonged to these people long before we came, and it will still belong to them long after we are gone." For that reason, we decided that we wouldn't make changes, add new programs, and so on, without the consent of the congregation, and that the work would be delegated to those faithful men who were experts in their field. We would keep our opinions to ourselves.

My husband believed in this idea so strongly that he wouldn't vote on the style, type of buildings or the architect when our present congregation voted to build a new church plant. The decision went to the congregation without anyone knowing how Dwight felt, though he was asked a number of times. Not until this book is read will anyone know that he would have voted differently. However, we happily and gladly acceded to the plans, knowing that they were what the church wanted. Now that the buildings are finished and being used, we are glad that he never said a word, for nothing could improve on what we have now.

However, when a matter of doctrine or plain Bible teaching is being violated in the church, he expects every elder to back him in making a God-directed change. But if a pastor has a board of men who "want peace at any price" or who aren't Christians, there is little hope that he will be backed in what might make some church members angry.

Another type of persecution that is hard to take is to be stabbed in the back and betrayed by others—Christians you trusted the most, and who acted the nicest to your face. For some reason this seems harder for the woman to bear than the man. Maybe women are naturally more trusting and more easily deceived.

On occasion I have discussed a few of my problems only to find my private affairs common church knowledge. One leader who seemed so nice was telling me one thing and others a different story, until finally I caught him in outright lying. Perhaps the greatest burden I have borne as a pastor's wife is to be bitterly disappointed in those who make such a profession of being mature Christians, and then I have seen them act like children of the Devil. God meant what He said in Jeremiah 17:9: "The heart is deceitful above all things, and desperately wicked." While this verse is generally used for salvation, it applies to Christians, too. My experiences have taught me never to trust anyone completely. We all have the old nature in us, even though we are saved, and human nature can never be trusted. It has taught me to turn my problems over to the Lord and not discuss them with any church member or officer. It is easier to deal with an unbeliever—from whom I expect nothing, with whom I can be on my guard—than to deal with a Christian who might act as a carnal man at any time without notice.

We made the serious mistake in our second pastorate of making close friends without realizing what we were doing. Dwight likes to relax Sunday evenings with friends and we accepted invitations to a number of homes of members. Naturally, I returned the invitations. The group began to grow, and all a couple had to do to join was to invite all of us to their home, and they were included from then on. Behind the scenes, a balance of power between two men whom we trusted and respected was teetering back and forth. Though they were Christians, each was jealous of the other. Each thought the other fellow was controlling the church through my husband. Nothing could have been further from the truth, as no one runs a church through Dwight. He is a firm believer in rule by the ruling board, elected by the people of the congregation. After these two men found they couldn't fight each other, they joined forces to fight my husband, each still thinking that the other had the leading hand in church affairs. Fuel was added to the fires of jealousy each time we had an informal gathering in a home after evening church. There we stood between two ambitious leaders and were perfectly innocent of what was going on, not even knowing about the situation until after all the church folks knew. These men did their best to wreck my husband's ministry; as a result the church was torn apart until one group that followed one man wouldn't speak to another group that followed my husband. The hurt feelings were never completely healed.

We really, unknowingly, brought this on ourselves. Now we believe it is best not to have any close friends in the church, and we never have time to find others. The church work keeps us so busy that we don't have time to be with the few other friends we do have. It is better to be lonely than to run the risk of causing trouble in a church.

Persecution takes other forms of behind-the-scenes, cowardly ways of hurting the pastor and his wife. Criticism of the minister in the presence of children and young people has done a lot to injure a church work. It is little wonder that young people lose respect for the best of pastors when they have "roast preacher" served so often in their homes and constantly hear criticism of the way the church is run. I am not talking about the people who deliberately do this, but the active Christian members who can't seem to sense what they are doing in subtly influencing their children against the church and pastor. We can usually tell how a couple feels about us by the way their children react to the Sunday school and church. Children reflect their parents' opinions very openly. What parents thoughtlessly say, and soon forget, the children take seriously and later the feelings of the parents become very evident to us. We often wonder if our congregations thought we walked around with our ears closed and blinders on just because we didn't gossip, and we didn't scold them and tell them exactly what we thought of their actions.

The type of persecution which is most insidious and hardest to recognize is psychological. Many times even the people who are causing it don't know the real reason why they are making trouble. To a certain extent, we are all guilty of taking our feelings out on innocent people. For instance, you will have a hard day with the children or at a women's meeting, and find yourself snapping at your husband as soon as he enters the door. He hasn't had time to do or say a thing to deserve such treatment. When someone bawls me out on the telephone, I often yell at my little daughter the next time she is naughty rather than speaking softly. The pastor's wife seems to come in for much criticism and crossness which she doesn't deserve because she happens to be a handy one to take one's feelings out on. She must listen and be polite, and people consciously or unconsciously know that she will be kind and won't strike back. She can't!

While such incidents are common to everyone's life, I am talking about far more serious troubles. As soon as we arrived in our second church home, we realized that an elder and his wife were openly against us though we hadn't gotten to know them and had done nothing in the church. Often they refused to speak to us. He took every opportunity to criticize Dwight openly and behind his back. She did the same thing to me. They stuck a knife in our backs and kept it there the entire five years. If we seemed to get used to it or ignored it, they would give it a good twist to keep us assured that they were fighting us as best they could. The nicer we tried to be to them, the worse they treated us. We invited them to the manse, and they openly refused with rudeness.

After several years, one man told us quite unexpectedly how the church got such a good buy on the manse. The house had been built by Mr. and Mrs. X., the elder and his wife. They had saved, worked hard, and planned that house. Finally, their dream house was a reality. They were very happy there, but during the depression he lost his business, and then the house. When they moved out, they vowed they would never again enter the door of that house until they once more owned it. There was our answer. We had noticed that any mention of the manse agitated them, also that she walked by it every day and stopped to look at it. But not knowing what we later learned, we soon forgot the reaction they showed about the house. In their minds, they still owned that house and persecuted anyone who lived there. The couple who bought the house were so constantly annoyed by the X. family that they sold it cheaply just to get away from them. When we found out that the same things had happened to the pastor before us and the one who followed us, we knew the problem.

This chapter would be very one-sided if I omitted a word of caution to the pastor and his wife. It's possible for them to cause their persecutions. Perhaps the mistake that causes the most trouble is taking over the work of the church. The wife is often prone to do this. She feels better trained to be president of the women's work. If she is musically talented, she often dominates the choir and expects to play the organ or piano. If she takes over such duties from others, it won't be long before she is criticized and experiences open opposition. On the other hand, the pastor often comes to a church with a headful of wonderful, new methods of improving the Sunday school, the young people's work, and the social program of the church. The minute the people sense that the church is about to be taken away from their control, they are apt to rebel. I believe that a large part of the persecutions caused by the congregation can be traced back to this fundamental cause. It is, of course, very possible that there is great scriptural need for changes, but people resent being pushed into a change without their consent.

The mistakes of the pastor's wife are fully discussed in another chapter, so we won't go into them again here.

There is often a great gulf fixed between the clergyman and his wife and the church members because of a failure on both sides to make an earnest effort to correct troubles as they arise, in a scriptural method. (See Matthew 18:15-17.) If the method the Lord Jesus Christ gave for settling troubles were faithfully used, there would be little cause for continued trouble on either side. When something goes wrong and there is a misunderstanding, the offended one is to go privately to the one who caused the trouble and talk it over in a Christ-like manner. If such action fails to straighten out the trouble, then the offended one is to go with two or three witnesses and talk the matter over again. In case the matter still can't be settled, it should be brought to the attention of the church, or, in most cases, the ruling church board, who are duly elected representatives of the congregation and have the authority to take care of such decisions. If the trouble isn't then corrected, the person guilty of offense should be removed from the church fellowship until what is wrong is made right.

If a church member feels that the pastor or his wife has done wrong or has offended in any way, that person should go straight to them and talk it over. Most of the troubles would stop right there, as the ministerial couple wants to be right. But the average church member is either too cowardly, doesn't have anything to go on but what someone else has said which can't be proved, or prefers to gossip and criticize behind their backs rather than trying to get the trouble cleared up. The reverse is often just as true; the minister will grumble, and his wife will complain to others and let bitterness and barriers go up between them and the laymen. This is a sinful disgrace in a church, no matter which side is responsible. It is definitely not God's will for misunderstandings in the flock to go on and on. I admit Christ's way of clearing up trouble is the hard way, but it is the manly and godly way and would make such a tremendous change in church relationships that unbelievers could really see the difference Christ can make in a life. Church quarrels, church splits, stories of accused pastors, and lawsuits among church members are often thoroughly aired in the newspapers and are a great disgrace to the cause of Christ, a poor testimony to an unsaved world.

An irate lady aired her grievances against her pastor to a Bible conference speaker instead of trying to straighten it out with the pastor. She said, "I've prayed and prayed that that man would change, and nothing has happened. What can I I do?" "Go home and pray just as long and fervently that the Lord will change you," suggested the speaker. Later, he received a letter from her stating that the trouble had all been her fault. As soon as she started praying that she would change, the Lord took her at her word, and now she greatly loved and respected the minister.

Open persecution, while hard to bear, is much easier to take because you will know what is going on and who is causing it. The behind-the-scenes type of persecution is usually more dangerous, for often the pastor and his wife are the last persons to hear about it. Lying, gossiping, criticism, and thoughtlessness of all kinds are like holding a handful of feathers in the wind. Once they have been blown away, they can never be retrieved. Once these forms of troubles are aimed at the pastor or his wife, there is no way for them to be corrected. Many people start a rumor either because they wrongly interpreted an innocent act or just to add spice to their otherwise dull lives. They are also driven to these things in order to get attention for themselves. They have nothing in themselves to attract others so they have to find a way to get people to want to listen to them. The best way, they find, is to give out a juicy piece of gossip, especially about the public target—the minister's family.

There is very little a pastor can do in a church when his board members aren't Christians or if they refuse to give reasonable cooperation and assist the pastor in his plans and necessary changes. In some cases, it is natural for some members to feel that they can't back the pastor's plans, but they should give good reason for their feelings at the board meetings and not gossip about it outside the board meeting. Pastors take this graciously and are usually willing to drop the subject. But when the elders or deacons will not stand behind the minister when he is doctrinally or morally right in what must be done, their failure is inexcusable. His ministry will always be limited when he has to stand alone, or even against the anger and criticism of his board members.

By far the worst kind of persecution has it roots in psychological causes. This kind of persecution is most difficult to recognize and almost impossible to cure. The only consolation of the person who suffers from this type of persecution is to be able to see the reason behind it and realize that though you are hurt and blamed, the person causing it is in need of medical help and does what he is doing because he can't help himself. As long as you are able to type the kinds of persecutions, realize that most of them are not caused by you, or are not personally aimed at you (though they always seem to be), it will be much easier for you to take persecution.

In some cases, through ignorance, lack of experience and haste in making changes, you may feel that you have the best answer to every situation in the church, and you will bring on yourself persecution that you can't blame on the others. In a very few cases, the pastor or his wife have stepped out of line morally, or have not "avoided the appearance of evil." They themselves are responsible for the outcome of such conduct and, while God will forgive and often restore to usefulness, the Bible principle still holds, that "whatsoever a man soweth, that shall he also reap."

If the pastor and his wife will consistently use the Bible method of taking care of misunderstandings, there is great hope that many of the church will gradually follow their example.

CHAPTER 13

"In Sickness or in Health"

THIS IS A DAY when both the church and the pastor's family must face the serious problem of the "sickly" minister's wife. The increasing number of always-tired wives in the manse, those who have nervous breakdowns, those who are semi-invalids and are chronically ill, has made such an impression on the public in general that lately a number of articles have been published on the subject in secular magazines written by counselors or medical men. Unfortunately, they merely quote statistics and results of surveys, but have given few workable or helpful suggestions for a cure. So far, the subject seems to have been ignored from the Christian viewpoint and has not been publicly discussed by any ministers' wives who have faced and overcome this problem.

This increase of wasted energy and much unnecessary suffering might often be avoided if there were a real understanding of some pertinent facts on both sides of the question. If the minister's wife, her husband, and the members of the congregation could see the problem in its true perspective, much could be done by the individual churches in helping to avoid illness, or to assist when there is sickness and, at the same time, to keep a happy relationship and sympathetic understanding between the manse dwellers and the church members.

Even more can be accomplished by the pastor's wife if she can honestly face the difficulties and see them for what they truly are. Then she can get needed help to correct the physical or emotional problems as they arise. Equally important is keeping a careful check on her spiritual life to be sure she is constantly controlled by the Holy Spirit and in fellowship with the Lord,

222

cheerfully following His will and not her own or that of any church member.

As in any family in other walks of life, there will be times of illness, operations, perhaps some prolonged periods of hospitalization and even emotional problems. God does not see fit to exempt the minister's family from such suffering. The attitude of the church folk can either add greatly to the suffering or be a tremendous help.

A number of years ago, a mistress of a manse, Mrs. Belling, was told that she had tuberculosis. As the church and manse were in a poor section of a town full of steel mills puffing out dark clouds of dirt into the air, the minister decided that the only way he could give her the proper air so essential for lung trouble, was to rent a home on top of a nearby hill just outside of the town. The church people understood that this was a necessary move and rented the manse in order to pay the rent on the second house. The pastor procured an excellent nurse and was able to continue his work in the church.

A friend of ours received his doctor's degree from the seminary while my husband was a student. He served a number of long, successful pastorates. An operation showed that his wife had a malignancy, but the doctors felt that there would be no return of the trouble. She was soon well again. However, when Phil went to candidate, he felt it was only fair to tell the pulpit committee of his wife's recent operation. Every congregation that planned to call him changed their minds— and one withdrew their call—when they heard this. For fifteen years his wife has been in perfect health, and he has been a successful engineer. Several churches have missed having one of the best preachers we know and his life has been a serious disappointment all because some churches felt that they must be sure the pastor's wife would be able to work in the church beside her husband.

Is it fair to require a minister's wife to be in perfect health? Factories, offices, and stores do not restrict a man from working for them because his wife is sick, or might be later on. They know that a man will do his work faithfully—perhaps more so— because his wife is sick and they need the money so much. It is confusing to see why churches are afraid that the minister would not perform his duties as faithfully as if his wife were able to work along with him. If they can trust him to guide them spiritually, why can't they trust him to do his work faithfully? Most pastors put in far more hours of church work than they are required to, anyway.

Mr. and Mrs. Chester were serving a growing church in central Pennsylvania when she was forced to have a serious operation. From that time on, she was a permanent invalid. He continued his pastorate for a while, with a nurse attending his wife, but he sensed that though the people appreciated his ministry they did not like the idea of having a sick mistress of the manse. Shortly afterward he felt led to resign and made no attempt to take another church. The Lord opened up a much greater ministry for him in his being a traveling Bible teacher and in doing much needed Christian camp work for boys near his home. His wife's prayers have so covered his ministry that I doubt if any man has been more used and blessed of the Lord. The church they left had chosen to take second best when they could have had the best. God's ministry for Mrs. Chester was prayer, and the only way she could be free from unnecessary church duties was to be put to bed permanently. That church could have had his outstanding ministry and the added blessing from her prayers had they not been so determined to have an active minister's wife.

But the purpose of this chapter is not so much to talk about the attitude of the church toward a sickly minister's wife, as to talk to the wives themselves about the problem. We need to see if we are allowing unnecessary illnesses. We need to find our limitations and to have the backbone to live within them. We also need to see how we may avoid getting sick or being chronically tired.

The number of ministers' wives that have broken down, sup-
posedly because of the extra duties and strains imposed by their
position, is greatly overemphasized. The thousands of women
of the manse who are happy, useful, and well are seldom mentioned, so an unfair picture is often shown to the public. This is
probably one reason so many of the wives of ministerial students are frightened at the prospect of entering the pastorate
with their husbands.

Dr. William Douglas, Assistant Professor of Psychology of
Religion at Boston University School of Theology, believes that
80 percent of ministers' wives find fulfillment and joy in their
work, though it may take a period of years for them to feel
completely at home in their varying situations.

Granted that there are unique pressures and demands on a
minister's family, even beyond those of families of other professional men, breakdowns seem due primarily, say the doctors,
to the personality of the wife or husband, rather than the nature
of the ministry. The women involved would probably have
broken down whatever the husband's vocation. So it is very unfair for anyone to say that illness on the part of the minister's
wife is always caused by the church situation.

Another factor should also be considered. What causes pressure on one mistress of the manse might not bother the next
one at all. Personality and background enter very greatly into
the response of a person to her environment.

For example, we believe that our present church is the finest
we know and much, much nicer than any we have previously
served. While everything is not always perfect for me, I am
wonderfully happy and satisfied here. Certainly that is the way
the Lord intends it to be. Many times differing attitudes toward
the work make the difference between happiness and misery.

Some pastors' wives retreat behind the congregation as a
cause for every trouble they have because they will not face up
to the fact that they are often the cause of their own trouble.

A number of years ago, I met a ministerial couple at a Bible conference. Though we were strangers except for an introduction, she started telling me all the things that were wrong in their church; she criticized the parsonage, the ladies, the boards, and at great length told me that she was so nervous she couldn't stand a pastorate much longer. Partly because of her attitude toward his ministry, her husband later took a job teaching at the same school where my husband was. They just happened to move near us. Every time there was a social function at the school, we drove into town together. She began from the first to complain about the demands that the school made on her husband's time, how little salary he was getting, and how many weekends he had to be away preaching. Finally, I could stand it no longer and always found a way of getting to the city without going with her. Later, I discovered that the root of the whole trouble was the meddling of her mother, who lived with them. The wife bitterly resented her mother's actions, and transferred her resentment to whatever work her husband happened to be doing. No matter what he would find to do, she would be unhappy because the matter of her mother was not settled. Finally, after we moved to Dallas, she had a breakdown. I hope that the doctors have shown her the real source of her trouble so that it can be corrected.

Many pastors' wives are nervous and sickly because they feel inadequate for the job that is before them, and just give up. One assignment I gave for the girls in my class for future pastors' wives was to answer questions about themselves like the following: Who am I? What kind of personality do I have? Do I have physical, emotional, and educational limitations that might make my adjustment to a church difficult? What is my attitude toward serving a church? These, along with some other questions, were designed to cause the girls to face some facts about themselves and make some definite decisions before they were suddenly plunged into the complex work of getting started in their first church. The questions were also designed to encourage them, while they still had time, to improve; to correct any problems possible; to seek medical care; to enlarge their education where they felt weakest; to accept cheerfully any limitations they had which could not be changed; and to know where their talents and personalities would best fit into a church program. They still had time to face any tendencies toward temper, jealousy, bossiness, and attempts to escape responsibilities and blame others for their problems. Many of the girls confessed that the class gave them a completely new picture of themselves. Had they gone into the pastorate without this appraisal, they would have been apt to blame the people of the church for their troubles. Now they are working to change their ways while they are still here at school.

One girl wrote a thank-you note, telling me that she was shy and timid, and very fearful about being a pastor's wife. She disclosed she had already begun to develop some unpleasant emotional symptoms. She said she had already made a list of excuses to get out of what she thought she would be asked to do in a pastorate. When she took a good look at herself after she had heard me tell how shy, introverted, and frightened I had been at first, she did a complete turnabout and determined to overcome these traits before she went into the pastorate. I predict she will make a good minister's wife.

Young ministers' wives do feel inadequate for the job that is placed before them, and no one should be surprised. The lectures we hear and the few handbooks published for the minister's wife present such an impossible standard, any woman would be apprehensive. God's Word presents a high enough standard for us, along with all other Christian women, without all the responsibilities man-made rules have added. I counted the things suggested in books for us to do to help our husbands personally until I lost count and gave up hopelessly. We are to protect his study time at any cost, answer the telephone all the time, and keep from disturbing him. (Some writers have not had much experience if they think that people will be held off like that! When they ask for the pastor, they want the pastor—not his wife. Their problems are too urgent to wait.) We are supposed to screen out those who want appointments, and those who come to the manse to see him. We are supposed to talk to those who are just complaining, and listen to those who are bored and just want someone to talk to. No wife would have time for all of that even if she gave her full time to it and completely neglected her children, home, and church work. I head a one-woman campaign to give the church back to the men. After all, they are the ones that are trained, called, paid, and given the authority in the church. No manly parson wants to hide behind the skirts of a woman, and I see no purpose in a feminine bodyguard for a minister. If he cannot take care of his work, then he should resign in favor of someone who can do it. No business or professional man takes his wife to the office to protect him. The Bible says that we are to be home-makers, lovers of our husbands and children first. Each church expects the pastor's wife to fulfill special duties, and the handbooks and lecturers add to our confusion by telling us that we are also to be our husbands' bodyguards, even in the home. No wonder some personalities cannot adjust to such a life!

Many pastors' wives, usually unconsciously, escape the pressure put on them by getting sick. They have felt trapped and tricked into a hopeless situation from which there seems no escape. The subconscious mind then presents the only foolproof way of escape—sickness. Certainly a pastor's wife cannot be expected to function in the church when she is sick.

One timid, shy and untrained minister's wife in New Mexico developed some severe chest pains. Since there was no specialist nearby, the family doctor put her in a small, poorly equipped hospital. There she stayed, with a heart condition, for nine months. It was later discovered that her heart was perfectly normal, and a trained counselor was able to show her that she had unconsciously developed the heart pains because she could not face the demands of pastoral life with her type of personality. The pains and discomfort went away as soon as she saw, on the conscious level, what she was doing and made a definite decision that these problems would be faced in reality and dealt with accordingly. Some things she was never able to do; others she excelled in; and she did still other things with the knowledge that her work was far from perfect, but she did the best she could. She never had heart trouble again.

Catherine Marshall, well known as the wife of the famous Presbyterian minister who was chaplain of the U.S. Senate until his sudden death, confesses that she was a shy, timid person, and so inactive in their church that many of the people who attended did not know whether Peter was married or not. She took her proper place primarily as a homemaker and a companion to him. Such a situation is ideal, but usually will only be found in a large church that is well staffed with assistants and secretaries. In my opinion, the larger the church, the easier is the job of the pastor's wife, and her services are seldom sought except in a social nature.

In the book, *To Live Again,* which Catherine Marshall wrote to tell of her life after her husband's death, she reveals how her shyness and habit of living in the background affected her when she was suddenly thrown into the limelight of public appearances, autographing parties for her books, and the showing of the movie depicting the life of her husband, Peter Marshall. Because being with people so much and traveling, with little chance for a good rest, were so contrary to her usual pattern of life, her subconscious mind found a way to help her out. She began to notice that when one of her public appearances was due, she was too often stricken with flu, viruses and other sickness that we associate entirely with germs and contagion. One would not link these things with a fear of being surrounded by people. However, Catherine did finally see that there was a definite connection, and her doctor confirmed the fact. Her illnesses were just another way of escaping something that was fun but at the same time frightening. She was put into a conflict she could escape only by illness. Some way had to be found to get her out of her dilemma. When she fully recognized these small illnesses as psychosomatic (caused more by the mind or emotions), she found that half the battle was won. "The rest was done through prayer, applying a little humor to the predicament, and resolving firmly that when I had made a date, it would be kept—period." The flu and the viruses just disappeared.

Do you want to be a healthy, happy, well-adjusted and useful pastor's wife? "Of course, I do," is your response. Yet there are many, many sickly wives who think they want to be well more than anything else in life, but they are using their sickness to shield and protect themselves against something in the church that they find very difficult. Perhaps all of this is done on the subconscious level. There is no way of knowing what is causing any trouble you may have. You and you alone are the one who has to face the issue honestly and find out if sickness could be a way of escape and retreat from something you resent or find too hard to do.

Start your program of getting well by praying "without ceasing," asking God to show you the answer to your problem. Ask to be given the ability to face reality honestly and to unearth any problems that may be the basis of your troubles.

If such a program of prayer and self-examination doesn't take care of your problem—and it probably won't completely, as we are such experts at fooling ourselves, go to a good doctor and tell him the complete story of all you have discovered about yourself. Be sure to describe in detail your physical illness. He can easily and quickly rule out the genuine physical troubles and cure them, or help you find out how to live with any limitations. Whatever he tells you—DO IT! I have little sympathy for those who come to me for advice after they have been from doctor to doctor and have done nothing they were told to do. It is utter nonsense for me to try to help people who will not take their own doctor's advice.

If you have been reassured by a competent doctor, after you have gone through all the tests he thinks are necessary, that nothing is physically wrong with you, then you know that your mind is playing tricks on you. All your aches and pains, dizziness, heaviness in your chest, shortness of breath, rapid pulse, and constant headaches can be attributed to nervousness. And in the final analysis, in very unmedical terms, nervousness is the result of the mind and emotions in conflict between the demands of your life and your desires. In short, you are being pulled into so many directions that you have become a one-woman traffic jam. Something has to give, and up come the unpleasant nervous symptoms as a warning that there is serious trouble.

Your doctor will decide if he can help you or if it is necessary to seek the help of one who specializes in nervous disorders. He should be a Christian, but even if you cannot secure the services of a Christian psychiatrist, your doctor's help and the help of your husband with any spiritual needs will be necessary. But *you* are the one who has to be willing and in earnest or no doctor can heal you. As long as you feel it necessary to hide behind your symptoms, they will never go away, no matter how outstanding the medical care.

There are a great many fine Christians who feel that no person living in fellowship with the Lord will have nervous or emotional disorders. No one has ever been able to prove that statement to me from Biblical truth. God has not drawn a line between mental, emotional, and physical sickness. He chooses what type of suffering He wants to send His child, and it might come in any of those areas. There are many born-again Christians in mental institutions; I say that on the authority of several psychiatrists who have worked with such persons both in and out of such institutions.

Usually II Timothy 1:7 ("But God has not given us the spirit of fear; but of power, and of love, and of a sound mind") is used to show that it is never God's will to let a Christian suffer mental illness. The verse has been taken out of its context and does not refer to mental disabilities. The words "sound mind" mean "serious-mindedness" or "soberness." Paul is exhorting Timothy to preach the Word with power and love and without fear, with all seriousness and earnestness, in spite of persecutions that would come as a result.

There is another fallacy among some Christians. They believe that this kind of illness is always caused by sin of some type. They encourage the suffering one to confess, to read the Word, and to pray more. It is obvious that those who give such advice have never gone through any serious nervousness themselves, for when the mind and nerves are upset, praying and reading the Word are almost impossible. The mind is in a whirl! Going round and round the problems and even forcing oneself to read the Bible brings no real results. Then the sick person feels an added sense of guilt because prayer and Bible reading are so hard to do. Some, for this reason have even felt that God has failed them. The Bible cannot heal a confused mind any more than it can knit together a broken bone. It cannot reach into the subconscious mind and deal with problems and circumstances that are beyond memory. Neither can it deal with troubles of a disturbed mind that is unable to reason, or to accept facts and truths. The mind must be healed first and then the Word can come in with full force and power to show if and where there are spiritual problems which need to be corrected.

There are very few cases where the illness of the pastor's wife goes to the extremes I have described, though every church has its share of people who suffer this way, and an understanding of these truths might help in counseling such.

So let us go on with the assumption that the doctor is helping with your difficulties, even though some can't be cured, even with his help. Nearly everyone has some kind of physical or emotional troubles, and they live peacefully with them most of the time and are usually able to carry on an active life if they refuse to let the disabilities turn them into self-pitying, sour, unhappy neurotics.

I find it very encouraging to read of the men God used so wonderfully in Bible times who were not blessed with good health. Paul carried "a thorn in the flesh." He thought that he could be much more effective for the Lord if that thorn were removed, but God did not answer his prayer in the affirmative. Rather God promised him extra strength to overcome his physical weakness by telling him that His strength would be made perfect in Paul's weakness. There would be little doubt, at least from the human standpoint, that Paul did the greatest work for God that anyone has done. (See II Corinthians 12: 7-10.)

Another man God greatly used was Timothy, and the words of Paul about him were most complimentary. Yet Timothy, even though a young man at the time, was plagued with some physical infirmity. This is suggested in I Timothy 5:23, where Paul advised Timothy, "Drink no longer water, but use a little wine for thy stomach's sake and thine often infirmities." Perhaps the doctors today would diagnose his trouble as an ulcer. We have no way of knowing for certain, but have reason to believe that he often suffered pain and was troubled to the point that Paul heard about his physical ailment.

When the Apostle John wrote one of his one-chapter books, the letter to Gaius, who was probably a minister, John took four precious verses to speak of Gaius' faith and exemplary Christian life. In verse two John said, "Beloved, I wish above all things that thou mayest prosper and be in health, even as thy soul prospereth." It is certain that there was nothing wrong with his spiritual life, but he did have ill health. Epaphroditus was "sick nigh unto death" while ministering with Paul. Others could be mentioned, but these will suffice for our purpose.

If there is a psychological or physical infirmity placed on you, there is no need to worry that you will not be able to accept the responsibilities of being a pastor's wife. After you have done all you can to correct your infirmities, or are in the process of correcting them, commit them to the Lord as often as necessary. He remembers that we are dust and knows that we live in a corrupt, mortal body. He has allowed any troubles you have for a good reason. With His guidance, if you are willing to follow Him, you will find it possible, usually, to live a normal active life even under the strain of constant church activities.

The most important thing you must do in order to have peace and happiness is to accept your limitations cheerfully. "Even so, not my will, but thine be done" should express our continuing attitude toward our disabilities.

For example, if you must have more rest than is normally taken by others, arrange your schedule so you get that rest regardless of your church program. If you have to be out in the afternoon, arrange for a nap time in the morning. If you have to take a certain kind of amount of exercise, do it in the morning. You may be tempted to let it slip, but if you leave the necessary housework until last, you'll always manage to do that.

If you have preschool children, take your naps when they do. If some of your children are beyond the nap age, they can play where you have arranged for them to be safe. Be sure to give them suggestions for things to do. If necessary, rest in the room where they are playing, and you can catch catnaps between interruptions. I have learned that children can easily be taught that Mother needs to rest. My girls learned quickly, and now do what they can to keep the house quiet when I am resting.

If your activities are limited because you don't have perfect health, God intends that you live according to your strength, whether your family and church people understand or not. It is useless for you to pray for strength when you deliberately and knowingly overwork your body and nerves. God promises strength for what He plans for us to do—not for everything that we might *want* to do.

"When a person accepts and admits his limitations, he finds

peace within himself," says Dr. David Fink in his book, *Be Your Real Self*. He no longer carries a heavy load of pretense and sham on his back. He no longer concentrates upon his limitations, but goes ahead to do the best he can with what he has. At least, he says, I can do a few things well."

To live with physical limitations, it is often necessary to learn the meaning of "no" and stick to it. If in all honesty, you have shifted your schedule around and have done your best to take part in all the activities of the church but simply can't do more, then it is time to apply the "no" treatment. When I reach this point, my husband and I talk over the situation. Usually we list what we consider the least important things and decide that I will have to give those up until I have more strength or time. Long ago, I gave up civic and community affairs such as canvassing for fund drives, the PTA, school plays and open house at school unless these directly affect one of my children, and volunteer charity. These things are fine for ministers' wives who have the time and interest. (Incidentally, when I read the handbooks that tell about the contributions pastors' wives can make in community affairs, I want to howl! What do they think we are? We can barely manage the double work of homemaking and church work placed on us now without adding work that can easily be done by those who are less interested in the church or do not come at all.)

This year there were extra strains put on me so that it was necessary to drop more outside activities. My husband and I decided that all outside speaking engagements would have to be declined. The other things that had to go were Christian banquets, and meetings of organizations that were not directly connected with our church, even though to decline might mean offending a member who invited me to these things. By eliminating as many outside activities as possible, I can still keep up with my usual church program. No matter who might criticize, I am not bothered, as I know I am doing God's will under the leadership of my husband, and with his consent.

Occasionally, in spite of keeping a datebook and not scheduling events too closely, I am caught with three meetings a day. Since I find this physically impossible, I cancel the least important engagement or the ones in which I have no part.

Pastors' wives often make two mistakes that contribute to poor health. First, our earnest desire and real interest in all of the church work makes us so anxious to help that we offer our help before we think through our schedules. I have often found that when the time came to deliver on my promise, I was not feeling well enough, had a sick child, or was swamped with regular meetings and activities from which I couldn't withdraw. My zeal so often runs ahead of my strength. But I always do what is promised though it might put me to bed for a few days, make me tired for a week or send me back to the doctor's again. This is definitely not wise and I am sure this is not what God expects of me.

The second mistake is more subtle. When someone calls to say that she or a member of her family is sick, or needs special attention, usually our first thought is *What does she expect me to do about it?* Instead of *What can I do to help them?* It is the tone of voice and the feeling of demand we detect, or the position of her husband in the church, that often govern what we do about the situation. Our own families may need us far more than the woman does, but we go, or do something, because we feel the pressure of the church members. This is the place where we have to apply a kindly but firm "no" if we are not to be driven by the needs and whims of the church people, whether they be members or visitors. Turn the situation over to your husband, and let him decide what is to be done. They are his members. Unfortunately, it is difficult to turn down a member of the congregation, no matter how trivial the need. Often we let our husbands and children suffer, or we let our own physical needs be neglected. It is easier to get our families to forgive us than a church member. We take our sickness out on our loved ones rather than run the risk of being criticized by a parishioner. This is not right.

Seldom does one find a minister's wife who is not tired most of the time. Psychologists tell us that there are three reasons for tiredness. The first is pathological fatigue: any early symptom of serious organic disease. The second is a physical fatigue: from chemical reactions in the blood of healthy people that leave the muscles exhausted. The third fatigue is a psychological feeling that comes from prolonged emotional conflict, anxiety, and boredom. The first kind will show itself quickly for what it is. The second is not often the cause for the tiredness of a minister's wife, and one night's rest will cure it.

So it is obvious that we should look into the third classification of fatigue for the answer in most cases. Without doubt most of these wives, unless exceptionally happy and well adjusted in the pastorate, are often living in periods of prolonged emotional conflicts. Nearly every chapter in this book shows some ways in which the mistress of the manse is under conflict while she is trying to live for her husband, family, and home, trying to please several hundred church people, and yet trying to find a little time for herself. Often she can't meet the constant demands on her time. Many times they overlap and double-overlap until anxiety mounts to the point where she can't take any more pressure. Naturally she becomes tired and is tired all the time. She is as tired when she gets up in the morning as when she went to bed at night, and finds it is all she can do to struggle through another day.

Speaking of similar cases, a Chicago psychiatrist says, "Anxiety warns them that something must be done; while their frayed nerves and tired bodies scream that something must be stopped. Since both sensations are operating blindly, there is real conflict and desperate fatigue."

"Psychological fatigue is an illness due largely to having been caught in a trap," is what Dr. Walter Alverez says. "This may come from having the wrong kind of job, and the best answer is to change your type of work." But that is the catch for the pastor's wife. She has no choice in the matter. She is married to her husband's work as securely as she is married to him, and there is no possibility of making a change. She can't even use her home as a place of escape for a change, as a large part of her church activities revolve around her home. She may be bored to death with the endless round of meetings, teas, dinners, picnics, committees, telephone calls, and counseling, but she has no way of escape except an occasional vacation outside the city.

Mrs. Marguerite Clark, in her book, *Why So Tired?*, says, "The world's weariest, most overworked and least appreciated person is the American housewife." To that I would like to add, "and the minister's wife."

If this is often true of so many women who felt led or called into their position as a pastor's wife, it is easy to see what suffering is being caused for the women who married a parson and gave little or no thought to the kind of life they would live in a parsonage. We can quickly see why so many pastors' wives are tired all the time and others are easy victims of psychosomatic illness.

As strange as it may sound, a Philadelphia doctor who works with many ministers' wives suggests that much of their tiredness comes from the lack of proper exercise. I can just hear you now! "I hardly have the strength to get my clothes off and fall into bed. I can't possibly exercise." That is what I said, too. He suggested a mile walk a day, alone. While we are walking, we must clear our minds of grudges, hurt feelings, resentments, worry, discouragement, and so on, and leave those things outside when we return home. The fresh air and exercise will clear out mental cobwebs, sweeten our dispositions, and generally tone up our entire systems. If you follow this advice, your work will be more pleasant and go faster when you come home. I have also added daily setting-up exercises that have been a great help to strengthen me, though it took a church member a year to talk me into trying because I thought I was too old and tired.

There are two national TV exercise programs right now, and you will find it is fun to exercise with an instructor, knowing that there are thousands of others doing the same things with you.

This may be the best time to sit down and take careful stock of yourself. Try to determine if you are sickly because you really can't help it, if too much is demanded of you from the church, or if your attitude toward what you think is expected is at fault. It is easily possible to fool yourself into believing that all of your physical troubles are coming from the congregation. Many things you consider demands may be demands only in your own mind.

A recent seminary graduate and his wife returned for commencement last spring. When she gave me a list of the things that she was doing in their church, I must have shown my surprise. She was doing everything but preach the sermons, conduct the board meetings, and do the janitor work, even though she had a small baby. It is certain that no church could demand that much of the pastor's wife! She and her husband were concerned for their homelife and the baby's care, and asked me what to do. I suggested that she go home and withdraw from every possible activity unless she enjoyed it and had the time for it. I also told her to be sure to save plenty of time for her family life. (I learned later that she followed my advice.) After thinking the problem over more carefully, I remembered that she had been a Christian education major in college, had taught in Christian grade school and had been very active in our church during her husband's seminary days. Perhaps she was so used to assuming responsibility and so well trained that she had mistaken these feelings as an insistence on the part of the church people.

We have found a few rules of good mental hygiene to be a necessary part of our living in order to keep the pushing and stretching and misunderstandings of the church people from making us emotional wrecks. We realize that many of those who cause us the most distress are the least conscious of it, but nevertheless we must fortify ourselves against the damage and unhappiness and hurt they cause us.

One of the first lessons I learned is that you cannot think clearly and intelligently when you're feeling sorry for yourself. Befuddled by the gray web of emotion called self-pity, you go off on tangents, make mistakes, become a nuisance to yourself and your family. If you are going to be any good to your family and the church, you'll have to pull yourself together and think honestly and realistically. Also when you let yourself wallow in self-pity, you are doubting the wisdom of God's will for your life and forgetting His promise that "ALL things work together for good" and that He will never leave you nor forsake you.

Never mind feeling sorry for yourself because of the way people treat you. Just try to return kindness and understanding for their thoughtlessness. Keep busy helping others as much as possible. When our children hurt themselves, we dust them off, administer first aid, kiss the hurt, and then send them back to play. Why don't we learn the truths we practice on our children? They soon forget the hurt by having their minds turned to something more pleasant. We don't encourage them to sit around crying about being hurt and feeling sorry for themselves; we direct their attention to something else, and the matter is closed.

Learn to live one day at a time, is an axiom my mother holds before me all the time. I think every pastor's wife who wants to be emotionally healthy and happy has to live one day at a time and take one task at a time. We use as much energy dreading a job which must be done as doing it. So don't face a job until you are ready to tackle it! Whenever you have a job to do, give it your complete attention. Work slowly and deliberately, and at the end of the day you will have accomplished more work, and you will feel fresher, more relaxed and less harassed. It isn't the hundred and one small tasks that exhaust us. What does exhaust us is the feeling that I *must* do this, the hurry, the torn-apart desperation of not being able to get all your work done, the worrisome *I must do this now.* Constantly running through our poor brains is the thought, *I must hurry, hurry to get that done.* Mostly we are ahead of or behind ourselves in thought, seldom right up with ourselves in attention. Thus our minds are in a state of turmoil, and we forget many important things, and blame is added to our already overloaded minds. No matter what you do—whether you answer the telephone, diaper a baby, prepare a Bible message for the women's association, or cook a meal—do it with your undivided attention, slowly and carefully as though that were the only thing you had to do all day. It will be hard to slow down your mind, give your attention to interruptions such as the children and the telephone, and think carefully on just what you are doing, but the habit is worth forming. If you do these things, you will find that life is happier, you will not be nearly as busy as you thought you were, and you will find that the work goes faster.

One factor which contributes to emotional problems, especially among ministerial couples, is to have hurt feelings. When we started in our first pastorate, I had a thin skin and a chip on my shoulder. Of course, I never would have tolerated this had I realized it was true. I have always been conscious of my supersensitivity, and I found it hard to conquer. Now if a person wants to insult me, he or she will have to make that intention very plain or I won't take it that way. Now I can look back to the many times I suffered and even cried over things that were said or done and then later events proved I had misunderstood. I was needlessly harming myself by indulging in self-pity and holding grudges against church people. The few who are trying to hurt me don't bother me any more, as I never expect to please everyone.

I've found that hurt feelings always have been my own fault anyway. At the bottom of the trouble is pride, conceit, and the weakness of letting other people's actions affect me adversely. Also, when I let my feelings get hurt, there is no allowance for the fact that others can make honest and unintentional mistakes, and often judge me without knowing all the facts that govern my behavior or the state of my health at that point. Life brings enough serious difficulties without my deliberately creating petty grievances. Harboring hurt feelings is futile, time-wasting, often dishonest, never pleasing to the Lord, and is really a refusal to face one's self-ness.

There is one kind of hurt feelings for which I have never found a cure. Maybe some of the rest of you can; I doubt if I will this side of Heaven. I am talking about the hurt and shock of being disappointed or hurt by a person you thought was one of the finest of Christians. We all have feet of clay and slip into the carnal ways of the flesh at times, so we really shouldn't be surprised, but we can't help being hurt. We can forgive and try to forget, but every time something like this happens, it leaves a scar. It is a part of suffering for Christ's sake. Just remember that our precious Saviour was betrayed by one of the twelve who lived closest to Him.

The churches and the pastors' families must face the difficult problem of how to handle the pastor's sickly wife. The church people seem to resent having a wife who is not in excellent health for two reasons: (1) because she can't share in the work of her husband and (2) because they are afraid that if his wife is sick, he will not faithfully do his church work. This is not fair because other employers take men to work for them even though their wives may be sick or might be sometime in the future. What a sad and very poor world this would be if everyone took the example of the Christian church in this matter. Perhaps this is proof that the average church member considers the wife as a team mate of her husband's or as an assistant pastor, and expects her to work along with him in spite of her lack of an official title or pay.

In some cases, wives are unconsciously pressured by either their duties, or the thoughtlessness of the members, into escaping by getting sick. This may also be caused because they don't feel adequate to the tasks set before them, they feel inferior, or too much is required of them. Sometimes the demands can't be met by the wife because she is not trained or does not have the type of personality to meet them. At other times, persons in the church have habits and ways of treating her that make her life miserable, and she must have some good excuse to get away from them. Some wives who honestly want to be well and happy are being tricked by their minds into being sick in order to escape the harder and more painful problems that being active in the church bring.

Whatever the situation may be, we must have the help and advice of a good doctor and then follow through with his instructions. If physical or emotional limitations are placed on us, we must accept them as God's will for our lives and take the necessary rest, care for our families properly, and carry on the church activities. This can be done by alternating our attendance at meetings, if necessary, or missing those that we must, or completely dropping off activities that are not connected with the church unless they happen to minister to you in pleasure and relaxation.

Most important of all, we have to learn to live within our limitations without self-pity, without getting a sour outlook on life and letting it make neurotics of us.

Several suggestions that will help are: (1) Learn to live one day at a time. (2) Do each task deliberately and carefully as though it were the only job you have to do right then. (3) To conserve energy, don't let your thoughts run ahead to what you must do next, or lag behind, thinking of what should have been done. Keep your thoughts concentrating on your present work. The habit of feeling hurried and pushed; of feeling you must do something for others, even though your family may need you more; of dreading something that must be done later, will drain your joy as well as your strength.

Several things to avoid are: letting yourself indulge in hurt feelings, becoming so interested in the work and success of the church that you promise to do more than your strength allows, or giving others time that should be reserved for your family or for your own rest. Driving yourself to the edge of your strength or beyond is wrong in God's sight and may eventually lead to serious illness.

Learning to say "no," when necessary, in a pleasant, unoffensive way is the greatest lesson a pastor's wife can learn. And along with that she needs to learn to ignore any misunderstanding or criticism.

Remember that whatever your limitations are, they usually need not keep you from leading an active church life if you really want to. So often the true secret lies in wanting to. God used many people in Bible times who were in poor health. He still does. Sickness will give you a real understanding of those who suffer illness, and enable you to comfort others who are going through trials and sickness.

CHAPTER 14

Are Your Attitudes Showing?

MOST CHURCHES RECOGNIZE that the minister's wife can be a genuine help or a hindrance to her husband's ministry. For that reason, congregations are reluctant to call a pastor until they have had a chance to take a good look at his wife. This is the time when a great many questions about her are asked. Unfortunately, many times the wrong questions are asked, and others that should be asked are overlooked.

The most important question every pulpit committee should ask and get a full reply to is: "What is her attitude toward her husband's work?" The right answer to that question will make a world of difference in the kind of ministry the church will receive from their new pastor. She may appear to be charming, she may be well trained, and have a good educational and social background and still be a tremendous hindrance to her husband's effectiveness in his pastoral work if she has a wrong attitude toward the church or her husband's calling. A pastor's wife can be so far from being a suitable helpmate that she actually becomes a stalemate to her husband's ministry.

Attitudes are thoughts and feelings we have toward others or our work. A motive is that which prompts one to act in a certain way. Attitudes and motives are closely related. In the light of a dictionary definition of an attitude, one can see at a glance that the way the pastor's wife feels will affect everything she does in the church and also gradually, in subtle, undercover ways not seen by the congregation, affect her husband's attitude toward his work. Being human, as we are, probably most of us are a wonderful help to our husbands at times and a real detriment at others. It is important to remember that as long as our attitudes and motives are right, the few mistakes we make that hinder the work will soon be forgotten and the work as a whole will not be hurt.

Every pastor's wife must ask two questions about her attitudes: What is my attitude toward the church? What is my attitude toward my husband and his calling to the ministry?

I asked all the seminary girls in my class on "Aid for Future Pastors' Wives" some serious questions about this subject. One was: "Do you look for fulfillment or frustration in your future work as a clergyman's wife?" Most of them answered very realistically by saying that they expected mostly fulfillment and a little frustration. Some said that they expected an equal amount of both, and one girl frankly admitted that she looked only for frustration. Her husband was called into the ministry after they were married; he was a successful businessman and they had a lovely home. However, as long as she anticipates frustration, probably that is just what she will find. The attitude she carries into her role as mistress of the manse in their first pastorate is apt to be the one she will carry through all of their pastorates.

Starting out with the wrong attitude reminds me of a cartoon I saw in the *Saturday Evening Post*. The picture shows the husband in smock and beret, with oil paints mixed on a palette, and a blank canvas ready for use on a nearby easel. The wife, with her hands on her hips, says, "Already I don't like it!" Some ministerial students' wives have adopted that feeling before they have given the Lord's work a chance to grasp their hearts and interest their abilities.

When a girl marries a man in the ministry only because she loves him but does not like the work he is doing, her attitude will be that of the wife in the *Post* cartoon. Starting out with this attitude of not liking the church work will gradually make her resent any demands that are made on her time and energy, and any time she considers overtime or things that shouldn't be asked of a minister. She will start from the beginning to demand "her" rights and "his" rights. There are many things that a ministerial couple can justly feel are their rights, but this is the last profession where they should be manifested. In fact, the Bible teaches us that we as Christians have no rights of our own and should always give the preference to others. This should be especially true of the pastor and his wife.

If the wife thinks of her husband's work only as a business in the sense that the wife of an executive does, there will be trouble that will gradually influence the minister whether he realizes it or not. Even the church members may not see how her attitudes are driving him to the wrong motives for service. This feeling on her part may cause her to be much more concerned about the size and outside influence of the church he serves than the work in the church. She will be doing those things that will help put her husband in the limelight and will call attention to him in larger churches so that he might have a chance to candidate in more prominent places. Her ambition for her husband will not be the faithful ministry of the Word in the present God-assigned church, but she will keep pushing him until he finds a larger church. If he doesn't, he will feel he is a failure in his wife's eyes. She will constantly insist that he be given all the honor due him and that each outstanding thing he does should come to the attention of the leaders in higher groups of the denomination. I have even watched wives working on the moderator of Presbytery for the purpose of getting their husbands a chance at a better church.

If her attitude is that of not being able to stand the manse unless it is perfect, there is bound to be friction that will jeopardize the harmony in the home. Many parsonages are not perfect, and many are truly difficult to keep, we admit. But if a minister is compelled to leave a church for another just because his wife can't stand the manse, a pattern will be set from that time on. They will have to pick each church largely on the condition of the parsonage, and not on whether he can do his best work in that place and whether the Lord has called him there. This is more common than the average church member might think. It is easy for ministerial couples (or any of us, for that matter) to rationalize and to see other things about the church that make it appear to be God's choice for them, when all the time they are either consciously or unconsciously choosing this place of service because it has a lovely manse. If they do this and are out of God's will, there will be very little blessing on the church or the couple, even though the pastor might preach marvelous sermons from the Bible.

Another insidious and treacherous way that the wife can sway her husband from giving his best to the Lord is by her feeling about money and worldly possessions. If she thinks of her husband's ministry as only a means to a meal ticket and the extras in life, she will make every effort to see that he makes plenty of money to satisfy her whims. She will nag until she drives him to ask for a salary increase or improvements on the manse. She will spend her time and attention on those who have money or authority in the church, and even drop hints that she and her husband are suffering for lack of funds, even if this isn't strictly true. The more they get, the more she will crave. It won't be long until she sees other things that she would like to have, and there will be no peace until she gets what she wants, even if it means moving to a bigger church which pays more salary.

No man can hold to the high standards of his ordination vows for long without the constant help and encouragement of his wife. She should be one who cheerfully accepts all circumstances and makes life as smooth and easy as possible for her husband. On the other hand, if she is a weight on him, with demands for larger pastorates, more money, better homes, high social levels, and more prominent places in the denomination, it won't be long before God's best for him is lost in a maze of rationalizing and pleasing a worldly wife.

A few ministers' wives choose their husbands because of their profession—not because of any spiritual reasons. They know that a minister is respected, well known, and usually liked, and invited to some of the most exclusive places in his community. For the social-climber wife, this is one sure way of reaching the top of the social ladder in Christian circles. She is tempted to give more time to her position than to helping in the church work. She will only want to entertain and be entertained by and be seen with the social leaders of the town. She will consider contacts with people in a lower social level a waste of time and will often make excuses for ignoring these people.

The reverse can sometimes be just as true. A timid, introversive wife is often found doing the same thing on the lowest level. Because she is insecure and feels inadequate or frightened by the well-educated and/or wealthy people, she will constantly seek the company of the poorly educated—those on her own social standing or below because then she feels safe, and sure of herself. As a result, she never learns to associate with people of all kinds and in all income brackets and how to act with professional people as well as those of her own intellectual standing. This minister's wife is neglecting a large part of the congregation just as definitely as the social climber. This is why, in naming the basic requirements for a good pastor's wife in chapter 15, I have listed "being able to work with all kinds and types of people, making them feel at home with you; and an obvious interest and affection for all the membership of the church equally" as a basic requirement for a good pastor's wife.

There are wives of clergymen who feel that their husband's churches are a wonderful opportunity for a career for themselves. They are the ones who promptly begin to systematically change everything in the church they don't like, often with little consideration for people's feelings. Such a woman walks around with this attitude: "I know it all and am determined to see that the best is done for this church." Needless to say, she is soon ostracized and criticized by the women, who might even find it hard not to hate her. She insults their abilities, their tastes, their education, and their well-established ways of carrying on their work; she drives roughshod over their beloved leaders who have to retreat in defeat before a harsh, outspoken parson's wife. A woman like this is usually unkind in her remarks and takes pride in telling the blunt truth to anyone she happens to dislike or who stands in her way to success. It is odd that so often a minister's wife of this type also frequently complains of being overworked and tired and giving her "all" to the church without proper appreciation (whatever she considers "proper" consideration). The ladies in the church become so confused by her actions and words that they finally give up trying to understand her and just ignore her. Some members who have pastors' wives like this say they can't wait for her to persuade her husband to resign. They would rather give up a much-loved pastor than to have to continue with his wife any longer.

Another similar attitude that can be disastrous is shown by the wife who feels that she is the assistant pastor and has equal rights in running the affairs of the church along with her husband. Women in this category are most dangerous and are usually at the bottom of most serious church troubles, church splits, and requests for pastors to resign. We all know pastors who can't get calls to churches because their wives are like this. Their wives' reputations go before them. No church will knowingly call a man whose wife is a trouble-maker, who might spilt their church or cause them to lose members.

A pastor's wife of this type believes she is well prepared to do good works in the church, and in order to do that she must have the authority to dictate policies and church actions. She must have the right to make decisions which she thinks are best for the church, through whatever organization she might be most interested in at the moment. She is overlooking the God-appointed place for women in the church. Women are told to keep silence in the church and not to usurp any authority over

the men. When she overrules the board members or her husband, her actions are directly contrary to the Bible, and disaster
is usually the result. She can easily run the church without
making an open stand against a board decision by acting in her
own right before they have a chance to make a decision and then
conveniently forgetting to change her actions. She can also work
slowly and thoroughly through her husband if he does not
realize what she is doing or if he doesn't have enough resistance
to refuse to take orders from her. Or he may be driven to do
what she wants, in order to have peace in the family.

This also shows a serious weakness and failure in the husband-
minister. A man should be head of his home in God's sight, and
if he can't control his own wife or teach her the scriptural ways
of doing church work, his qualifications for running a church
may well be questioned. If he is so weak in yielding to the
whims or demands of a woman, even the one he loves most,
then he is a poor risk for a pastoral candidate. It is certain that
a Casper Milquetoast kind of man doesn't have the fortitude to
direct his own church. It will be just a matter of time before
it is decided who will dominate the church, his wife or some
other strong-minded person or group in the congregation. This
may lead straight to a church split or a request for the pastor to
find another place of ministry. The pastor may think of his
failure to assert his leadership as meekness, or God-directed
action to live in peace, but if he is honest, he will see he is nothing but a coward! His own insecurity and his fear of trusting
himself to make decisions may let him feel that it is all right for
his wife to do it. He may have had a domineering mother who
ruled his life for so long that he hasn't known anything but
having a woman overrule him. Whatever the cause, he gives
little promise of being a good organizer, executive, and preacher
and should be passed over by churches who want the best type
of godly man.

Beware of the parson's wife who is frustrated or neurotic.
She may keep fairly quiet and in the background, but her in-

fluence is definitely felt by the congregation, and even more by the pastor. If self-pity governs her life, she will resent what is expected of her and be a constant complainer. All that she does will be with this attitude: "I'll do it because I can't get out of it. I'm trapped because I'm the pastor's wife." Too often she deliberately shows this side of her feelings to all who ask her to do anything in the church.

She is sensitive about every remark made about her and takes it wrong. She feels that the way people act is a deliberate attempt to hurt her feelings. If her suggestions are not carried out according to her wishes, she feels she is mistreated, and she pouts and refuses to help with the ideas and activities of others. On the other hand, she always expects the ladies to immediately and cheerfully work out her plans and comment favorably on them. A neurotic wife of a pastor is usually on the defensive, and no matter what is done, it is always taken wrong. Years ago, we had a pastor's wife like this, and in spite of our patience, explanations, and efforts to help her, she took everything as an insult. The women even prayed that she would stay away from the services and meetings, which she often threatened to do if her ideas weren't carried out. They wanted the minister, but they soon started looking for another because of his wife.

This type of person is also often a source of sorrow and perplexity to her husband. He hates to see her feelings hurt over things that he well knows were not intended or are, in her view, magnified out of all proportion. Try as he will, it is very difficult to smooth things over, and she may accuse him of standing with the church ladies against her. He may try moving to another church, only to find the same pattern repeated. Moving is not the answer to the problem. She needs special medical care, and the sooner she gets it, the quicker there will be peace in the home and harmony in the church. In spite of her spirituality, constant Bible reading and prayer, she may not be able to conquer these traits if they have come from things in her background, and things that have happened which she cannot recall.

Only a mind specialist can help her remember these and then show her how to adjust to her place in the church and home. Such treatment may seem costly, but far more costly is a ruined ministry, to which God called the husband, which might be cut off at any time because of the wife.

No one can advise a church, when they are interested in calling a new pastor, on how to find out the motives and attitudes that will lead a woman to act in wrong ways. These are the hidden things of the heart that are seldom evidenced in a visit or two to the new church. It is best to have a good talk with the wife privately in some informal way to see how she feels about her part in the church work and how she reacts to the demands that a pastorate puts on her husband. It is even best, if possible, to do this without the minister being present, as there are times when he will answer for her, and he might attempt to cover some things he would rather not have known. Or he could speak up out of habit of being the family spokesman. As a result, you will not really get her viewpoint at all. No worthwhile pastor's wife should resent being asked how she feels about certain things, even though she is not to be employed by the church. We all know that we have an important place in the allover work and success of the church, and we should expect members to be concerned about the kind of persons we are.

One of the best ways of getting to know a couple is to have them visit your town for a week, if possible. During that time, you will not only have a chance to hear the minister preach twice and conduct a prayer meeting but you can have some informal meetings where both the couple and the boards can express what they expect of each other. The ministerial couple can be entertained in some of the homes and at small social gatherings. During this time, the wife is apt to discuss their present church. Notice if she is critical, see what she doesn't like about the church, how anxious she is to leave, and why. There will certainly be enough discerning people who can piece together her conversation and her answers to your questions so that you can get a fairly clear picture of her motives and attitudes and be able to classify the kind of pastor's helpmeet she will be. Since none of us is perfect and most of us probably manifest many wrong attitudes at some time in our lives, you will have to decide which attitudes are most important to your church and which you think can be overlooked in your type of work. Please remember that at such a time she is very conscious of your watching and judging her. Naturally, she may become nervous and do things that she does not normally do. Put yourself in her place and then you will understand what a strain she is under while being interviewed and being entertained in members' homes.

It is well to take into consideration that while you are questioning the couple, they are forming opinions of the congregation and the boards and may see a lot of things that they don't like in your attitudes and expectations. It is wisest to have the church hear one candidate at a time, and then vote on him. If he is rejected, then consider another until you agree on one. Such a procedure is better than voting on several candidates, with the possible result of a completely split congregation. Most pastors are afraid of churches where the members can't make up their minds in a reasonable length of time, and of split votes. The pastoral candidate may fear that these are people who aren't capable of making good decisions. He may also question the possibility of uniting a church that has been divided by too many candidates. Under such circumstances, the best ministers will probably refuse a call.

To the ministers' wives, I would like to make a few suggestions. It may be well to study over the motives I have written about in this chapter and others you may think of which I did not discuss here for lack of space. You may have been letting these things have their way in your heart without honestly facing the issues and doing something about them. "As a man thinketh in his heart, so is he." Someone has said that "motives are congealed attitudes" and "motives are attitudes in practice."

No matter how well a parson's spouse may be able to hide her emotions when the couple first arrives in a new pastorate, before long she will act according to her attitudes and motives. In reality, no other way is possible for her because these are so much a part of her being that they must express themselves. A food company once had the slogan, "You are what you eat." God's Word says that you are what you think. Good, pure motives can't come out of a mind of distorted, ungodly attitudes.

If you put too much emphasis on material possessions, such an attitude must be straightened out with the Lord in honest confession. The Bible says, "Love not the world, neither the things that are in the world. If any man love the world, the love of the Father is not in him" (I John 2:15). In Philippians 4:11-12 Paul says, "I have learned, in whatsoever state I am, therewith to be content. I know both how to be abased, and I know how to abound: everywhere and in all things I am instructed both to be full and to be hungry, both to abound and to suffer need." And again Paul tells us, "Set your affections on things above, not on things on the earth" (Col. 3:2). These verses should be your standard for living.

If you are carried away with the idea of making the church your career, then study your Bible carefully to learn God's place for women in the church. Also see God's plan for your place in the home. Most women who work constantly in the church neglect their husband and children and have messy homes. Such women are usually cross and impatient with their families and take little or no time for the spiritual training of their own children. Put first things first in your life, and you won't have the time or energy to try to control the church. I would highly recommend *The Place of Women in the Church* by Dr. Charles C. Ryrie (Macmillan Co.) for all Christian women, but especially for the ministers' wives. This book does not give just one man's opinions, but is based almost entirely on God-given principles as stated in the Bible. Dr. Ryrie also discusses practices in the early church in order to give added weight to his presentation of woman's proper place in the home and in the church. There would be much less trouble in the churches if women would find their proper place and heed Biblical teaching on the subject.

Encourage your husband to be head of the home and leader in the church as you make certain that you put yourself in the background. No matter how much pressure is exerted to have you make decisions (and remember we all have experienced such pressure, even though we may never have yielded to it), insist that matters requiring a decision be taken to your husband or to the board members.

Enlist your husband's aid in correcting some of the things you have been doing wrong. When he tells you the truth, don't get angry. Remember, you asked for his help! Many husbands have come to us in distress, knowing that their wives are developing wrong attitudes. These husbands ask what they can do. They don't want to hurt the one they love, but feel that their ministries will be affected if the wife continues in her wrong attitudes. Some wives misunderstand, cry, or refuse to listen. If you are truly a godly woman, you will appreciate your pastor-husband's advice, I know, even though it really hurts at the time. If you do your best to correct the trouble, you will see in time that your husband was right.

If you have sincerely tried to conquer your faults before the Lord, with your husband's help, and still have emotional problems you can't handle, then suggest to your husband that you seek medical help. Cut down on other expenses and little luxuries, if necessary, in order to get the care you need to be a happy, useful person. Most people will not know that you are seeking the assistance of a psychiatrist, and even those who do will appreciate your effort to be a better pastor's wife. The few people who misunderstand only show their lack of knowledge of a new science that is doing so much to help mankind.

Even the most consecrated wives of ministers have some attitudes that are felt personally but seldom shown to the congregation. There will be periods of resentment, often with just cause. There will be times when we feel like expressing our outrage at having all our rights taken away from us without permission. Though such feelings are a normal reaction, it is not wise to show them to the church.

The feeling that we are expected to do too much for the church or people is usually more in our minds than a reality. If you wish to be entirely honest about this, I have found a way to quickly cure myself of unjust feelings.

First, take a piece of paper and fold it in the middle. On the left-hand side, make a complete list of everything you do just because your husband is a pastor. Be very truthful about this! Then on the right-hand side of the page list the things that you would probably do in any church as a lay member. You will probably be surprised, as I was, to find that as a proper Christian church member you would be doing most of the same things even if your husband were a plumber, repairman, clerk, or lawyer. If you study this book, you will be helped in making these lists without my further restating many items which might appear on such lists.

Second, cross out each activity on the first list that you would be doing as a lay member. See! There are only a few things left that you do because of your position as first lady of the manse, UNLESS you have deliberately taken on too much of the church work. If you have, quietly and gradually slip out of your jobs, unless you are sure that what you are doing is the Lord's will. Don't be concerned about what the church folks think about your action. Things done in the energy of the flesh are not acceptable or blessed of God and are a useless waste of your strength. Furthermore, overwork may affect your emotional stability.

Most people just go around in circles as they think about their problems, but never come to grips with them and do something about them. If you truly face your difficulties, written down where you can have a good look at them, you will find in most cases, that it is not what is demanded of you or the amount of work you do in the church that makes you feel so overworked and mistreated as the trapped feeling you have. This attitude has made your motives for church work a feeling of compulsion and a desire to please church people rather than serving the Lord with a joyful spirit.

Third, bring the entire matter of your attitudes to the Lord. Come before Him with a true willingness to cheerfully do whatever He shows you to be His will. He can straighten out your attitudes including your feeling of being overworked and having too many demands put on you. He will show you if you have undertaken more activities than you should and have neglected your family and health. There are activities that each of you must engage in because of your position, but with God's help and under the Spirit's direction you can let these activities become a labor of love, and you can find fulfillment in your position as a parson's wife. You will be a better church leader, wife and mother and more pleasing to the Lord. Your health will probably improve too. Then keep your thought life patterned after His directions given in the Word. The wrong kind of thoughts and attitudes can wreck a couple's ministry, cause psychosomatic sickness and neurosis. In fundamental circles there isn't nearly enough said about the thought life. I have discussed this subject thoroughly in my book, *My Pursuit of Peace,* so it can't be repeated here, but you can get all you need on the subject from a study of the Word, with a good concordance, and a heart willing to be convicted.

Speaking as a pastor's wife who has run the gamut from an overwhelming love for the church people to the bitterest resentment of others, I would like to suggest the two most important forces that guide the attitudes and motives of the pastor's wife to bring about the utmost effectiveness both for her and her husband. Happy and blessed is the church who finds not only a good preacher but one whose wife is motivated by a godly love for and a genuine interest in each church member and who daily prays for them and the work of the church. No matter what other desirable qualifications she may lack, these will make up for what is missing, since such a woman will put her husband's ministry and the good of the church first in her life and his.

Loving the members of a congregation is often easier to talk about than to do and can't be done in human strength. Such love must come by God working through us. I am not talking about the "I-love-them-in-the-Lord-but-don't-expect-me-to-like-them" attitude. If you love your people, you will suffer with those who suffer, rejoice with those who rejoice, comfort those who are in sorrow, and seriously take to heart the burdens of those who have problems.

This is not easy; it takes a terrific toll emotionally and physically from the pastor and his wife. Many times my husband and I have prayed together in tears for the members of our congregation and have lain awake half the night bearing and feeling their burdens. But there is no substitute for the reward that comes from helping people.

It never ceases to amaze me how many people need the interest and affection of the pastor and his wife. Even the most successful and the wealthiest people, and those with the finest families, need the sympathy, love, and understanding that come from God's special servants. There are so many lonely people who, though surrounded by friends and busy in many activities, need our support.

In a recent article by Dr. Murray Banks on "How To Live With Yourself," he lists ten essentials for emotional health. One is to have a person who truly cares and one in whom you can confide. He states, "Every person—no matter how young, how old, how rich, how poor, or how successful—needs someone who cares to confide in, to talk to freely and without fear of being double-crossed."

Usually people find a doctor, a friend, the pastor or his wife—someone they feel will keep confidences, someone who is personally interested in them and cares enough to help with their problems.

The finest Christian worker will find it difficult to help the church people unless they know that he is interested in them personally. We all hate to go to a doctor who treats us like we are Patient Number 9999. When we leave his office, we wonder if we are going to be helped by his advice. He may have made a brilliant diagnosis of our trouble, but, on the other hand, he may have been so reserved and distant that we lack confidence in him because of his reserved manner.

How many of you have friends who will stand by you, pray for you daily, help in financial need, give counsel when you have problems, serious illness, and trials? If you do, you are unusually blessed. Very few have such friends. For this reason members of the congregation lean on the pastor and his wife for support in times of need. Then people's hearts are open to the ones they know have a true affection for them. If you miss these chances, you are missing many of your best opportunities to help bring people to salvation or to Christian maturity. Many ministers' wives resent any interruptions in their work, but they are missing great opportunities to accomplish what their own Bible messages and their husband's sermons might never attain in these lives. Don't think of emergencies and telephone calls as intrusions or unpleasant duties. Try to think of them as open doors to hearts and a useful part of your ministry for the Lord. My husband and I believe that the people who have been helped by one or both of us through some trials get the most from the pulpit ministry. They know that the ministerial couple understand their needs and care about the things that concern them.

Prayer is probably the hardest ministry to which we are called. There is always pressure from our church work that keeps us busy getting things done. It takes self-discipline and self-denial to labor in prayer. The fact that there seems to be little immediate benefit tends to take away the incentive to pray. Something outstanding done in the church brings praise and honor to us; prayer seems dull and hard in comparison.

We also have to be quiet in spirit as well as in body to pray. We must be free of interruptions and distractions. Since everything seems to be against our prayer ministry, we must be convinced that it is imperative. You are all probably giving mental assent that prayer is important, but I doubt if many of you live as though you believed it is essential. Possibly you will have to learn the indispensability of prayer through some hard experience the Lord may send in due time.

Why don't we pray as much as we should? You can give a long list of reasons. Let's put them in one sentence. We don't really have a strong enough desire for a close communion with the Lord, and we don't really believe that prayer is absolutely necessary.

If we are honest, most of us will have to admit that we are so busy planning, organizing, and even scheming that there is little time left over for prayer. It is usually the last thing we do. In the little time that is left after we have done everything else, we take time to ask God to bless the plans that we have already made. Then we become discouraged and frustrated because there seems to be so little blessing on the things we have planned and done. We are acting on the assumption that we know what is best for the church instead of first taking all the needs, problems, and work to God in prayer and asking His direction.

Neglecting to give prayer its rightful place in our lives is like trying to work for an employer we seldom contact. We all know that in business the boss supplies the working materials and the plans for production. He supervises the work and makes changes and gives suggestions and help constantly. We talk about working for the Lord, when in reality we are often working for ourselves in our own strength and in our own wills. Such service, the Bible makes plain, will be fruitless and lack God's blessing. Christ said, "Without ME, ye can do nothing." Your work may look good to you, but how does it look to God?

Only through prayer can our lives be so in tune with God that we can pray about everything first and then wait patiently for Him to show us His will and let Him work His purposes in His own time. This is the only way to blessing and growth.

Perhaps the most important ministry the pastor's wife can have is that of prayer. Our husbands need our constant prayer support more than they need our work in the church. The church people are always in need of much intercession. Much will be lost if we don't carry on this essential work. A prayer ministry will not bring glory to us, or put us in a place to receive honor, but it will bring wondrous results in spiritual work accomplished. Only eternity will show what changes have been wrought by even one pastor's wife who has faithfully lived a life of daily, earnest prayer for the congregation and her husband.

If you read through the Epistles with thoughts of a genuine and godly affection for the congregation and a life of constant prayer in mind, you will be impressed with how often Paul speaks of his love for the ones to whom he is writing and of his daily prayers for them. Many times Paul had to correct evils among the people, and at times he spoke sharply, but they listened and heeded. I believe that much of Paul's success with these people was due to the fact that his ministry was conceived in prayer and given in love. It is my prayer for you, that your work as a pastor's wife will be well received and blessed because it will be born in prayer and administered in love.

Your reaction after reading this book might be one of hopelessness and discouragement. You might feel that I have set too high a goal for any woman to follow. Perhaps that is true. I have set this goal for myself. I know that unless we set a standard higher than we think we can reach, we will never rise any higher than we are now. Most of you will be helped by only a few of the suggestions; others will need to make changes in one or more areas of their lives; and some will rebel against all that I have said and prefer to go on in their stubborn, unhappy ways. It has been necessary to cover as many needs and problems as possible in the space allotted me and, therefore, it was impossible to clarify many of these with more illustrations, and many questions and problems had to be ignored entirely. It is impossible for any one book to meet the needs of thousands of pastors' wives in thousands of churches, scattered all over the country. If your situations don't happen to match those that I have used from my experience or the experiences of fellow ministers' wives, don't decide that we are wrong.

Maybe a few of you will feel that I have not shown enough sympathy.

However, I do understand your problems and am experiencing some of the same perplexities you are facing. Therefore, I feel a real sympathy for you. This book is written from my heart with the fondest hope that you can sense my sympathy and be comforted by it.

CHAPTER 15

Can You Help Me?

THERE OUGHT TO BE a twelve-volume encyclopedia on how to be a successful pastor's wife. It would take a set that big to answer all of my questions. Just when I think I have found the answers for my needs, a new set arises or we move to another church, and everything is different," said one minister's wife. "Why doesn't someone with experience write a book to help us with our problems?" She expressed a desire felt by many of us. To my amazement, when I started research for this book, I found only five books on the market written just for ministers' wives, and one was written by a man in a rural pastorate. Several of these books are over ten years old and one was published over twenty years ago. (A new book was just published as this manuscript was finished, but was written by a man who is not in a pastorate.) It is natural to wonder why there are so few books, because ministers' wives have written many other books. Many of these women have the ability. It may be because only in the last twenty-five years has the minister's wife in her relationship to the church work become so important, or because circumstances and people vary so much from one church to another that it truly would take twelve volumes to begin to cover the needs of all. It is probably mostly because none of us, no matter how experienced, feels adequate for giving advice to others.

Since so little has been written on the subject, including all novels about preachers' families, and articles in both secular and Christian magazines, I decided that the best way to make this work practical was to go straight to the pastors' wives to find out

CAN YOU HELP ME?   265

what their problems are. I have written to and questioned hundreds of clergymen's wives and ministerial students' wives from all denominations to find out what situations and difficulties they found most perplexing. It is, of course, impossible to deal with all of these. Those that seemed most urgent and about which most questions were asked, are answered to the best of my ability in the preceding chapters of this book. The other questions are answered in this chapter and the next.

Please define the terms we are hearing so much about lately such as: the role of the minister's wife; duties of the wife; and the image of the minister's wife. Do they mean the same thing?

These do not mean the same thing, though many use them to mean many different things, and sometimes interchangeably. Since there is no church-defined meaning of these, it seems best to stick to the meanings given in our standard dictionaries.

The *role* of the pastor's wife is being a helpmeet to her husband, whether in the home, personally, or in the church. A helpmeet is a suitable helper for the husband. This is a God-given definition (Gen. 2:18-20). The *duties* of the minister's wife constitute what the couple themselves, or the church members, think is the work that she should do in the church or for the congregation. The *image* of the wife is the preconceived picture in the minds of the church people of what the wife should be from her personality to her activities in the church.

Many conflicts arise between the mistress of the manse and the church folks because the ideas of the role, duties, and the image of the minister's wife are so confused. One reason for writing this book is to try to bring about a clearer understanding of these things between the family in the church home and the people of the church.

Besides the spiritual qualifications, what do you think are the basic requirements for being a good minister's wife?

My list of such requirements includes the following: A dedication to her place as first lady of the manse; an obvious affection and interest in all the members of the church; showing that she is backing up her husband in all his work; living peacefully with all kinds of people; cheerfully living within the family income, including the home provided; keeping confidences strictly; always using good common sense; a sense of humor; and the ability to let her husband give his time to the church work without resentment or complaint.

I would hasten to add that having a pleasing personality (that can be developed if one truly wishes to); being properly groomed at all times (which includes in the home, too); keeping a neat church home; and refraining from any gossip and criticism are almost as essential as the basic requirement. Higher education, Bible school training, social graces, ability to entertain beautifully, talents, and good health are real assets but not necessary.

While these may sound like very high requirements, they represent, I think, what the Lord expects from us and what every worthwhile woman wants in her life. It is important to have a high standard, even if we never attain to it!

I was brought up on a farm where we paid little attention to the social graces. Now my husband is serving a wealthy city church, and I am afraid all the time that I will do something wrong. Can you help me?

Being brought up on a farm does not necessarily mean that you have missed the social graces. I was reared on a farm, too, but we lived as graciously there as we would have in a town. However, I understand your feeling of insecurity in a completely different environment.

Just be your natural self, and try to relax in every situation! Being nervous often causes one to make mistakes or say the wrong thing. If you should say or do the wrong thing, just let it go without talking about it and over-apologizing; that only draws more attention to something that might otherwise go unnoticed or be soon forgotten. Remember everyone makes mistakes, no matter how perfectly trained. Just dismiss your mistakes, and others will do the same.

There are two words I would suggest your remembering in your struggle to adjust to your higher position in life. They are "observation" and "practice." After all, that is the way most of us learn everything. You know certain people will always do the right thing; watch them and then follow their ways.

Keep yourself out of the limelight as much as possible. Many times the minister's wife is asked to serve herself first out of honor for her, but often I have been able to let an older woman go before me. If you don't feel sure of yourself, perhaps you can be far enough away from the serving table so it would be inconvenient to make you first, or you can see that an older person gets the preference. However, once you have been told to serve yourself first, go right ahead no matter how uncomfortable it might make you not to see how others serve themselves first. To hesitate and make excuses will merely draw other people's attention to what you are doing and will give them an occasion to watch you. Using the silverware that is provided beside the dish, take dainty portions of food (there is no law that says you can't return for a second helping if you really want it). At a dinner, the hostess is supposed to start eating first, so keep an eye on what she does, and you will know which piece of silver to use, and so on. In case you are still uncertain about what you are to do, you can always take another drink of water or coffee, or speak to your partner until someone else starts eating, and you can copy that one.

Being a good listener is an art that is appreciated in every guest. The more you listen, the more people will like you and think you are taking a personal interest in them. Also the less you talk, the surer you can be that you won't be saying or doing the wrong thing. In almost every case, the constant talker is a nervous person or one who is unsure of herself. Her chatter not only betrays her insecurity but soon becomes very annoying to others.

One of the best confidence builders is to be sure that you are properly and correctly dressed—and as attractively as possible. Some will wonder why I took an entire chapter to discuss the way the pastor's wife dressed. While I put the emphasis on good grooming for the sake of her testimony, I believe that good grooming has a wonderful psychological effect on the woman herself and will help her through many trying situations. If you are sure that your clothes are appropriate for the occasion and make you look your best, your mind will be free to concentrate on the social function you are attending.

Etiquette is little more than doing things the easiest and most gracious way, as becomes a Christian lady. Someone has said that, "Etiquette is just kindness and consideration for others."

Most ministers' wives are asked to "pour" at morning coffees, teas, and receptions. This is an inescapable duty, so the sooner you learn by practice to feel at home with the tea things, the easier life will be for you. These are the things I have learned that helped me enjoy this privilege: First, I find out just what the hostess wants me to do and how. When seated in front of the tray, I arrange things so they are the most convenient for me. Since few of our ladies drink tea, I put the teapot at the back, and the coffee pot at the front. The cream and sugar are put to the side with the sugar closest to me because our ladies seldom use cream. I ask the ladies to come to my left, since I am right-handed. I take the cups off their plates, put them on the tray, and then pour. That way if anything spills, the table cloth is protected by the tray. I take the cup by the handle with my right hand and put my left hand on the other side, partly holding the bottom and return it to the lady's plate. I have found that passing a full cup from one hand to another is a dangerous practice. Ask each lady who comes by whether she will have tea or coffee, and then whether she will have sugar and cream—or lemon, if she asks for tea. Put a scant spoonful of sugar, and enough cream to color the coffee in each cup unless someone instructs you otherwise. Be sure to smile at each one, and make some personal comment. Or ask questions, if you can, which show your interest in those you are serving.

Many hostesses place a dinner-sized linen napkin beside the silver service for the person who pours to put in her lap to protect her dress and use in case of emergencies.

Standing in receiving lines is also a necessary duty of most pastors' wives. This can be distressing at times and very amusing at other times. I think that there are more dumb and embarrassing remarks made at receptions than any other place. It is easy to understand why such remarks are made, because they are usually caused by nervousness. Where there are a hundred or more people gathered together, many of whom don't know others in the group and no one person is acquainted with all in the crowd, there is a degree of discomfort on the part of both those in the receiving line and those who are passing down the line. Don't feel that you are the only one who has any troubles along this line. My husband and I have been at receptions for over twenty-five years, and they are still somewhat of an endurance contest to me.

In theory, the one next to you is supposed to introduce you to the next guest coming down the line; you are supposed to remember his name, make a pleasant remark and greeting, and then introduce him to the one on the other side of you. Therein lies great danger. Sometimes the guests move down the line so fast that my husband doesn't have time to introduce a guest to me. In that case, I extend my hand and give the guest my name. He should then give his name, but if he doesn't, I never press the issue as he will be quickly moving on again. The reverse is often just as true. Some further down the line will stop to chat, thus leaving a group of strangers stranded in front of those they have already greeted. Everyone on both sides of the line is trying to think of something correct to say. That is when most of the dumb remarks are made. When you have nothing to say—just don't say it! No matter how miserable you are, so are the others! And the line is bound to start moving in a minute.

When my husband and I entertain in our home we both stand at the door, and the one least occupied at the moment opens the door. Unless the person or persons coming in are well known to both of us, the one of us who knows their names uses them as soon as possible, thus giving the other one the names. People like to hear their names, anyway, so use them even if all in the group are familiar.

You can feel quite at ease no matter what you are asked to do at receptions, dinners, teas, coffees, and weddings, as each community has its own way of doing things that varies according to customs and different parts of the country; and each hostess has a different arrangement for her entertaining. When I am asked to take part in any of these affairs, I find out, in spite of my years of experience, just what is expected of me, in detail. This way, there is no chance of my making a mistake. There is no reason why you can't do the same. You really should, even though you might be asked to do something that is not just right according to etiquette. I can never say often enough that the pastor's wife should know and practice the ways of her church and community regardless of her knowledge of good etiquette. It is more important to please your congregation and not embarrass or correct them than to be able to quote Emily Post by heart.

If your discomfort continues in spite of time, observation, and practice, try to find a friend or church member you can trust and confess your difficulty and ask her to help you. She will be delighted and will probably assure you that your conduct is perfect and that only your mental attitude is at fault. Be sure that you aren't hurt if she finds it necessary to make some suggestions. Remember you asked for advice, and what she tells you to help you will all be for the good of the Lord's work.

Do what she tells you and, before you know it, you will be thoroughly enjoying all social functions.

If you are shy about entertaining in the parsonage because of table settings, decorations, and how to serve, then the same friend can probably help you in this, too. A good cookbook—one that includes menus, table settings and decorations—and a recent, good etiquette book are a must for you. Study these and the women's magazines for the answers to questions that haunt you and for new and attractive ideas. Start your entertaining on a small scale, and gradually work up to dinner parties and open house. Use the same tried and true menus over and over for different groups until preparing them is second nature to you. You can cook the same meal for the family if you are a new bride or not too experienced a cook. They won't mind your practicing on them first.

If decorating is not one of your talents, a few dollars will buy a lovely fresh-flower ararngement, if you are not too choosy about the kind of flowers and if you take one of your own containers. That is all that is really needed. Artificial flowers can be a real help; they are so real looking now that they are accepted in the most well-to-do homes. Try to make a hobby of gradually collecting seasonal decorations that can be saved and changed a little from year to year. Magazines abound with these ideas, and you will find that there is nearly always some holiday near the time you are entertaining. I have gathered a closetful of such decorations in a few years, at very little expense.

Women seem to love to help in the manse, so I know that there will be some who will be delighted to help with "open house," serving meals, and preparing the decorations if they realize that you want their help. They don't often run the risk of being considered nosy or critical by offering, so you will have to let them know that you would appreciate anything they want to do.

I have chosen this question to discuss because its answer also answers numerous other questions that were sent me. Insecurity in the matter of social graces seems to be an outstanding problem, especially of the new pastors' wives, of those who have moved up the social ladder or have moved from rural to city churches or communities that have much social life.

Do you advise writing thank-you notes every time we are entertained?

Emily Post says that as long as one has thanked the hostess at the time, it is unnecessary to write one's thanks. However, this is an especially nice gesture for the minister's wife, as in most cases it will not be possible to return the kindness. There are two difficulties involved in doing this. Once you start writing, you will have to be sure that you write everyone without fail or run the risk of hurting some feelings. The other problem arises because the same groups are usually the ones who will entertain you the most, and before you know it, you will run out of different ways of thanking them. It is nice to mention what a nice time you had at a person's home the next time you see that one. That gives them double thanks without writing. Please don't phone your hostess the next day (which used to be considered the proper procedure), for in these days of servantless homes, the hostess is apt to be resting or struggling to wash the dishes and put away her good china and silver. Constant telephone calls will be such an interruption that she might wish she hadn't entertained. When I travel with my husband, and we are entertained in any way from luncheon to an airplane ride, I always write a note after I reach home because I may never see these people again.

While we are on the subject of thanks, let me add another suggestion. Be sure to write promptly when you receive a gift from a church member. When a money gift has been given by the congregation, be sure to put a note in the church bulletin, or have your husband express your feelings from the pulpit. Emily Post states that when a guest brings a gift to your home, even though there are others present who did not, you should open the package and thank the giver, and then quietly put the gift away. Proper etiquette also decrees that if a gift is opened in the presence of the giver and she is thanked then, whether in your home or at a shower or birthday party, it is not necessary to write a note of thanks. However, since everyone in Dallas also writes her thanks, that is what I do, too. Practice whatever your church members do whether it seems strange to you or proper. Otherwise, you will seem to be critical of their ways and give them the impression that you consider them poorly trained.

Why don't members of the congregation invite our children to dinner with us since they know our limited budget doesn't allow much for baby-sitting?

Children are very distracting to people who are not used to having them and a hostess often dreads what children might do to her good china and carpeting. I have had ministers' children sitting on the drop-leaf part of my antique table and carrying around my two-hundred-year-old china syrup jug as though it were a football. Few people bother to correct their children as long as they aren't doing something that is exceptionally bad.

Even if children sit perfectly still, without handling precious items, they constantly distract people's attention and this is especially true at the table. Their presence is often a restraint on the conversation for fear they may understand and repeat something personal that is said. The host and hostess usually invite the pastor and his wife to dinner in order to have a quiet uninterrupted conversation with them. Often people wish to entertain a larger group at the same time, and if the children come there would not be room for them all. Even when I entertain, in order to have my children out of the way I often send them to my mother's or a baby-sitter's home.

I will probably never forget the embarrassment caused when we went to a dinner planned for six couples and one couple arrived with three children. The hostess had only the correct number of broiled chicken halves for the adults. Somehow she managed to feed the children in the kitchen, but her plans were obviously upset by having to prepare for extra people at the last minute.

Never take your children anywhere you are invited unless the hostess makes it very clear that they are invited. The little children should be fed at their regular time and put to bed at the proper time; the older ones should study and then go to bed. It is putting unfair pressure on your children to expect them to sit unnoticed in an adult group, to behave perfectly, and to stay up far beyond their usual bedtime.

You also mentioned the small amount of money you have for baby-sitting. That is a problem for so many that we might pursue that further right here. There are nurseries in most churches during every meeting. If not, start one where you are. Let the mothers take turns caring for the children if your church can't have paid workers. Nearly every minister's wife told me that she could find church women who would baby-sit for her for little or nothing.

In our first pastorate, no one offered to sit for us, but in the second, a teen-ager did all our baby-sitting free, even when it meant missing a date or a party of her own. In our present church several have offered to help, but since the members of our congregation are scattered, it is nearly impossible to depend on them for such help. Also I have my mother here, and she is glad to baby-sit for us.

My mother used to baby-sit for free for the pastor's family when she lived in Washington state. When she baby-sat, she cooked their dinners, bathed the children and put them to bed. Then she did everything she could find that needed doing such as ironing, mending, and cleaning up the kitchen. She considered this her contribution to the Lord, since she couldn't be active in the church during the week because of her working hours.

If you are certain that you cannot afford a baby-sitter, then you will have to decline the invitation to dinner on the grounds that you can't get someone to keep the children. Never mention that money is involved, or you will make some of the church people angry. Somehow, I believe that if you are careful with your money, the Lord will see that there will be enough to take care of the times when you need a sitter. Also remember that you are being saved the price of dinner at home, and I doubt if the sitter would cost more than that.

May I ask the wives who have this problem one question? (And I hope that you will search your hearts in all honesty and not get mad at me.) Are you certain that you lack means or ways of getting baby-sitters, or do you feel resentment because of having to use money you would rather spend other ways, in order to go to a meeting or dinner that you feel you are compelled to attend?

Is it right for me to take an office in the church, women's work or Sunday school?

Without exception, everyone of whom I asked this question said that they thought that a minister's wife should never take an office, though they did feel it would be all right for her to teach a Sunday school class. Those asked included many lay members, too. They felt that she should give devotional talks, lead Bible studies, and participate in activities of a spiritual nature. Some pastors' wives admitted that in small churches with poor leadership they had taken jobs in the women's organizations, and a few had done other things because their husbands felt they were the only ones they could trust to do them right. Most of the pastors' wives said they would not take an office where there is trained or experienced leadership among the women.

In every church there are too many women who want places of leadership who would make excellent leaders with the help and encouragement of the pastor's wife. As long as the parson's spouse will do the work, there are many who will never be trained and will remain in the background. As long as the wife takes a leadership part in organizations, there will be one group of women who are jealous because they want the job themselves, another group who will feel that she only took the work because she thinks that she can do it so much better than they (and that is far too often true, and the women sense it quickly), and still another group will never learn leadership because they feel they can never do things as well as the pastor's wife.

As soon as you take an office in the church, you immediately open yourself to much criticism, as you can never please all of the women even if you were an angel straight from Heaven. One veteran minister's wife from Pittsburgh gave me this piece of advice: "Never take a job in the church work. If you do, you will have hundreds criticizing everything you do. If you stay out of everything, they can only criticize you for one thing—that you don't take an office." As time goes on, I see the wisdom of her advice, and I wish I had heeded it before I took the presidency of the women's organization in our first church.

There we consolidated a number of dying old-fashioned women's organizations into one such as the Southern Presbyterian Church has. Since I grew up in that church and organization, I let the nominating committee present my name for president. I was elected. It was one of the biggest mistakes I made in church work. Evidently, it showed that I thought I knew it all, and many of the ladies resented it immediately. The Lord put a stop to it all in three months by putting me to bed for nine months. The vice-president took over, and the work ran beautifully without my attendance. I had made the serious error of insisting on using a set of rules and activities because they had worked so well in other churches. Instead, I should have let the ladies work out their own needs and ideas under the general plan of the women's organization. What I did was the result of no training for my work and my lack of experience.

Most of us have found it wisest not to tie ourselves down too tightly in any one organization, then we will be free to visit, and assist as needed in all organizations. Many offices take almost full-time work outside of our homes and child care, so we will be neglecting a large portion of the church if we give all our time to any one group. We have to adjust our schedules to meet our husbands' needs and be good mothers, and to be ready for emergencies that arise in the church. We must be free to counsel when a person is desperate, visit the hospital, go with our husbands when necessary, care for our children, and entertain guest speakers and missionaries on short notice. These things are almost impossible to do if we are committed to an office in one of many organizations. Few pastors' wives have time and energy for everything, even if no special needs arise.

Is calling on the church members a part of my work?

No, calling is not a part of your work unless you make it so, though you will find churches who feel that it is. There are many different feelings about this matter, both on the part of the ministerial couple and the members. All you can do is consider some of the pros and cons, and then think the situation over and make your decision in the light of your circumstances or time.

My husband does not want me to go calling with him. If we go together, the call becomes purely a social call, and while that is nice, he seldom has time for social calling. He tries to make every call a spiritual one. No one with a special problem or secret sorrow will want to share it with anyone but the minister. The presence of his wife puts a restraint on those who otherwise would unburden their hearts. Dwight also calls on many unsaved people with the express purpose of trying to lead them to Christ as Saviour. No matter how much the wife may be loved and respected by the people, they still want to talk to the pastor privately. There is always the danger of the wife unintentionally changing the conversation and the fear that what is said might be repeated by her to others.

If possible, do as much social calling together as you can when you first enter a new pastorate. Seldom does a member confide in a new man right away unless he is desperate, and in that case he should be willing to make an appointment to meet with the pastor in the church office. By calling in the homes, you will get to know the people, their tastes and backgrounds, and connect the parents with the children. They will also have a chance to get to know you, which is difficult in just a brief greeting at church. A call in the home shows that you are interested in them, even though you may never have occasion to call in that home again. It always makes a closer relationship right from the start if this type of calling can be done as soon as possible after moving into a new community.

At present we have a part-time assistant who calls on visitors, the sick, and those who request a call. He does a job of screening out those who do not need my husband's attention. He finds those who are members of other churches in the city and those who are not interested except for one visit, and then turns in the names of those who want the pastor to call, need help with spiritual problems, or who want to join the church, and Dwight makes these calls. We also have in our women's and men's fellowships several active visiting committees who are willing to call on anyone the pastor suggests. Usually they call on all the women who are new in the church. In the case of a couple, a husband-and-wife team usually makes an evening call. This not only relieves us but makes the newcomers feel wanted and welcome in the church. Often the general attitude is that "the pastor is paid to call." But when church members call, the newcomers consider that call evidence of a sincere interest in them personally. Many people who have joined our church said that they first became interested because they felt welcome through the call of someone other than the pastor. If you don't have visiting committees, I would strongly advise starting some.

Whenever my husband is out of town, I call in his place, when possible, in homes where there is a real need such as a

death, a sudden tragedy, an urgent request for counseling, and
sickness, or I stay with a family during an operation, if they want
me. Somehow I still feel such calls should be cared for by the
elders, and I might say they often care for these calls. When
my husband is home, he does all of this calling.

There are so many burdened, chronically ill, brokenhearted,
and lonely people in every congregation that a pastor's wife
can carry on a tremendous ministry of comfort and help if she
has the time and is able to get to these homes. In our first
pastorate, we had many shut-ins and semi-invalids. Since I had
no children, and we lived in such a small town that I could
walk to any home, I spent much of my time calling on people
in this special group. They were so grateful, but I truly felt
that in our visits together I was more helped by them than they
were by me.

Now our situation is entirely different. We live in a city of
700,000 people, and our membership is scattered all over the
city and several surrounding cities. Except in a few cases, our
nearest members live over ten miles away from our home. I
have a large home, two children (one who is sickly and requires extra help and gets out of school early in the afternoons),
so it is impossible for me to do any calling.

A cross section of church members shows that the active
people really don't care for the pastor and his wife to visit except in times of special needs. Most of our women have cars of
their own and are away from home during the day. They are
active in many organizations, teaching or attending weekday
Bible classes, or are out calling on those in need, and hence they
seldom have time for just "visiting" with the minister. The shut-
ins and lonely—and new people—appreciate calls more. One
close friend of mine, a member of another church, said frankly
that she didn't want her minister to call. She was too busy to
be bothered. She feels that the day of routine calling by pastors is over, because people get away from home so much that

they don't depend on visits from the clergymen as they did in olden days.

Considering the needs of the people in your church, what they really want, how your husband feels about your calling, your own circumstances and transportation, and the leading of the Lord, you will have to decide what to do about calling on the members of your church. Every church and community has different expectations; insofar as possible, do accordingly. There can be no standard rule in this matter.

Please give me all the help you can on weddings.

This is a large order. I wanted to write a chapter on the subject, but there just wasn't room. In fact, I secretly hope some day to write a book about the weddings we have had.

In a large city, like the one we live in, the pastor and his wife have little to say about the wedding. Bridal counselors from one of the department stores usually take entire charge of the arrangements, so the pastor's wife has nothing to do but attend.

In our other pastorates, the happy couple came to the church for the rehearsal without the least idea of what they wanted or how to plan the service. That left all the planning in my husband's hands. This is usually easiest, because then he can conduct the rehearsal without any discussion and give directions for a lovely wedding. Occasionally, a mother may give an odd suggestion of something she did at her wedding or something she read about, but mothers can be handled with tact if their ideas won't work, or if my husband senses the couple resents the intrusion.

It is, of course, necessary for the minister to have a good idea of how weddings are conducted, especially if he is new in the ministry or the community. A good book on etiquette, and especially one on weddings, is a must. Many large cities have books of local wedding customs, which we always procured ahead of time and studied thoroughly. This book should be taken to the church for the rehearsal so it can be referred to when a question arises. Since customs vary from one locality to another, it is best for the new pastor, if he isn't completely sure of himself, to talk the wedding over with the organist or a neighborhood minister ahead of time.

My husband begins the rehearsal period by having each member of the wedding party stand where he or she is to be in front of the altar. Then he has them practice their walk for timing and spacing, with the organist playing the accompaniment. After that each member of the party goes to the place where he should be just before the wedding starts. The organist plays; the mothers are seated (the bride's mother last, as her being seated is the signal for the wedding march to start). First the minister, groom, and best man come from some door near the front of the church. Then the bridal attendants start down the aisle, with the maid of honor immediately preceding the bride. I always had the privilege of holding the bride's train and starting the other girls down the aisle at the right time. At the receptions, I did whatever was requested, like pouring punch or helping with the cake, but usually we were seated at the bridal table. In a few cases, where the wedding party was very large, we were seated at a second table with members of the family.

A home wedding, and especially one at the manse—perhaps with little notice—takes far more cooperation from you. It can be a lot of fun if you will let it be. It is best to be prepared ahead of time. If you keep at least the front of your home in good order, your house shouldn't present a problem except for a quick dusting and a glance around to see that the children haven't left something there that would be very much out of place for a wedding. If you have plenty of warning ahead of time, you can give the rooms a thorough cleaning and put as many nice decorations and flowers as you have in the rooms which will be used.

You can improvise a nice altar out of inexpensive lumber that can be saved for use each time, or use a table or a card table.

Cover with a white tablecloth that reaches to the floor, if possible; or buy red velveteen as a covering to reach the floor. Keep plenty of white candles on hand, and use your best candle-holders. Place them on the front corners nearest the wedding couple. If there is room for flowers, put them in between. In these days of such real-looking artificial flowers, you can feel perfectly free to use them. You can use a nice arrangement you already have. If you can afford it, by all means have a fresh floral arrangement of white flowers. If you live near the church, borrow the pulpit Bible, ribbon and all, and leave it opened in the center front nearest where your husband will stand. Or use the largest Bible you have at home and place a ribbon in it, preferably one that is red or purple. If it is customary for couples to kneel during wedding services, you can make a long pillow from an old pew cushion, a folded quilt, or two bed pillows covered with white satin. Put a zipper on the end if the inside is something you must use regularly. Put this on the floor in front of your improvised altar. If the couple is away from home or the wedding does not have the approval of their parents, their wedding can be very lonely. If they have no further plans, you can make the occasion happier by serving cake and coffee and, perhaps, ice cream. In these days of cake mixes, and ready-made frostings, it shouldn't take long to make a cake. At the dime store or a bakery you can buy a miniature bride and groom to set on top of the cake. The variety and hardware stores have sets of four pans in graduated sizes for making a tiered cake. For this you will need two boxes of cake mix. If you don't have any other decorations, use the cake for the centerpiece on the dining room table. You can also suggest that any bridal attendants who have flowers put them around the cake, and you can also quickly move the candles from the altar to the table if you need them. I also use as the center decoration a small-sized bridal veil of white nylon net sewed on a ten-cent hairband, covered with a ten-cent spray of white orange blossoms. Inside this, I place a white Bible with two white artificial carnations or roses. They are even prettier if they are tied together with some narrow white ribbon, with small white flowers tied to the ends. This arrangement is also used for wedding showers, and anniversary dinners. Always offer the top layer of the cake and the miniature bride and groom to the couple. They take them so gratefully and sometimes timidly ask for the white carnations, which I gladly give them.

My husband and I love weddings and consider them an important part of our work. We really enter into the feelings and joys of the couple getting married and do all that we can to make this day the happiest memory of their lives. My husband lets them change any part of the service possible, and add anything they want, and carefully goes over every detail of the service to be sure that they understand. He assures them that he is responsible and will repeat anything necessary during the exchange of vows, giving them advice if needed, even during the service. A pastor can speak softly to the bride or groom without anyone in the congregation knowing it. At one wedding, after the father had given the bride away, he stepped back, but in so doing, stepped on the bride's train. It had been so securely fastened to her hair that her head was jerked back and the congregation gasped. A word of assurance from my husband that she looked all right saved the day for her, she told us afterwards.

Members of our second church sponsored a Chinese couple who were studying medicine in this country. Naturally they wanted to be married in our church. We soon found out that in China things are done very differently. A Christian couple is not properly married unless there is congregational singing, and a sermon is a part of the wedding. My husband gladly consented, but suggested that they sit on the front pew during the sermon. They preferred to stand. To our surprise, our own young people liked the idea of a sermon so much that from that time on my husband had to preach one for every wedding.

While a wedding fee is usually given, and this traditionally goes to the wife, don't let the thought that the fee may be small influence the way you treat the couple. We have usually put the most work on the couples who have given the smallest fees. Our experience is that wedding fees are no larger now than they were twenty years ago. This work is a true labor of love, and the fee is incidental.

Neither Emily Post nor church etiquette requires that the pastor's family give a wedding gift. Even though they should always receive an invitation, a gift is never expected unless you have made it your custom to send one. If I am invited to a bridal shower, I give as nice a gift as I can afford, and then I only send a congratulation card or a note to the couple at the time of the wedding. Because my husband is so well known and has taught at two schools, we are constantly receiving invitations to weddings in other parts of the country, too. We try to acknowledge them all by letter or card but never send a gift. To give gifts to all would be financially impossible.

In one pastorate, we had so many weddings that I used the fees to buy gifts for the brides, new babies, and graduates of both high school and college. Such gifts, while appreciated, take more time than I can spare now, and we have so few weddings that there isn't any reserve fund to use for that purpose. You will have to decide according to local customs and your budget whether you will give a wedding gift or not. Many times what you have to spend to have a nice wedding in the manse will cost more than a gift, and the couple will take that into consideration, I hope.

Is it all right for the pastor's wife to have outside employment?

The wife has a right to do as she chooses. But she must be very careful not to do those things that will hinder her husband's work, or she will not be a proper helpmeet. We are back to the matter of the rights of the ministerial couple again, and again I say we had better forget most of our rights, for insisting on them usually causes trouble. Since you are not employed or paid or assigned any part of your husband's work, you are free to do what you think is best for your family and the church.

Most church members feel a strong resentment against the wife who seeks outside employment. They feel that it is a reflection on their church and the amount of salary the pastor receives. The wife's employment nearly always leads to misunderstanding and difficulty within the congregation. People from other churches also make remarks, wondering why it is necessary for a pastor's wife to work. So her employment affects the church's testimony, too.

Certainly, only a superhuman woman can be a good employee eight hours a day, a good pastor's wife, mother, wife, and housekeeper. Something suffers! Whether this is a fair criticism or not, the people in the church feel that she is neglecting her church work. The husband needs a quiet, well-run home in which to relax, a rested wife to share the burdens—not a tired wife who has to do the housework at night and weekends, when they might have a little time together. The children need a mother in the home all the time no matter what their ages! There are adjustments and temptations and needs for love and counseling at every age, and since the father is often not available, an extra burden of these parental duties rests on the mother.

Two main reasons for working have been given me. First, some wives take jobs because they say that housework and the work of the church don't give them an outlet for their talents or energies. This is obviously an excuse, in my opinion, as any woman can find outlets in the work of her church or community where the effect will count for Christ's sake or the betterment of others. I also wonder whether these women should have married at all or whether they have really felt a call to help a minister in his work if they can not content themselves with making a happy home and channeling their interests and talents within the church group. There is always a need for any worthwhile ability and talent in every church.

Second, most working wives said they needed to go to work for financial reasons. Many of them have children in college, and the days of generous scholarships for ministers' children are over. The pastor's income was not enough to meet the extra strain of education, even though the student works part-time, too. This is sometimes questioned in my mind, too, as there are over two hundred married students in our seminary, and many of them support families as well as go to school. In these days of great job opportunities in most college communities, it seems that a young person who really wants higher education can get it by himself if necessary.

One mother who was working for this reason told me that her children didn't need her any more, that the father was often in the study in the church next door. They have three school-age children at home. Some time later, I asked one of the girls why she didn't date one of the minister's sons. She replied, "He smokes, he drinks, and is entirely too free with his hands." Of course, his parents don't know this, and because they are very spiritual people they will be brokenhearted when they find out. The mother will learn, too late, how dearly she is paying for not staying at home and checking on her children and giving them guidance. If she were close to her son much, she could easily detect the fact that he drinks and smokes. Drinking and smoking leave an odor that can't be completely hidden.

We live in a well-to-do section of the city. The people around us have very expensive houses, two cars, and full-time maids. Yet last year, two unwed high school girls in this block had babies. Both mothers were working because they wanted to and said their children didn't need them any more. All of this misbehavior was going on right in their homes while the mothers were at work.

Before considering outside employment, make absolutely certain that you *must* work. Poor management in money matters, trying to keep up with others, or a discontentment with what God has provided for you are some of the underlying reasons why a wife feels she must work. If you are sure that working is necessary for the good of your family and husband, try to take work that can be done in the home, where you can supervise your children at the same time. Teaching music lessons, tutoring school children, caring for children of working mothers, typing, sewing, handcraft, baking, and writing are just a few of the possibilities that I am sure the church people would not criticize. There are a number of widows who help young mothers get caught up on their ironing, who bake and help with special dinner parties, and even help with cleaning. In these days of a servant problem, even for those who can pay well, there are many women who would pay almost any amount to have a little help with the housework and ironing.

CHAPTER 16

What, How, and Why?

What can I do with gifts that I don't want to use?

YOU HAVE A PERFECT RIGHT to put them away and never use them. However, by doing so you run a great risk of offending those among your church members who have given things to you. This will be especially true if a woman who feels you don't like her sees that you are not using her gift.

My husband and I use everything that is given us. It means far more to us to be remembered by members of our congregation than to have our house perfectly decorated. Happily, we have always found sooner or later, just the right place for each thing so it has been displayed to the best advantage and has added a pleasant touch to our home. The show of affection of our members is far more precious than having a perfect gift.

When a young couple is starting out, in most cases they really need and can use a lot of odds and ends to help furnish their homes. Later on, they will probably move to a church where nicer and more appropriate gifts are given and they can discard the earlier ones, if desired.

Our present church has the nicest custom of all. I heartily recommend it to all churches. When the people of our church want to do something for us, they take a love gift secretly among the people and present the money to us, to be used any way we wish. Except for once when we all needed winter coats badly, these gifts have always been used for something permanent by which we can remember the church. All of our good china came from one church, our silver from another. Our television set came from my husband's Sunday school class, and our typewriter and an air conditioner and all the trees and shrubbery around our new house came from our present church. All these were things we needed and probably could not have had but for the generosity of the people in our churches. Many smaller gifts would have been nice, but not really needed, since our house is fully furnished after many years of collecting.

I never have enough time. What are some of the shortcuts you have found that save time?

Magazines abound with articles by experts on how to do housework more effectively, and many utility companies have issued numerous booklets on this subject, so it seems foolish to waste precious space rehashing such suggestions. You can find them for yourselves. Personally, they have done little to help me. The idea of learning to dust with both hands at the same time just confuses me and takes as much time as the old-fashioned way, to use one illustration. Anyway, I need my left hand to move objects aside while I dust with the right one. Also, making a time schedule of each duty done during the day is a foolish waste of time for the pastor's wife and/or the mother of small children. It is impossible to control all the conditions that will arise. Telephone calls, a distressed visitor, a sudden death in the church, a necessary, unplanned hospital call will put the best household experts in a tizzy—not to mention the interruptions that small children make, which we all know only too well. However, there must be some organized way of getting the work done, and I believe every woman must find the best way for herself.

Rather than checking on the time you work, it is often better to check the time you are wasting to find out where your time is going. Visiting-type telephone calls, coffee breaks, visiting over the fence with the neighbors, stopping in the middle of a cleaning job to read an article, watching television, and getting sidetracked from one job into another before the first one is done—all consume more time than most of us realize.

Training your children to be neat and to take care of their own rooms and baths is probably the biggest time-saver I know. When they reach school age, every boy and girl should be taught to keep his or her own room clean. That includes making the bed each morning, putting all toys and clothes away, and a thorough weekly cleaning. It takes a lot of patience and endurance, and many mothers give up before they accomplish their goal. My seven-year-old girl is learning these lessons right now. It really takes more time for me to wait for her to get things done than would be taken if I took care of her room, but she soon will be able to do a good job herself. My younger daughter helps by setting the table and putting the food on the table. The older daughter completely takes over as soon as the meals are finished when she is at home. When she was younger, she helped me clear the table and wash dishes.

Any possessions, suchs as toys, games, and clothing, that have been left in any part of the house have to be put away before the children go to bed. I leave the kitchen in perfect order and pick up the odds and ends, straighten chairs and pillows, and remove the newspaper before we go to bed, so when we arise in the morning, our house is ready for any visitor who might want to take a tour. Our beds are made the minute we crawl out, so it is not necessary for me to return to the part of the house where our bedrooms are unless I have plenty of time.

The blessing of the automatic washing machine has saved us from the old-fashioned "wash on Monday; iron on Tuesday" routine. If you don't have a clothes dryer, then put the clothes as near the washer to dry as possible. In the North where there are basements in the houses, there is a good place for drying, when the weather is bad, but it takes time to hang clothes up and take them down. I don't have a basement, so I put my clothes on a wooden rack in the furnace closet that is one step from my washer, and they dry from the heat of the furnace and the water heater in a few hours. I wash at night, at noon, or morning, or whenever I am doing something else that enables me to take a few minutes off to hang them up. I have no special days or time to wash. I wash when there is a need, and always when I can be doing other things at the same time. The biggest time-saver is to have the washer and/or dryer as close to the kitchen as possible, or in it, no matter how nice a basement you might have. Such an arrangement will save thousands of steps and much time. I fold, separate, and iron the clothes in the evenings while I help with homework, visit with my husband, or watch television. This arrangement for laundry releases two mornings a week without sacrifice for me or my family. Usually this is the time that I am able to do my writing.

My daily straightening and dusting is a small item since we constantly keep our house in order. This is usually done while I am preparing a meal, waiting for my husband to return, if he is away, or for him to finish a phone call or an interview and come for a meal. Normally, such periods of time would be wasted. By using this general method, housecleaning in the spring and fall is so simple that it can be skipped or done one room at a time as I have the time. In this country of no soil from coal and oil heating, cleaning is not such a problem. We just have to remove a lot of dust.

I have heard many wives complain that shopping consumes a large part of their time. I have found it is best to do all my weekly shopping on one day, in a center where everything we need can be bought in a few stores. It is easier, faster, and in the long run just as cheap to do all your grocery shopping in the same store. You can waste precious time, energy, and gasoline running from store to store because this week they carry one or two items a little cheaper than other stores. When you become a steady customer of one store, the clerks and manager appreciate your patronage, and tell you of the good buys, often save things "on special" that they think you will want, and give you the best cuts of meat. In the store I patronize, a clerk in the meat department selects my meat for me (after we decide what is "on special" and what I need), while I do my other shopping. That way, I get the best cuts of meat at less expense, with no waiting. You can easily train yourself to get all your weekly food needs in one trip unless you have an unusually large family or a poor refrigerator. What I forget that one day, we go without unless it is a necessity.

I have my own car, but because I didn't use it enough, I had a lot of trouble with carbon and with the battery. Now my husband and I trade cars so that my car is used enough. I have learned that taking the car out, no matter how short the run or how small the errand, will frequently ruin a morning's work.

Arrange your kitchen (where you do most of your housework) so that everything you need is placed exactly where you use it most. There is no rule that says you have to keep all of the pans or bowls together, or in a stack. The spices don't have to be on one shelf. Spread out your utensils as much as space will permit so that you won't have to move several things to get to the one you want. Probably many of you will have to be content with an old-fashioned kitchen, but that does not mean that meals can't be prepared as well and as quickly as in one with the latest gadgets. The way the stove, sink, and refrigerator are placed in relation to each other will save more steps than any other plan. You can do a lot to make your kitchen more convenient.

In the first home we had in Dallas, we had a small, long kitchen sandwiched between the dining room and breakfast nook. The sink, surrounded by cupboards, under the only window, was on one end and two alcoves were used on the other end of the room for the stove and refrigerator. On one side wall was a built-in ironing board and on the other a much too small broom closet. It was ten steps from the stove to the sink, and because my pans had to be stored there, I had to make three trips to cook and serve any food, not counting the many ten steps I had to take back and forth to the refrigerator. There was too much waste space! We brought the stove up on one side, covering the ironing-board closet that I never used. We took the door off the broom closet and put the refrigerator in front of it. The two shelves that showed on top made two nice knick knack shelves. The door, with some facing around it, was used to cover one alcove, which made a generous-sized closet that was large enough for the vacuum cleaner, ironing board, brooms, etc. The other alcove was the perfect place for the automatic washer. I have never had a more convenient kitchen, though I have had three prettier and more modern ones. With a fresh coat of paint for the entire kitchen, I felt as if I had a new room.

Unless you have an unusually small house, have an extension telephone. This is a must if you live on two floors, as running up and down steps all day is nothing but a "woman-killer." (Though we live on one floor, our house is large, and we have three telephones, two outside lines and one extension. We have to have those to keep up with our calls since we don't have a church office.) Learn to save as many steps as possible in a two-story house by placing things that must go downstairs or upstairs on a step until you are making a necessary trip anyway. Let the children run as many errands as possible for you. If you have a baby, have part of his clothes on each floor to save carrying a baby up and down stairs for changes.

I might add that we now have an eight-room house, three halls, three baths, a large patio, two porches, a two-car garage, and a large storage room. I take care of my house without a maid or cleaning woman, do my laundry, care for my husband with three meals a day, do my church work and carry on a writing career, with a limited amount of physical strength. Anyone can do what he really wants to if he exercises self-discipline and some systematic planning of how to get things done.

I am always late. Usually my husband and I go together, but because he was taught to be on time, he gets very upset at me. I can hardly stand his impatience. What can I do?

Being late is nothing but a habit. That sounds cruel to a busy minister's wife who perhaps has several children to dress and feed, but it is true nevertheless. If you will look at your question again with understanding eyes, you will see that you have answered your own inquiry. You say that your husband was "taught" to be on time. There is your problem. You can teach yourself to be on time, too, if you really want to.

Before going out, plan what you need to do. For example, on Saturday night, be sure that the children are scrubbed well before they go to bed, lay out their clothes for Sunday where they are easy to find. If possible, have your children dress themselves. Be sure that everything is clean, mended, and ready for use. Be sure to do the same thing for yourself! Right along this line, we find it best not to take any Saturday night engagements unless we return home very early. This keeps us from being sleepy and overly tired on Sunday. If you are out late Saturday nights, you will find it difficult to get up early, feeling fresh and rested for your hardest day of the week.

Set your alarm clock so as to allow yourself at least a half hour more than the amount of time you think you will need. That way you won't have to be cross, rushing the children, throwing your clothes on at the last minute and starting off to Sunday school and church late and in a vile mood. You are truly hurting your husband's ministry more than you realize if you don't have a quiet, well-ordered household, especially on Sunday morning when most ministers are under extra pressure because they are facing their responsibility of preaching two sermons and maybe teaching a Sunday school class. There should be plenty of time for a good, well-balanced breakfast and family worship before departing from home. Have a set departure time for each service so that everyone in the family knows the car is leaving then and they had better be ready.

When you are going somewhere alone or out to dinner with your husband, plan for the children first. Start well ahead of time, leaving some things undone, if necessary, so that the children are well-fed, bathed and ready for bed (if your baby-sitter doesn't do these things). Then dress yourself. If you have little ones who hinder your dressing, have the baby-sitter come a half hour early and take over the care of the children. Then you can dress quietly and calmly, in peace. Don't waste priceless time rehashing the same old instructions to the baby-sitter. This procedure usually prolongs the leaving, gets the children upset and leaves the baby-sitter feeling that she is considered a moron. Such treatment is our oldest daughter's biggest gripe about baby-sitting.

I have cared for my babies, answered telephone calls, taken interruptions, and still have arrived on time for a six o'clock dinner appointment. If you start your preparations earlier and have a real desire to be on time, you can do it.

My husband and I were invited to a dinner where there were to be six couples. The minister and his wife were an hour late. Their late arrival was not only rude but stole time from everyone present. Each couple paid for an extra hour of baby-sitting, and the hostess had to pay extra for her maid to stay longer. Ten hours of time was stolen from the group, which is a priceless commodity these days. We find it hard not to resent the many hours we have wasted waiting for latecomers, as we never have enough time for important work anyway. Hostesses will soon tire of ruined meals and stop inviting you.

It seems to be considered fashionable around Dallas to be late to dinner. When I invite church members to meals at the manse, I let the group set the time that is most convenient for them to come so my dinners will be eaten when they are ready and at their peak of flavor. Allowing my guests to set the time helps some, but there are still some who are a half hour late, so I plan meals composed of foods that will not lose their goodness if not served immediately. We serve some kind of juice and appetizers to keep those who come on time from getting too hungry, and we give them something to do. If some couples are more than a half hour late, I start with dinner, and the latecomers just skip the first part. In one church, when I was entertaining a very large church board and their wives, one couple was an hour late. Everyone agreed that they must not be coming, though we waited. After we were all seated and eating our dinner, they arrived. They were very much offended because we hadn't waited for them. It is pure selfishness for a couple to think that they have a right to keep a dozen or twenty people waiting and have the dinner overdone and dried out. Emily Post advises hostesses to wait only ten minutes beyond the time set, and then start the latecomers with the course that is being served at the time they arrive. However, since it is customary in Dallas to wait for people, I feel that I must wait, whenever possible.

What can I do about a girl or woman who is obviously trying to attract my husband?

First of all, be very sure that what you think true *is* true, especially if you have reason to believe that your husband returns her attentions. Many a wife has made a mess of her life and a church work by letting a jealous imagination get away with her.

Never listen to gossip, even from your so-called good friends, who are telling you tales "for your own good." Cut them off immediately in spite of your curiosity, even though you might have to do it sharply. If you lose their friendship because of it, you haven't lost anything, for a true friend would never report such a rumor because she would realize how hurt you would be. Such people are just busybodies who want to see your reaction, to see if what they say is true, or to check on whether you have already heard the rumor, so they can pass the latest gossip on to others.

Above all, never admit to anyone that you believe any of the stories that are going around the church even if you have cause to think they are true. Believe in your husband to the last moment, until you see that the tales being told are true.

Before making a move of any kind, and through it all, be sure that you take nothing into your own hands. Don't move according to your wisdom. Lay the entire matter before the Lord and ask for His guidance, with a determination to do His will. Delay any action until you get your marching orders from the Lord.

Never go to the woman involved no matter how angry and resentful you are, no matter how anxious you are to give her a piece of your mind. Such conduct is a very serious mistake and immediately puts you on the defensive and suggests to her that you are at her mercy which really isn't so). If you talk to her you will just prove that you believe all that is said, that you are desperate, defeated, and insecure in your husband's love. Fuel will be added to the fire and the other woman will be spurred on to greater efforts when she sees that she has the advantage over you. She will also have more gossip to pass around to her friends and church members. She will twist your words around to mean something entirely different as she repeats what you say and adds to it. Facing the woman seldom does any good and usually ends in a fight, for which you will always be given the blame. Remember, it is only your word against hers. Since she is the kind of person who will try to steal another woman's husband, and especially a minister, she will stop at nothing to gain the advantage over you, even if she ruins your reputation along with your husband's. You will have lost the battle before you go to her. But, worst of all, you will humiliate your husband. This shouldn't happen to the worst of men!

When you are absolutely certain of your facts, then go to your husband—not even a best friend or a member of either family! Pick a time when you know that the children will not be around and when you are certain there will be no interruptions. Take the telephone off the hook, if necessary. Then quietly tell him what you know and how it is affecting you and the church. Ask him to correct the matter. Ask him to do it for your sake and for the sake of your children first; then show him that to continue in this way will ruin his ministry. All but the most hardened hearts will respond to such a plea.

All marriage problems are caused by both partners, so don't put all the blame on him. Find out in what way he feels you have failed him and made it easy for him to seek other feminine companionship. Work out the problems that stand between you, and together ask the Lord's forgiveness and direction in starting anew. When he is truly sorry, then really forgive him! This is a very important step you MUST take if all is to turn out right.

Then decide how the "other woman" is to be handled. Your husband should avoid being seen with her at any cost. He should never call in her home unless another person of high standing goes with him, and he must let his wife or secretary take all of her telephone calls and say that he is too busy to speak with her. It may be best for your husband to meet her face to face and tell her bluntly that the affair is over, so that there can be no mistake about it. He can also explain that he can no longer be a pastor to her but will send an assistant or an elder if she needs any help. However, a scorned woman can do much damage, so a trusted elder or friend should make the call with him in order to be a witness to what goes on, since she might tell a terrible lie about it. She can still make a lot of trouble for the pastor and heartache for the wife and children who are old enough to understand. God has said that what we sow we shall also reap, and the minister has only himself to blame.

So many innocent people are hurt for the rest of their lives when a minister goes astray—his wife, children, relatives, church members and friends—that it is hard to see how a pastor could let himself in for such a thing.

To the one who sent me this question anonymously, let me say this: You are not suffering alone. But please don't despair, for things will turn out right after a while. I could name quite a number of nationally known Bible-preaching ministers who at some time in their lives, and to various degrees, have been attracted by a scheming woman. But you will never learn the names of these men from me. Since each has made things right with his God, his church, and his wife, he has been forgiven.

Each of these men (except one) has learned hard lessons by his experience and failure, and God is using each one in the ministry to His glory. If God forgives and forgets, why can't we? Remember that ministers are only human, too, and subject to many temptations of this nature.

Is it really true that ministerial couples need hobbies? I don't have much time for them, and most of them are just like another job to me. What are your hobbies?

Yes, I feel that what doctors are telling us about the necessity of having hobbies is especially needed by ministers and their wives. We need a complete change from our church work and household duties in order to recharge our energy and relieve the tensions that build up from church pressures.

My favorite hobby is writing and the research reading that goes along with it. I seldom read fiction, though for some of you, that might be best. Study books are my main interest. Even after these many years of experience, I feel it is important to read all that I can to help me as a pastor's wife. My special attention is given to books about ministers' wives, counseling, and psychology, and helps on writing. In a few years, my type of reading interests may be entirely different. These hobbies are the ones that keep me mentally alert and give me pleasant things to think about rather than worrying about church affairs. At the same time my hobbies help me keep up with my husband's mental abilities and up to date on things that will make me a better minister's wife.

For relaxation, I do handwork such as knitting, and embroidery, I watch television, and listen to good music. Sometimes, I lie on the floor flat on my back with my feet on a chair while I listen to music. To me this is most refreshing and relaxing. I learned to relax in this way years ago when I had a leg complication. A doctor told me to pretend to be a rag doll and consciously loosen all my muscles, one by one. It takes weeks of practice to be able to relax all your muscles and have them stay relaxed. Sometimes I go to sleep doing this, or am so relaxed that as soon as I get in bed I fall to sleep, when normally I have a great deal of trouble going to sleep. Another way to relax which I like is to sit outdoors day or night, and look at God's wonderful sky no matter how cold or hot the weather is. This usually leads to prayer and praise and a blessed communion with our Lord that is the most refreshing experience any Christian can know.

Walking is another activity that refreshes me and keeps my body alert and feeling better. Somehow that is the time I can clean out the cobwebs of resentment and hurt feelings that are bound to accumulate in the mind of a pastor's wife. As I walk alone and just look at the things of nature, I find myself praying to God and confessing all to Him. When I return home I feel that I have had an internal bath, and a spiritual cleansing. I often walk to and from school with my younger child, thus combining my giving her my undivided attention with getting necessary exercise at the same time.

The Albuquerque Tribune, a New Mexico newspaper, devoted its women's page to interviews with six outstanding ministers' wives of that city. They were asked what they did for hobbies. Their answers might help you. They collect rare, foreign objects, collect tea cups, read books and give book reviews, give time to counseling, music (singing and playing instruments), gardening, horseback riding, writing, cooking, and sewing.

Just in case the husbands are interested in my husband's numerous hobbies, they come under the heading of working with his hands. He enjoys refinishing furniture, remodeling and redecorating a home, building a cottage, cutting down trees, painting, wiring, and decorating our homes. He also enjoys good music, television programs now and then, and reading news magazines. He enjoys people most of all. He likes to travel, especially to see historical places. In a very real sense, his church work and teaching bring him such pleasure that they are more like hobbies than work to him.

Perhaps your biggest problem about hobbies is that you have been told to have some, but the ones suggested to you don't interest you. Also, you may have a number of ways of relaxing or enjoying yourself that you don't classify as hobbies. Just do what you really want to do—even if it is nothing! Don't try to conform to someone else's idea of what would make a good hobby for a pastor's wife. If you are finding such fulfillment in your position as homemaker and wife of a minister that you don't need other activities, then forget the whole idea. If you are really too busy for hobbies you know you need, take immediate steps to give up all you can, and arrange for the care of your children, so that you will have some time to do just what you want to do, even if it's just taking a nap, shopping or visiting a friend.

I find it very difficult to call at funeral parlors and in homes where there has been a tragedy. What do you consider the proper things to say at such times?

I almost omitted answering this question, though it was asked by many, for fear some of you may try to copy my way of doing things or the expressions I sometimes use. There is a real danger in using the "proper things to say" or pat Christian answers when you talk to the brokenhearted and suffering. A kind of parroted professional jargon will ruin a ministry of comfort. If there ever was a time when you must be led momentarily by the Holy Spirit, that time is when you are in the presence of sorrow. I doubt if any of us ever feels that we are adequate for situations such as this, but we can be assured we always have the undying gratitude of those we go to see.

Two days after my husband left for a West Coast conference, one of our active church ladies died. I was notified and in turn

phoned the part-time student assistant pastor. We arrived at
the funeral home at the same time. As we were going up the
steps, he asked, "What does a person say at a time like this?"
This was his first funeral. I felt sorry for him, but told him that
after twenty-three years of these experiences, I still couldn't
answer his question.

The biggest lesson I've learned over the years is that you don't
have to say much. You don't need a prepared speech. In every
case I remember, the bereaved person has spoken first, and a
natural answer always came to my mind.

Be prepared for any reaction. Usually the bereaved one will
wring your hands, or hug you and thank you over and over again
for coming and tell you how much it means to have you there.
I have even had men who normally would be horrified at the
idea of touching the pastor's wife, throw their arms around me
and weep on my shoulder. There can be no harm in such a
momentary show of gratitude and grief, so accept it for just what
it is.

The Apostle Paul said, "Rejoice with them that do rejoice,
and weep with them that weep." If weeping is what the person is doing, and you feel a kinship in his sorrow, then weep
along with him. That keeps him from being embarrassed by his
show of emotion and makes him feel that you are entering
into his suffering along with him—helping to carry his burden.

Another lesson I have learned is to let the brokenhearted one
set the pace. If that one wants to talk about the circumstances
of the death or suffering, let him talk. If he wishes to speak of
other things, let him be the leader, and you follow. In most
cases, the suffering one will want to do all the talking. It is an
emotional release that all doctors encourage. Just be a good
listener.

In my experience I found one exception that probably proves
the rule. During World War II, a widow in our church lost
her only son. I went to call on her at home, as his body was
not returned. We embraced, wept a little, and I sat down and

expressed my sympathy. She stared straight ahead of her and said nothing the entire time. Needless to say, I was in agony, wondering what to do. Every time I tried to say something, it got choked in my throat. After a half hour, I stood and said I must go. She turned to me and thanked me for my comfort and sympathy, and added that I had helped more than anyone who had called on her. That is the first time I knew that for some people there is more comfort in silence than in words.

Last, but most important, we can relay the comfort of the Scriptures and of prayer. This usually has to be done in an informal, quiet way, especially in a funeral home where others are around, including, perhaps, directors trying to line up the details of the burial. But a few well-chosen verses of comfort and a short prayer just before you leave are always in order. Often I say something like this: "We sorrow with you in your loss, but rejoice with [name of deceased] because she is in the presence of the Lord. Just think, she has seen the glory of the Lord! She is with Christ. She will never have any more pain or suffering. She has really begun to live! Even if we were given the choice we could never ask her to return to this earth after she has had a glimpse of Heaven." A number of people have come to me months later and have said that a remark something like that at the time of the death of a loved one had stayed with them. It woke them up to the fact that their grief was not for the dead, as they had supposed, but for themselves and their children. Theirs was a selfish grief. After seeing this truth, they soon learned how to live a full life again.

How can I stop women from making sly remarks and suggestions about what they think should be changed in the church as they look straight at me as though they were blaming me? This is always done before a group of women.

This seems to be a universal problem in churches. It has been true in all of our pastorates. For a while it had me baffled and very uncomfortable, but finally the pieces began to fit together. You will notice that the ones who do this are usually complaining about the same thing each time, and it always concerns something in which a member of that family has a special interest. Their actions are typical of human nature and demonstrate that these people are expecting you to report the things of which they complain to your husband, and in that way get a change. For a while I did tell my husband what was said, and in most cases where there was a real need of a change all that could be done about it was being done. In a few cases the most critical women had been asked to help with the work but had refused, using numerous excuses.

This is how I handle it. See if it will work for you. Do all you can to avoid the topic of conversation. However, a determined woman can work around to it no matter how far afield discussions may be. Then let her have her say no matter how much it bothers you inside, and just take it gracefully. When she has completely unwound, tell of any plans for a change that you are free to discuss, speaking loudly enough for the women who heard her complaint to hear you. If you are not free to divulge any secret plans, just say, "The pastor and board members are working on that problem." There is one response you can always use, if necessary, in replying to such a person (but please, PLEASE smile and speak in a gentle tone of voice): "Why don't you talk it over with my husband or a member of the board? They welcome any suggestions that would improve our church." I guarantee that will silence them. They are either too cowardly, have too selfish a motive or are not concerned enough if they are not willing to go to the pastor or an elder with the need. The very fact that they have to speak before a large group of people and blame the pastor's wife, shows they don't have the courage to present their ideas through the proper channels.

This is only a temporary way of handling the problem, as the same ones will bring up the same subjects at the next opportunity. The permanent way to stop women from directing complaints to you takes time, but is very effective. Never repeat anything you hear this way to your husband! At an opportune moment, casually remark that you never repeat things to your husband and that you don't make any suggestions about the church work; also that you have no more power nor authority in the church than any other church member. It won't be too long before they will realize that their ideas are not being channeled through you to the pastor.

In one church this situation worked for the good of our church. When a woman realized that her complaints weren't going from me to my husband, she and her husband took on a hard job that we had been begging someone to do for a long time. They did a wonderful work, and relieved us of something that was a problem and sorrow to us.

How can I remember people's names, especially when entering a new pastorate?

Remembering names takes real effort, especially for those of us who have so many things on our minds at once. Perhaps a few suggestions will help.

When my husband goes to a church to candidate, we memorize the name of the one who writes, his position, and the names of any others he mentions in his letter. When we receive a church bulletin, either before our first visit or when we arrive, we memorize the roster of names of board members, special officers in the Sunday school, the choir director, the organist, and the day's soloist. When we are introduced to any of those people, we mention in our conversation that he is Sunday school Superintendent, or an elder, and always their faces show obvious pleasure. Just remembering a few names and positions will give you the reputation from the first of knowing everyone and of being very friendly.

I will never forget the impression made on a soloist who sang the day my husband candidated in our last pastorate. With the bulletin before me, I had plently of time to learn her name as she sang. After the service, I called her by name, in a large group of people, and told her what a blessing her singing had been.

Once you are settled in a new church, the easiest way to get to know the people is to visit in their homes, or to have them come to yours. But you can't rely entirely on the latter way, for even if it were practical it is too slow a way to entertain all your church members. Many will help you out by inviting you to their homes soon after you arrive.

Attending small group meetings is a tremendous help. During an evening, you will hear the names repeated many times and you can give your attention to remembering names and faces.

I like to stand at the door at church, some distance from my husband and greet people as they go by after services. If one comes by that I haven't met, I tell them who I am, and usually they introduce themselves. If not, I ask for their names. Sometimes I pull some boners, but am now able to apologize and laugh at myself, and so far everyone seems to have taken it good-naturedly. If you realize that you will make some mistakes connecting names and faces, you won't be embarrassed and flustered when you do. Don't give up trying to know all your church members just because you might make an error.

In our other churches it was an easy job to learn the members and pick out the visitors for special attention. Our present church presents an entirely different problem. About a third of those who attend with fair regularity are not members. We have about fifteen new visitors each Sunday, some from various parts of the country, and some from our own city and other churches. Many seminary couples attend our church while they are at school, and we have to learn the names of new students each fall. You can imagine better than I can describe what happens to my poor brain as I try to connect the faces and names of those who are potential members and those who are passing through who expect us to remember meeting them in another part of the country or a foreign country.

We arrive at church early for every service, and I start talking to people as they arrive, giving special attention to strangers. In the largest couples' Sunday school class, which I attend, visitors are introduced. I write down their names, and something that will help me remember them. Then I speak to as many as possible between Sunday school and church, calling them by name. I try to reach the others as they pass me after church. We ask visitors to sign cards, and these are given to my husband at the door. I might add than an elder and his wife who have lived in Dallas all their lives also greet people, and when there are any people that we don't know, this couple usually can tell us.

Occasionally there are people who come regularly whose names slip me. I ask several others if they know them. If they don't, I request someone to speak to the couple and then let me know their names. That often saves me the embarrassment of having to admit that I don't know someone.

Apparently our church hadn't heard of ministers having Mondays off. How can I inform them of this?

To begin with, *you* don't inform the church or any of its members about anything. This is not your responsibility. Your husband, as pastor, is the one who should talk any matter over with the board members and get it settled. If you don't stay entirely out of a matter like this, you'll find yourself in trouble.

Our friends and acquaintances, as well as we, have found that the minister's day off each Monday is more of a myth than a reality. During our twenty-five years of ministry, there was only one pastorate where we could even plan to be away Mondays. Those we spent visiting my husband's family. Sunday was the day when my husband learned of sick ones, those who wanted him to call, those who wanted interviews, or were in the hospital. Problems and sick calls just don't wait until it is convenient for the pastor's wife. My husband generally spends his Mondays getting caught up on his correspondence, straightening out his office, laying out plans for board meetings, etc., and starting on his sermons for Sunday and a message for the Wednesday prayer service. Somehow when he takes Monday off, he seems a little behind all the week. There is so much to be done that he needs seven days a week to do it all.

This question has more to it than appears here, I believe. It implies that she was determined to hold on to their "rights," no matter what was involved. An attitude like that is apt to show in other ways, too, and cause much harm in the church. Human nature being what it is, people will be reluctant to give you what you wish when they feel they are forced into it.

"They phone us on Mondays and ask us to call, or they spend an hour talking on the phone. They even deliberately schedule meetings that one or both of us must attend," continued the wail.

We have found it better to forget our rights in the matter of having one day a week off and continue with the necessary work. Rather, we just wait until we have a free day and take that one off without announcing the fact. We also let our Mondays accumulate and then go somewhere interesting that takes more than a day's trip.

Unfortunately, the only way most church leaders find it possible to get a day off is to leave home. So few church members remember that this should be your day off that to visit friends or relatives, or shop, to enjoy outdoor sports may be the only way you can be sure that your time won't be disturbed. We find it easier to relax for a few hours at a time on many different days than to rigidly hold to any one day. If we were suddenly compelled to hold our hands every Monday and do nothing for the church, we would be miserable.

Our family's answer came twenty-five years after we were married. We bought a cottage at a nearby lake, and when the phone rings too much and the pressure of church activities gets too much, we go up there. Our cottage has only one room with a screened-in porch and has no water, but the main omission is a telephone. This gives my husband the chance to remake a house, put in water, chop down trees, and exercise physically, which he needs as a change from teaching and preaching! Even so simple a place might be beyond the budget of young couples, but the day may soon come when you can find the perfect solution to your problem of relaxation, too.

Since the churches are now demanding so much training and work from the pastors' wives, why don't they pay us a part-time salary?

You will have to ask some of the church members that one, for frankly, I have wondered about that myself sometimes. However, I do not believe that a plan of this kind would be feasible even if churches could be convinced that they should do so.

You are only supposed to do what any other wife and mother does in the church. What you do should be done as "unto the Lord" in the same spirit as many other workers in the church serve. There are people in our church who do a lot more work than I do. If I were paid, then they should be, too.

If you accept a salary, you are stepping into the official work of the church, which might put you in a very dangerous position. It would be difficult to hold to the scriptural principles for the Christian woman, and there would be times when it would be nearly impossible to keep from usurping authority over men, which is forbidden in the Word (I Tim. 2:11-12). You would be taking a part of what is rightfully your husband's work.

You would soon find yourself in more of a dilemma by taking a salary than you are now, because as soon as the people knew you were being paid, you would be worked as hard as your husband, and unless you answered every beck and call, regardless of your home responsibilities and children, you would be severely criticized. We have known a number of part-time church secretaries who have had to give up their jobs because everyone felt they should do their bidding merely because they were on the payroll. They found they were working a full-time job, including nearly every night, and receiving part-time pay. You would probably find yourself in the same position.

The average church member has no idea of the time that the wife devotes to church work because most of the work she does can't be seen by them. They will never understand the heavy burdens that you carry, even though I have tried to explain these things in this book. They would resent every penny you were being paid, and that would cause a worse breach between you and them than is already present in most churches.

An article in the *Saturday Evening Post* once told that some churches are beginning to employ the pastor's wife as church secretary. Since they had to pay for a secretary anyway, they felt it best to let the ministerial couple have the benefit of receiving the additional income. This was also done because they felt the two could work together better, since they knew the same people and problems. Also, it was thought this would prevent any secrets being released and would save any criticism of the pastor working alone with a woman or girl in the church. The pastor and his wife could work in their own home and save heating and cooling the church during the week, and yet the wife would have time to supervise her household and children. The writer did not say what was the reaction of congregations to this plan. Such a plan might be the answer to several problems—giving the clergyman's family more income to meet the high cost of living and in giving the wife a feeling of importance and reward for the work that she is doing. It might, in some cases, save the wife from having to find an outside job or the husband from taking a part-time job to meet the added needs of his family.

How can we make our pastor's wife happier and let her know we do appreciate her?

Since this question was asked in two parts, I will answer it that way. It was suggested to me as a closing question by a church member who has done much to keep before me the layman's viewpoint of the problems of the pastor's wife.

Let your minister's wife live! Don't suffocate her with too much work, criticism, advice, or even attention. She wants to be herself and not just an image. She wants to be a real person and not always "the preacher's wife." Let her be a good mother, a helpful wife, and a church member, just as the rest of you are. The fact that she married a parson should not set her apart as different from others any more than your being married to a clerk, a barber, or a business executive should make you different in the church. Try to accept the fact that she is doing what she thinks is best for all concerned in her life, which includes her family, too! Remember that you don't know all the facts that lead to the decisions she makes. If you did, you might be doing the same things you are now so prone to criticize her for doing. Don't be so quick to pass judgment on her for something you don't like; she might be carrying out what some other member has told her would please the women.

If, after a reasonable period of time, you are still not pleased with your minister's wife, then really start praying for her and for God to guide and help her. Also ask God to change any wrong ideas you might have. Don't blame everything on her, as you may be the very one who is driving her into doing things you feel are wrong. Really try to lay aside your preconceived notions of the role of the minister's wife, your prejudices, criticisms, and gossip. Try with an open mind to start anew by showing her your affection, interest, support and prayers. Show real friendship by doing something for her or the family.

We always protect our investments and usually after we work on behalf of a person, we take a great deal more interest in that one. Why not back up your pastor's wife when others are critical? Support her suggestions and actions, and before long, you will understand why she is the kind of person she is. You may even soon feel a strong tie to her, and a lifetime friendship may develop. This principle has worked a number of times, and it could work hundreds of times more if each church lady would sincerely try to be a sympathetic and understanding friend to the lady of the manse. Be honest now, and put yourself in her place and see if you wouldn't react to unkindnesses in just the way she does. I truly believe that the major trouble comes because the church folks are judging the parsons' wives on the superficial basis of the amount of actual work they do in a church without the least understanding of the unseen work, the heartaches, the unkind things that are done and said, the demands for unreasonable attention, the sharing of her husband with many others, the neglect of the children by the father, and so on. These have already been discussed. If the average church member had to follow the pastor's wife around and take part in every activity she has to for a few weeks, they would all want to get out, no matter how much strength they might have, and there would be almost no criticism of her.

In most cases, the lady of the manse is trying her best to please the church people. She wants to be liked and accepted, she wants her husband's ministry to be a success and she knows she is important in accomplishing that; she wants to be a testimony to the Lord and be used for His glory. She has every reason to try to please and no reason to want to upset people or anger them. When she comes to a new church, she is one new person standing against a churchful of people who already know and respect each other and have set ways of carrying on their work. In many places, the congregation seems to take the attitude of sitting back, as if to say, "We are just waiting for you to make us like you." The relationship between a church and the pastor's wife is a two-way relationship, and it is more important for the congregation to make her feel at home than for them to expect her to prove herself first. In pleasing one group, she often finds that she is being criticized by another. In some cases, it is impossible for her to be accepted by some if she is pleasing others, as two groups are already at odds with each other. A pastor's wife may find herself innocently in the middle of a church feud, being used as a football, kicked back and forth between the two groups. Try as we will to think of ourselves only as mothers and active church members, we are seldom allowed to forget that we are part of a team, called along with our husbands as servants of the church to do their bidding and never rebel or complain about anything.

Not one minister's wife who has contributed to this book by questions, letters, interviews, and opinions said she expected anything in the way of appreciation from the church. Each expressed her expectation of something intangible, a sense of feeling the support and appreciation of the church. All of these women said they needed to know that they are appreciated instead of being criticized. Most of them feel that they should get no more credit than any other working member of the church—nor any more unkindness or criticism. They feel that their work is unto the Lord, and from Him they will receive their reward.

But, since I have been asked, there are a few suggestions I would like to make that will make the parson's wife feel appreciated.

Every now and then arrange a luncheon, a meeting, or a party just to honor the pastor's wife and let her know that her efforts have not gone unnoticed.

Occasionally, on her wedding anniversary, her birthday, Christmas, or Easter, the church as a whole might send her some flowers or a corsage, with a note of thanks for all the behind-the-scenes work she has done to help her husband be a better pastor and for her help in any special project that year.

She will almost die of shock if some of the women would offer to baby-sit free of charge; to drive her around if she doesn't have a car; to sit with a sick child while she gets some rest or does some necessary shopping; and to help in her preparations when they see an announcement in the bulletin that she will be entertaining in the manse. I know she would appreciate finding some brave soul to care for her children so that she and her husband can take a short vacation alone. They might also pay her expenses so that she can accompany her husband on a special trip. There is an endless list of things that will help her morale, if you just watch for them and truly want to be a help. Most of them would cost very little except in time.

Though many churches give gifts—often money—to the pastor and his wife, the pastor is always the one who receives it and gets the words of praise and thanks for HIS work. See what a difference it would make if the wife is singled out just once to receive the gift for both and if the words of appreciation are given to her, too. While every wife appreciates these gifts and accepts them as partly hers, there is an inner voice that tells her she is only included because she happens to be "his" wife and no attention or interest would be taken in her but for that fact.

If church members like to be entertained in the manse, they might make a small allowance to help finance these occasions. It takes a week's food budget to entertain almost any group, so it is hard for the chief cook to juggle the money around to feed the family four weeks on the money that normally is used for three. Even if the family is willing to sacrifice without complaint, it is hard to manage.

If your people are in the habit of giving gifts to the ministerial couple or the wife, instead of giving just anything that comes to mind, try to find out what is needed and would be most appreciated. In many cases, it is nice for people to pool their cash and get one large gift. Gifts that will help the wife with entertaining will have a double purpose by indirectly helping the church, too. They will show your appreciation and greatly help in her service to you. She may need a large coffee pot for serving crowds, some trays, a silver service, punch bowl, hostess trays, and even additional silverware to entertain large numbers of people at once. It shouldn't take long for women who help in the manse to find out just what is needed.

I sincerely believe that if the church people are thoughtful in their attitudes and actions and in doing little extra things occasionally, the pastor's wife will be happy and feel liked and appreciated. If she will do her best to be the kind of clergyman's wife the church likes, and has a real desire to please the Lord first and then the people, most of the friction between the congregation and the pastor's wife will vanish or gradually fade away. The few wives who don't respond to this kind of treatment are those who would be a misfit in any place or have emotional problems they can't overcome alone. If possible, such women should be helped in these ways by the church people with the hope that these things might make the difference that is so needed in their lives.

To make the work of the pastor's wife a true fulfillment rather than a frustration, and to make a happy church family, all that is usually needed is a clear understanding of each other's problems and patience to work them out with the Lord's guidance.